THE CHURCH: A SYMPOSIUM

The Church

A Symposium of Principles and Practice

Edited by
J. B. Watson

JOHN RITCHIE LTD
CHRISTIAN PUBLICATIONS

40 Beansburn, Kilmarnock, Scotland

ISBN 0 946351 86 4

Printed by Bell & Bain Ltd., Glasgow

PREFACE

AN entire study by seventeen writers on subjects connected with Church doctrine, constitution and witness. This book has been prepared in the belief that such a book is timely and will serve a useful purpose, and it is in that hope of usefulness that it is sent forth. Church truth is a realm where many and deep differences persist and wherein are found divergent schools of thought: a realm wherein centuries of deeply ingrained traditions have made grooves in popular religious thinking which tend to interfere with the simple appeal to the testimony of Holy Scripture. We would only venture to ask that the chapters be read with Holy Writ as their testing standard and that a spirit of patience may prevail in regard to any criticism or in respect to points of difference.

As the subjects treated are diverse and the various contributors write without detailed knowledge of their co-contributors' views, it is necessary to make clear that each writer is responsible for his own chapter only.

A few notes on points of interest are printed as an Appendix. The first of these notes is by the late C.F. Hogg, and for permission to include it we are grateful to Mrs. Hogg. The other notes are over the initials of the respective contributors and for any unsigned notes the editor accepts responsibility. For his help in the reading of proofs and the compilation of the Index acknowledgements are due to Mr. G.C.D. Howley.

J.B.W.

PREFACE TO THE SECOND EDITION

A LMOST half a century has passed since this book was first published. The contributors have all been called home and perhaps are names which are not now known by many believers today. Why then reprint it? The material it contains and the purpose for which it was intended remain unaffected by the passage of time. It was deemed timely and needful when first published, and is even more appropriate as we cross the threshold of a new millennium, and increasing attacks on the foundational truths of the christian faith. The helpful subjects treated have proved of great benefit to many and our desire in making it available is that it will continue to upbuild and instruct believers of a later generation, and glorify the ONE who is central to all scripture.

September 1999

CONTENTS

INTRODUCTION

'HOLY Scripture containeth all things necessary to salvation'; so runs Article VI of the formulary of the English Establishment. It cannot be emphasised too much that Holy Scripture is the sole authority in all matters that concern the salvation of men, and it is equally true that Holy Scripture is the primary authority governing the personal and corporate life of the Christian. It pleases God to incorporate into the Church each person who receives His Son by faith, and no small part of the spiritual well-being of every Christian is bound up with the recognition of the obligations involved in sharing with others the common salvation and with the response he makes to the wise ordering by which God has seen fit to set the solitary in families. This being so, it is reasonable to expect that everything the Christian requires to know in order to obey God in these corporate relationships will be found in The Book.

The majority of ecclesiastical writers, however, do not agree that Holy Scripture is the sole fount of authority for Church polity in its local and visible form. They affirm, on the contrary, that such a view ignores the developments in the life of the churches since apostolic times; that it does not take account of the presence of the Spirit in each age and stage of the church's history; that it denies that the numerous existing forms of church government are parts of His varied guidance, and that it is putting back the hands of the clock to attempt a return to apostolic days for a pattern of church life and order. They give equal, yea, greater regard to sub-apostolic traditions, the writings of the Latin and Greek Fathers and the decrees of church Councils. They interpret Scripture in the light of history instead of interpreting history in the light of Scripture.

It is curious how in things divine the natural mind prefers to accept secondary authority when access is open to the primary source. Why should we base our practice on sub-apostolic times when that of apostolic times is before us? The apostles, divinely inspired, are surely to be preferred to the teachers of succeeding generations who had no such infallible inspiration. Besides, the apostles forewarned their contemporaries of the secret working of evils which would become more manifest in the churches after their day. It is easy to forget how quickly there was departure from the faith once delivered to the saints, and propose to ourselves as a pattern of excellence some later age in which there was deterioration and departure. To treat Holy Scripture as secondary and prefer to follow the intricacies of the traditions of the Church is surely to follow the error of those who in our Lord's day, by their regard for men's traditions, made the commandment of God of none effect.

Departure from apostolic principle and practice was, it is repeated, very rapid. 'They have turned aside quickly out of the way' was the true testimony of God against Israel when they made and worshipped the golden calf. Nothing is more remarkable in man than his propensity for moving rapidly away from the clearly expressed will of God and adopting as an improvement some self-evolved substitute. The mode of government—pure Theocracy —given to Israel of old did not long satisfy them. They desired, like other nations, to have a visible head rather than retain God as their invisible King. Their request for a king angered God, yet He gave them a king in His wrath and warned them how greatly they would be impoverished and oppressed by their new and self-chosen form of government. The analogy in church history is extraordinarily complete. Not long were the churches of the saints content each to depend upon an invisible Head in heaven, but desired, like other organizations, to have a visible head and government. Grieved, the Lord did not forsake His own, or withdraw His Spirit, though already in His Word He had forewarned the churches of the ravages and loss they would incur if they so acted.

Is Scripture incomplete? If not, why should Scripture be treated as insufficient for this so important a phase of Christian truth and life? Is it likely that writings which contain all things needful for ordering the individual believer's life, will afford only partial and inadequate instruction for Christians in their corporate relationships? Nay, we are assured that we may turn to the Holy Oracles for all needful instruction to enable us here, as elsewhere, to answer to the will of our Lord.

Therefore, if tradition and history be at all considered let them stand before the tribunal of the Living Oracles. As we see in history the simple churches of the New Testament passing to monarchical forms of government, see individual churches confederated into almost world-wide association, see that association recognized by the State, see its officers formed into a class standing apart from the ordinary Christian community, see ecclesiastical princes exercising jurisdiction over widely confederated communities, see this confederation broken and again broken, and see the sundered portions each arrogating to itself the name of Catholic, let us use the torch put into our hands in the sacred Word to enable us to discern and decide whether these things are developments having Scripture warrant or departures from Scriptural principle.

We start, therefore, from this point: that Holy Scripture is the supreme and sufficient authority and fountain of truth as to the constitution, nature and polity of the Church. And the enquiry to which this book endeavours to supply an answer is: What light is there to guide a seeker after the Lord's mind as to his obligations as a member of the company of the saved? Does Scripture teach certainties about the Church and the privileges and responsibilities of the individual within it? Enquiry along this line discloses that a surprisingly large part of the New Testament is devoted to the subject and that the relevant passages lay foundations, state truth and set forth principles upon which may be built an obedience pleasing to God.

This being so, let the mind be formed by the truth set forth in the Scriptures. Let us decline to be impressed by that which lacks the authority of a word of the Lord. Let us cease to be influenced by hoary traditions, by centuries of history, by claims to privilege, by learning, wealth, numbers or social eminence. Let no theory of development through the ever-present guidance of the Spirit be accounted tenable which justifies practices and associations contrary to the Word of the Lord. Instead, let us be ever asking 'is there any word from the Lord?' What word is there concerning the polity, functions, and witness of the companies of believing men and women meeting together in Christ's Name in this place and that? It is in this spirit that the theme of the Church is approached by the writers who have contributed to this book.

It is essential to a right consideration of this subject that the magnificence of the New Testament concept of the Church be apprehended. In the Epistles to the Ephesians and to the Colossians the view of the Church which is His (Christ's) Body is set forth. It is there seen as the ideal, invisible, indivisible, inviolable company of the redeemed of the present age. None but the truly regenerate have part therein; none save the elect partake of its blessedness. Failure and defection are unknown to it; into it the pretender and the hypocrite cannot come; breach or division it cannot know. Its unity is unbreakable; its calling and glory heavenly; its relationship to Christ holy and intimate and its destiny bound up in Him in splendour inconceivable. Through the centuries of our era each marching generation but brings a contribution to it. While historically its members are being called one by one and incorporated into it, in its completeness and glory it is ever before the eye of God. Indeed, it has been in His heart from before all time. From their heavenly vantage points the angelic orders observe it and are impressed and enlightened concerning the manifold wisdom of its divine Architect. Through the swift-ebbing years of this age Christ Himself is its builder, adding stone to stone to this Temple exceeding magnifical, Himself the while abiding that day when at last complete, sanctified, beautiful, spotless, and radiant with His heavenly glory it shall be presented to Himself and taken into the full enjoyment of an eternal association of blessedness, the features of which are at present undisclosed.

It is said that Cologne Cathedral took nearly a thousand years to finish, generation after generation of craftsmen adding each their own parts, spending their lives one upon this, another upon that portion of the vast structure and only the last of them were privileged to look upon it in its completeness. After this fashion are the gifts, given from the Risen Head, being employed in the building of the Church. Each servant contributes his little share and passes on: not one of them has grasped in its entirety the grandeur of the divine Builder's concept nor seen what the final perfection will be. His duty is but to spend himself in the task assigned to him as a steward responsible to the bestower of the gifts imparted 'for the perfecting of the saints, unto the work of ministering, unto the building up of the Body of Christ: till we all attain unto the unity of the faith, and of the knowledge of the Son of God, unto a full-grown man, unto the measure of the stature of the fulness of Christ.' This perfect (*teleios*) man is that one new man whose creation is spoken of in Ephesians 2. 15 as the purpose of the death of Christ: it is the Church, the Body of Christ, in its mature perfection.

No circle or federation of visible congregations can express this Church, nor does Scripture ever contemplate them as doing so. Even were all the Christian congregations in the world at any given time included in such an organized, visible unity, that unity would not set forth the Body of Christ. The very term 'body' demands organic completeness: it follows that until all the members are historically incorporated and until they are together manifested with Christ in glory, the glory of His Return, the Church which is His Body cannot be seen by the world. The aggregate of the saved who may be alive upon earth at a given moment are sometimes called in theology the Church on earth. Holy Scripture never so calls them.

What provision, then, has been made for the life of believers considered corporately? The New Testament answer to this question is The Church of God. This expression is applied to a company of believers gathered together in the Name of the Lord Jesus Christ[1] in the locality in which they reside, for worship, fellowship, prayer, mutual edification and evangelical witness. This name or title, which is found nine times in the New Testament is on each of those occasions used, we judge, to indicate a local congregation of believers, a conclusion verifiable by an examination of the various contexts. The churches in a district or province are not regarded as being confederated into one union forming the Church of that region, but each congregation is regarded as preserving its own administrative identity. So we read of the churches of Judæa, the churches of Macedonia, the churches of Galatia, but

[1] See Notes 1 and 2, pp. 209-211.

not the church of Judæa, etc., etc.[1] Each church is administratively autonomous, subject to no control by outside authority, Synod, Metropolitan or Hierarchy, but directly responsible to the Lord Jesus Christ for obedience to His Word.

But, it will be objected, is it conceivable that the founder of Christianity did not intend His Church to be a vast, powerful, world-wide organization influencing mankind by its united action and Christianizing civilization by its teaching and example? To such an enquiry the reply must be that Scripture never so presents the Church, never so conceives her purpose, does not legislate for such a society or provide for the ruling hierarchy which such a con-federation would render necessary. It follows that either the pro-visions and directions of Scripture are incomplete or that this idea of the Church on earth is foreign both to Scripture and the mind of God.

What, then, is the mind of God as far as the witness of the churches to the world is concerned? Surely this: That all the world shall be evangelized: that in each place those born anew through the preaching of the Gospel shall become the church in that place: that these churches, their lamp of testimony lit by the Lord, their spiritual endowments the gifts of His Spirit, their spiritual condition His care, their continuance in being His pleasure, shall be corporate witnesses to His presence, power and grace each in its own place; that through the spiritual labours of those who go forth in obedience to His command a people called out from the world for His Name shall be won.

If it be objected that a form of witness apparently so sporadic and uncentralized cannot hope to achieve the conversion of the world, the reply is that Scripture does not contemplate the con-version of the world in the Church age, but on the contrary clearly teaches that not until the age that succeeds the present, when Christ shall have returned in power and glory, will the world as a whole receive, acknowledge, and serve Him.

If the criticism is made that the plan indicated lacks legislative definiteness, the answer is that divine methods are always such as are practicable only to the spiritual. That is no reason for abandon-ing them and substituting human expedients whose machinery is obviously designed to make dependence on spiritual resources less needful. All through the Christian age a minority of believers has endeavoured to carry out in corporate life these Scriptural principles. The bitterest and most implacable opposition has come to them, not from the world, but from organized Christendom, that is the system men call The Church. By this powerful organization they have been in turn oppressed, misrepresented, persecuted, reviled, ridiculed, and ignored, but their persistence from century to century has supplied proof of the practicability of the principles they professed.

We hold that Scripture makes no provision for a central authority having jurisdiction over a circle of churches, but that each church should be administratively independent. The internal ordering of each church is to be the care of those within it, raised up and fitted by the Lord for this work. The company of the saved in each place is to be directly responsible to the Lord and His Word in all matters of doctrine and fellowship, but to decrees, creeds, encyclicals, or formularies imposed by external authority they shall not be required to submit. They will dwell in a fellowship of unity one with another, but its bond will be that of a common obedience to the same Lord and subjection to His Word, not that of conformity to decisions laid on them from without or that secured by creeds or governmental forms laid down by representative councils. The unity thus exhibited will be one of the Spirit the effect of which towards the world will be that which only the steady pressure of truth manifest in life can produce.

CHAPTER I

THE CHURCH: WHAT IT IS

ROBERT RENDALL

WHAT is the Church? In what relation does it stand to Christ? What is its nature and constitution? How is its fellowship expressed? Throughout successive generations these and kindred questions have occupied the minds of believers, and, despite wide differences of judgment regarding them, continue to do so. The subject of the Church is seen to have significant bearings on doctrine and practice, and therefore to give character and direction to Christian life. How then, if we are rightly to apprehend what the Church essentially is, ought the subject to be approached?

Let the New Testament mode of introducing it be considered. Take, for example, the following Scriptures:

'And He put all things in subjection under His feet, and gave Him to be head over all things to the Church, which is His body, the fulness of Him that filleth all in all' (Eph. 1. 22, 23: R.V.).

'To the intent that now . . . might be made known through the church the manifold wisdom of God, according to the eternal purpose which He purposed in Christ Jesus our Lord.'

' . . . unto Him be glory in the church and in Christ Jesus unto all generations for ever and ever' (Eph. 3. 10, 11, 21: R.V.).

'And He is before all things, and in Him all things consist. And He is the Head of the body, the Church: Who is the beginning, the firstborn from the dead; that in all things He might have the pre-eminence' (Col. 1. 17, 18: R.V.).

Is it not abundantly plain that the Church is here mentioned subordinately to the greater theme filling the apostle's mind—the Person of Christ Himself in all the plenitude of His risen and glorified state? Only when viewed in relation to Him is the Church seen in its true perspective. For the New Testament is not so much concerned with isolated church truth as with truth concerning Christ and the Church. To keep this continually in mind will give us, each in our measure, a balanced apprehension of divine truth, and help to preserve us from partial and limited views. Here, as in all else, Christ is all.

It is in the context of God's eternal purpose in Christ that the Church in its complete aspect is brought before us (Eph. 3. 10-11). Paul speaks of it as being connected with a mystery, something not made known in former ages, but now disclosed to men. For mysteries, in their New Testament sense, are not things *still* kept secret, and therefore mysterious, but things that once were hid in God. The central mystery unfolded in Ephesians is variously termed the mystery of His will, the mystery of Christ, the mystery of the gospel. This mystery was made known to Paul by revelation (Eph. 3. 3). It has its source in the good pleasure of God's will (which includes the thought of grace as well as of decree), and concerns the final issue of that purpose, namely, 'to gather together in one all things in Christ' (Eph. 1. 10). The wisdom of this divine counsel is carried into effect by 'Him Who worketh all things after the counsel of His own will.' There is an ordering of events in their appropriate seasons, and only when these have been fulfilled are the threads of God's purpose brought together. The rich bounty of God's grace will then be dispensed in fullest measure. This gives the whole movement the character of a dispensation, that is, an arrangement for administering the affairs of a household or of a kingdom. Although in its ultimate aim this dispensation cannot be reached until the appointed seasons have run their course, its provisions are operative even now. For unto Paul was committed a stewardship (dispensation) of this mystery (Eph. 3. 2), which he fulfilled by preaching among the Gentiles the unsearchable riches of Christ. Moreover, through the Holy Spirit of promise, the unifying process was even now at work, uniting Jew and Gentile in one as God's heritage (Eph. 1. 11-14, R.V.).

Eph. 1. 22 explicitly says that it is as Head over all things that Christ has been given to the Church, so that in some way, which as yet we are not able fully to comprehend, the calling of the Church is bound up with the ultimate subjection of all things to Christ.

It therefore follows that the relation of Christ to the created universe has a peculiar interest for those who are associated with Him in that relation. 'Do ye not know,' says the Apostle in another place, 'that the saints shall judge the world?' 'Know ye not that we shall judge angels?' (1 Cor. 6. 2, 3). The headship of Christ over all things (in their severalty: Eph. 1. 22) has in it the thought of established rule, involving the subjection of all things to His authority, and so leading to the summing up of (the) all things (as an ordered whole: Eph. 1. 10) in Him. This is borne out by the quotation from Psalm 8. 6, 'Thou hast put all things under His feet,' which in turn looks back to Genesis 1. 28, 'Have dominion . . . over every living thing' (cf. Dan. 2. 38). Man was the crown and glory of creation; all things had their centre of unity in him. In Adam creation came under the disruptive power of sin, but in Christ unity is to be restored (cf. Rom. 8. 20, 21). This will be brought about by the exercise of divine power, whereby He is able 'to subdue all things to Himself.' Two other passages in the New Testament quote Psalm 8. 6, and expand the same line of truth (1 Cor. 15. 27; Heb. 2. 8). That in 1 Cor. 15. 27 is strengthened by a previous quotation from Psalm 110. 1, 'until I make Thy foes Thy footstool.' This administrative unity must not be construed, however, so as to weaken the force of such Scriptures as Matt. 25. 46 and John 5. 29 (cf. Phil. 2. 10).

He Who is the Head of all principality and power (Col. 1. 16; 2. 10) is also Head of the Church (Col. 1. 18). His headship in creation is a headship *over* all things (Eph. 1. 22). For He Himself is before all things, and in Him all things cohere (Col. 1. 17). But in His headship *to* the Church (Eph. 1. 22) there is a vital relation between Him and those who are His members. Moreover, as the Firstborn of every creature, and therefore divine (Col. 1. 15), He *is* the Head of the created universe. But as the Firstborn from the dead, He *became* Head of the Church, even as it is written, 'that in all things He might (come to) have the pre-eminence' (Col. 1. 18). Thus while one divine Person is Head both of creation and the Church, a distinction is to be observed in His connection with each. His headship to the Church is an added glory, the result not only of what He is in His divine Person, but of His incarnation and redemptive work.

3

The metaphor of 'the head' naturally suggests that of 'the body.' Consequently the Church is frequently referred to under this figure. The variant forms in which it appears are instructive.

'THE BODY, THE CHURCH' (Col. 1. 18; cf. Eph. 5. 23) refers to a specific known entity, the Church in its heavenly completeness. The simple term, 'the body,' is also found in 1 Cor. 12, there used by analogy to denote the *local* church in its organic unity.

'THE CHURCH, WHICH IS HIS BODY' (Eph. 1. 22, 23; Col. 1. 24) contains the idea of possession. The Church belongs to Him, even as the body belongs to, and is one with, the head. (Cf. Matt. 16. 18, My church). This idea of the Church being His is latent, too, in the clause, 'that He might present it *to Himself* a glorious Church' (Eph. 5. 27). The Church exists peculiarly for Him, and subserves His glory. The words that follow in Eph. 1. 23, 'the fulness of Him that filleth all in all,' are epexegetical of the term. For that which makes the Church His body comes from Himself, seeing that He is the One Who 'filleth all things' with whatever they are full.

'THE BODY OF (THE) CHRIST' (Eph. 4. 12) is that by which is expressed the fulness that is in Him as the Christ. Cf. 1 Cor. 12. 12. The term takes meaning from the words that follow in Eph. 4. 13, 'till we come . . . unto a perfect man, unto the measure of the stature of the fulness of (the) Christ.'

'ONE BODY' is used in Eph. 2. 16 and Eph. 4. 4, but in different senses: in the former it refers to the union of Jew and Gentile; in the latter it means, 'there is one body, and no other.' Col. 3. 15 makes the unity of the body a reason for saints living together in harmony. The term is also applied to the human body as figurative of a local church (Rom. 12. 4, 5; 1 Cor. 10. 17; 12. 12, 13, 20—though in these passages it may also have a more general application).

'THE WHOLE BODY, ALL THE BODY' (Eph. 4. 16; Col. 2. 19, cf. Eph. 2. 21) is the sum of all its parts in harmonious combination, and in mutual interdependence. Growth is of the body as a whole.

'THE SAME BODY' (Eph. 3. 6). 'Of the same body' represents a single compound noun, literally fellow (members) of the body. Jerome translates it by a word of which concorporate is a near equivalent in English. It expresses equality of privilege between Jew and Gentile in that one body. Note the triple epithet: fellow-heirs, fellow-members, fellow-partakers. Paul's use of the Greek prefix *sun* (with nouns translated 'fellow,' and with verbs, 'together with') is characteristic.

By a discriminate use of prepositions Paul distinguishes various aspects of the connective link between the Church and Christ. Three call for our attention; all, it may be noted, are connected with growth.

'IN WHOM' (Eph. 2. 21, 22; cf. John 15. 2, and Eph. 1. 11, with its emphatic resumption in v. 13). The Church exists *in* Christ. But the term may also imply 'in (fellowship with) Him.' Standing and vital experience are not to be divorced.

'FROM WHOM' (Eph. 4. 16; Col. 2. 19). *From* signifies *out from*, and points to the Head as the source of the Church's growth and development. Nourishment not only comes to us *away from* Him, but *out from* Him.

'INTO HIM' (Eph. 4. 15). The increase of the body contributes to the self-expression of the Head. The term also connotes increased intimacy of fellowship with the Head.

Growth and edification are *in* Him, and *from* Him, and *into* Him. Christ Himself is the divine sphere in Whom the Church exists, the living source from Whom her nourishment is derived, and the grand end toward which she moves and in Whom she finds her glorious destiny.

Taken together, these Scriptures point to a real and vital unity between the Head and the members. Although the language is figurative, the thing expressed is not. The spiritual bond uniting Christ and the Church is organic, structural, vital. Christ, as Head of the Church, is the seat of her life, and the source of her nourishment and well-being. All the members function from the Head, and are united in harmonious action by their common dependence on Him. The nourishment ministered from the Head is supplied through the joints and bands (Col. 2. 19, R.V.). The joints are that which unites the body in all its parts and gives it structural unity, the figure implying the severalty of the members, but framed together bone to his bone. The bands or ligaments are that which secures common movement and activity, the sinews and the flesh. But organic completeness is not enough. The bones must live, and the sinews respond to the volition of the Head. The spirit of life must fill the whole body. The juxtaposition of one body and one Spirit in Eph. 4. 4 suggests a divinely-intentioned relation between them and this is confirmed by a like juxtaposition in 1 Cor. 12. 13, where, although the immediate application is, perhaps, more restricted, the wider aspect is not excluded. This accords again with Ezekiel 37, where the organic structure of the human body is used to illustrate the process of Israel's regeneration, the crowning point being reached in the words, 'and the breath came into them, and they lived.' This life has been secured for the Church by Christ Himself, in His death and resurrection, and is communicated to her by the Holy Spirit.

If these things be so, and they are certainly the way in which Holy Scripture presents the facts, it is plainly manifest that the Church is transcendental in her nature and hope, and that she is something far other than an earthly institution. For as is the Head, so are the members. Those that compose the Church are, as to their status, 'seated in the heavenlies in Christ Jesus,' and it is there that the Church displays the manifold wisdom of Him for Whose glory she has been called into being (Eph. 3. 10). Her vocation reaches far above 'this restless world that wars below,' and will only be realized in a super-temporal sphere (Eph. 2. 7). What thoughts of lowly reverence and of grateful adoration ought therefore to fill our hearts as we reflect upon the grace of Him Who has chosen us for such high ends. For the great ground of the Church's existence is that she might be 'to the praise of the glory of His grace' (Eph. 1. 6, 12, 14), and we are assured that that glory will be His 'throughout all ages, world without end,' to which faith adds, 'Amen' (Eph. 3. 21).

For teaching concerning the Church in its heavenly character we naturally turn to Ephesians and Colossians, but other Scriptures equally important and bearing on the corporate life of believers must not be neglected. The metaphors found in 1 Peter 2. 5-10, for example, must surely reflect through Peter's mind the Lord's own words concerning the Church (Matt. 16. 17, 18), and if, as 2 Peter 3. 15 suggests, Peter studied the writings of 'our beloved brother Paul,' may he not well have had Eph. 2. 20 in mind when he applied the prophecy of Isa. 28. 16 to Christ as 'the chief corner stone' of that 'spiritual house' of which believers were the 'living stones'? Earlier he had used the language of Psalm 118. 22, 'head of the corner,' when addressing the rulers of the people (Acts 4. 11). The structure of John 17, too, seems to indicate that it is an anticipative purview of a dispensation; for it takes in not only the work of Christ when here on earth, but its extension, first through the twelve, and then through those who should afterwards believe on Christ through their word, with special emphasis on the all-embracing unity of the whole. John also dwells on the gathering together in one of the children of God, irrespective of Jewish privilege (John 11. 51, 52, cf. Ezek. 34. 12), and in so doing but follows the Lord's own teaching. For the words of Christ in John 10. 16, 'other sheep I have, which are not of this fold: them also I must bring; . . . and they shall become one flock, one Shepherd,' anticipate the breaking down of the Jewish fold and the establishment of one flock under one Shepherd. This saying of the Lord combines in a very remarkable way two passages in the Old Testament, 'Yet will I gather others to Him, besides those that are gathered unto Him' (Isa. 56. 8), and 'I will set up one Shepherd over them' (Ezek. 34. 23), which therefore provide the background to John 10. Thus other figures besides that of the body, and other modes of presentation than that found in Paul's writings are used to give us a full picture of our corporate life in Christ.

The lofty flights taken in Ephesians do not lose themselves in clouds of mysticism. Indeed, it is not without reason that the epistle which sets forth in their sublimest aspects the great truths concerning Christ and the Church should also contain those practical teachings that are needed to balance them in our lives. Membership in Christ calls for corresponding spiritual character. This touches our lives as individuals, and also in our assembly fellowship. The Ephesian and Colossian epistles do not perhaps concern the ordering of church gatherings, as do the Corinthian epistles, but they deal with something equally important for the well-being of local assemblies, and without which all outward arrangements fail to secure their end, namely, the inward spirit and temper of those who compose such assemblies. For it would be a mistake to assume that the thought of the local assembly is altogether absent from these epistles. Paul is writing to Christian men and women in existing assemblies. While he addresses them as saints, and therefore as members of the body, he takes care to add that by which they may be recognized on earth, 'faithful (i.e., believing) brethren.' For it is a mark of a genuine local church that it receives only those who make a credible profession of faith. Pastors and teachers, too, while apparently given to the body, and therefore making the edification of that body the aim of their ministry, surely fulfil their service in local churches. The epistles themselves, though addressed to saints as such, were 'appointed to be read in churches' (Col. 4. 16), as they are to this day. For the great truths concerning the Church universal are intended to have a formative effect on the church local.

Just as in Ephesians and Colossians the fact of local assemblies is presupposed in Paul's mind, so in his former epistles, which deal chiefly with matters concerning local churches, the idea of *the* Church is not wholly forgotten. That this is so is shown by his characteristic use of the formula 'in Christ' or 'in Christ Jesus.' When he defines the church at Corinth as consisting of 'the sanctified in Christ Jesus' he is thinking of them as members of Christ. Thus the relation between the Church, the body, and its representation in a local church is assumed throughout his writings. 'All the saints in Christ Jesus' is practically equated with the Church. Nor is it surprising that the thought of the Church should ever have been present to his mind. For if we go back to his experience on the Damascus road (Acts 9. 1-4), are we not to believe that he himself clearly perceived in the words 'Saul, Saul, why persecutest thou Me?' that latent meaning which to later believers has been so evident in them? From the very first the apostle must have been deeply conscious of that line of truth—to use a modern idiom—that had been committed to him, even if its full implications were only afterwards worked out in his mind.

Local churches, in the New Testament, are designated churches of Christ, or churches of God. Doubtless they were so called in order to distinguish them from other and non-Christian assemblies (Acts 19. 32, 39). The stumbling block to the Jews was Christ, hence the appropriateness of the title churches of Christ in circles where a Jewish element predominated, and of churches of God amid the idolatrous superstition of a Gentile environment. But that the terms have a deeper and more spiritual significance is manifest when we consider the language of 1 Thess. 1. 1 and Gal. 1. 22. Local assemblies have their existence in God the Father and (in) our Lord Jesus Christ, and while the activities of such assemblies, as touching believers' responsibilities in them, are said to be discharged in the Lord (1 Thess. 5. 12), their actual standing and existence is said to be in Christ Jesus (1 Thess. 2. 14). They thus in some sense individually represent *the* Church, of which each may be said to be a microcosm. They are severally founded, as was the church at Corinth, upon Christ Himself (1 Cor. 3. 11), and derive their true validity as churches from that fact. In other words, they exist in virtue of a present relationship to Christ, Whose presence is manifested in their gatherings by the exercise of spiritual gifts under the guidance and power of the Holy Spirit. It follows from this that only those who are truly united to Christ can form a local assembly, and that only where spiritual conditions obtain can the proper functions of an assembly be carried out.

New Testament churches were founded by individuals or groups of individuals, through the preaching of the Word of God. These individuals were servants of God, and not the delegates of a mother-church. The churches which they founded, therefore, were not mere outposts of a central authority. The conception of the Church as an organized system binding together a number of congregations under one creed or rule is a development from sub-apostolic times. When a number of churches were conveniently grouped in one district they were sometimes addressed together on doctrinal and other matters affecting Christian life as a whole (e.g., the churches of Galatia, cf. also 1 Cor. 11. 16; 14. 33; 16. 1; 2 Cor. 8. 19), but *congregational* affairs were never subjected to the decision of a general council or synod of churches. In each individual church, elders were raised up by the Holy Spirit and to them was committed the care of the church in which they ministered. The Lord Himself, as we find from the letters to the seven churches, directly superintends each several church.

From this immediate dependence of each assembly on Christ flow several important consequences. First, that church gatherings in every place function from the presence in the midst of the Lord Himself, made known by the manifestation of the Spirit

(1 Cor. 12. 3, 11; 14. 31; cf. 1 Thess. 5. 19, 20; Phil. 3. 3 (r.v.); 1 Peter 4. 10). Thus the varied gifts of the Spirit, bestowed by the one Lord, are brought into active exercise, and operate through the power of God for the edifying of the church. The direct relation to Christ also ensures that fellowship rests, not on sectarian grounds or on adherence to a system, but on that same ground upon which a believer becomes a member of Christ. Faithfulness to Christ involves the loving recognition as one with us of all whom He has united with Himself. Anything less than this diminishes the glory of Christ. What is divisive is 'not according to Him.' Grace has broken down all middle walls of partition between the children of God, and forbids that we should raise them up again (Gal. 2. 11-14; Eph. 2. 14; 3 John 10). If churches so group themselves together as to think and speak of other believers who are equally in the body of Christ as 'not belonging to us,' they become sectarian, and virtually, if not openly, a system. But if we receive all fellow-believers sound in faith and godly in life, simply because they belong to Christ, then, although to our grief many whom we love as saints do not see their way to share with us in assembly worship and service, we are free from the reproach of sectarianism, however much it may be put upon us. Even such refusal on the part of any does not absolve us from our responsibility to love them as 'fellow-members of the body.' And we may well ask whether by giving such an impression of narrowness of heart we hinder them from seeking fellowship with us in our common privilege as saints. To counterbalance this truth, but not so as to diminish its force, the New Testament also stresses the importance of godly order for the maintenance of sound doctrine and Scriptural practice.

Then again the autonomy of local churches has an important bearing on the continuance upon earth, throughout the present dispensation, of churches of the saints. Historical continuity is secured for these through the ever-active power of God in Christ. What is sought for by the Roman Catholic church through apostolic succession (so-claimed), and in other confessions through historical creeds and formal constitutions, is seen in the New Testament to reside in Christ Himself. He is the living Lord of the churches, from Whom they derive their existence, and by

Whose present power they are maintained and upheld. The continuance of church testimony lies with Him Who walks in the midst of the seven golden lampstands: His it is to place as to remove (Rev. 2. 5). It is in His relation to the churches that the Lord is spoken of as being alive for evermore, and as having the keys of hell and of death (Rev. 1. 17, 18). Whether it be the continuance of existing assemblies, or their succession by others under different historical conditions, the government is upon His shoulder.

Churches after the pattern of the New Testament in the world to-day may not be able to trace their historical connection with those founded by the apostles (although there has always been a succession of such New Testament churches), but since they exist in virtue of a present relationship with Christ as did the church of the Thessalonians in the days of Paul, they have the same right to be regarded as divinely-constituted assemblies.

Paul's epistolary modes of address not only conform to the usage of the period in which he lived, as contemporary papyri show, but also serve spiritual ends. They are descriptive epithets—almost technical definitions—of what a local church essentially is. Their variety of expression, taken in conjunction with the uniform identity of the thing described, enables us to perceive more fully what he had in mind when he spoke concerning such assemblies. Consider the forms in which he addresses *single* churches.

To all that be in Rome, beloved of God, called (to be) saints (Rom. 1. 7).

Unto the church of God which is at Corinth, to them that are sanctified in Christ Jesus, called (to be) saints, with all that in every place call upon the Name of Jesus Christ our Lord, both theirs and ours (1 Cor. 1. 2).

Unto the church of God which is at Corinth, with all the saints which are in all Achaia (2 Cor. 1. 1).

To the saints which are (at Ephesus), and to the faithful in Christ Jesus (Eph. 1. 1).

To all the saints in Christ Jesus which are at Philippi, with the bishops and deacons (Phil. 1. 1).

To the saints and faithful brethren in Christ, which are at Colossæ (Col. 1. 2).

Unto the church of the Thessalonians which is in God the Father and (in) the Lord Jesus Christ (1 Thess. 1. 1).

Unto the church of the Thessalonians in God our Father and the Lord Jesus Christ (2 Thess. 1. 1).

How much Paul makes of the inclusiveness of Christian fellowship: all in every place, with all the saints in all Achaia, to all the saints at Philippi. And how he loves to reiterate that which gives *character* to a local assembly: sainthood in Christ Jesus. But these forms of address also delimit local churches. A local church is co-extensive with the locality within which believers can meet in one place (Acts 2. 1; 2. 44; 1 Cor. 11. 20; 14. 23). As obviously in a large scattered district this is impracticable, several companies come to be formed, each existing in direct dependence on Christ but all of which can fitly enough be called the churches (plural) of that district. Likewise in a large city, where it is impossible for all the believers to meet in one place, different assemblies come into being. Locality is incidental rather than attributive. Though in most cases, as in apostolic times, a city offers a natural area for a single gathering, the city-unit is not absolute. The phrase in 1 Cor. 1. 2, *in every place* equals *in every locality*, and therefore refers to areas indefinite, or at any rate undefined, in extent. The phrase is not general but particular (i.e., it is not the same as 'everywhere'), so that it would seem to indicate places as such—and therefore presumably, local churches. Compare with 1 Tim. 2. 8 (everywhere).

Moreover, the name of a locality is never used *adjectivally* in connection with single assemblies. It is always the church of God *at* or *in* a particular place, never the Corinthian church or the church of Corinth, as if the locality had some special significance. The R.V. rightly renders Rev. 2. 1, the church *in* Ephesus. The place is, so to speak, only the postal address. The church of the Thessalonians is no exception, since there *persons* are in view, and the qualifying phrase 'in God the Father' prevents any possible misunderstanding. True, we find churches of Macedonia, but here the *plural* rules out any necessary geographical delimitation of the individual churches. All this but re-affirms an old familiar truth, the simplicity of which is all too easily forgotten, that 'where two or three are gathered together in My name, there am I in the midst of them' (Matt. 18. 20). Local conditions vary, but the presence of Christ is the centre of the gathering in every place, whether in the large upper room of a city, or the humbler Emmaus-like meeting-places of a country district. But such assembly gatherings are not casual: they are regular and habitual, being held in known places like that of which it is written that 'Jesus ofttimes resorted thither with His disciples.' Thus again, in the practical conditions of assembly life as in what concerns the Church, His body, everything is related to Christ, and has its counterpart in some aspect of His Person or offices.

CHAPTER II

NEW TESTAMENT CHURCHES

An Introductory Study

ROWLAND C. EDWARDS

IN apostolic days, when people became Christians, they were gathered together to form churches (assemblies or congregations). This is our pattern for to-day. Only Christians were meant to be in these assemblies. They were not mixed companies of Christians and non-Christians. Hence they were called CHURCHES OF THE SAINTS (1 Cor. 14. 33). The believers were of varied ages and degrees of development in the Christian life, but the younger were not separated from the older, or the less learned from the wiser—they were all together. They were of various social grades, some slaves and some highly placed officials and there were what we would call University men as well as tradesmen. In an assembly, however, they were not separated into grades or orders, but were all together. Scripture knows nothing of the division of Christians into orders such as are described to-day by the words clergy and laity.

Just as individual Christians are variously described as saints, brethren, disciples, believers, so assemblies are described in various ways. These descriptions of New Testament assemblies are full of meaning for us to-day as we seek to model both our individual and collective practice on the New Testament pattern, which alone has divine authority.

It is no part of New Testament teaching that Christians in a locality should be divided from each other for segregation into denominations. Though in newspapers and books (even religious books written by learned and sometimes Christian authors) denominations are often enough called churches, yet it is necessary to appreciate that the word church in the New Testament never denotes a denomination. Unless this is clearly recognized, confusion of mind results to the impairment of spiritual life. The real lover of Scripture, the Christian true to his character, whether young or old, endeavours to read the Scriptures carefully.

Nor does the English word church in the New Testament ever mean a literal building, with the sole exception of Acts 19. 37, where 'churches' should be 'temples.' The term house of God, frequently applied in religious usage to so-called sacred buildings, is never so used in the New Testament.

The idea of national churches, such as the Church of England, the Church of Scotland, the Chinese Church, the Welsh Church, the Indian Church and the African Church is quite foreign to Scripture.

Further, it is needful to bear in mind that an assembly is not described in Scripture as joined to other assemblies so as to form, with them, a larger body. Thus, when you became a member of the assembly in which you are, you did not thereby become a member of any larger body of which it might possibly be thought to form a part. You did not enter any circle of communion, whether named or un-named.

The believers at Corinth in New Testament days formed one assembly. (There was another a short distance away, at Cenchrea). They came together into one place (1 Cor. 11. 20), but did not cease to be a church when they dispersed. They needed instruction. What they received is what all such assemblies need. Hence Paul said, in 1 Cor. 7. 17, 'so ordain I in all the churches,' and in 1 Cor. 4. 17, 'as I teach everywhere in every church.' No Scriptural authority has ever been given for departing from such teaching.

They were a CHURCH OF GOD (1 Cor. 1. 2; 10. 32; 11. 16; 2 Cor. 1. 1; 1 Thess. 2. 14). This implies that they were, as a body, partakers of God's provision, on the one hand, and responsible to Him, on the other. Everyone in an assembly, young and old alike, is meant to enter into this. For God is a living God (1 Thess. 1. 9; 1 Tim. 3. 15; 4. 10). It became necessary as it appears from 1 Cor. 11. 22, for Paul to ask, 'despised ye the church of God?' In using this term he was not referring to the aggregate of Christians scattered throughout the world, or to the sum-total of those in the Roman Empire, or to the general body of Christians in the province of Achaia (of which Corinth was one of the chief towns) or to any collection of congregations, but to the local assembly at Corinth. Some of the Corinthians were acting as if it did not matter what happened to the assembly, as long as they themselves were having what to-day is often called a good time. They had lost the sense of God, a fatal defect, acting as if God had nothing to do with His church at Corinth. This made the eating of the Lord's supper an impossibility. They could not intelligently break the bread and drink of the cup in remembrance of the Lord Jesus Christ as He had commanded His disciples to do.

Assemblies are also called CHURCHES OF CHRIST (Rom. 16. 16). Their very existence they owe to Christ, Who died for each member, to buy him unto Himself. They belong to Christ and are meant to function in willing and hearty subjection to Him. On no other basis can an assembly's business be conducted. For it is not an autocracy (dominated by one man), or an oligarchy (dominated by a few), or a democracy (with rights and privileges to be claimed by all). The mind of Christ must be supreme. Christ must be owned as Lord (2 Cor. 4. 5; I Cor. 12. 3). This is the way of the leading of the Spirit. Believers are called to fellowship, not to isolation, but this relationship to each other takes its character from God's Son Jesus Christ our Lord (I Cor. 1. 9).

It must not be thought that this term 'churches of Christ' is intended in Scripture to be a denominational title, marking off some congregations from others. Scriptural assemblies of Christians are all churches of Christ.

An assembly is also regarded as GOD'S CULTIVATED FIELD, TILLAGE, OR HUSBANDRY (I Cor. 3. 9). What is to be learned from this designation? A study of Hebrews 6. 7-9 is helpful. The passage tells of copious rains falling on a portion of land which is under cultivation. If it produces plants useful for its owners, it is said to be fruitful for them. This is a blessing to itself. But if it produces noxious weeds such as thistles, these have to be burned off. As God's cultivated field, an assembly ought to be bearing fruit for Him. What fruit? 'The fruit of the Spirit,' is the reply—'love, joy, peace, long-suffering, gentleness, goodness, faith, meekness, self-control.' Contrast this with the workings of the flesh. Read, for this purpose, Gal. 5. 16-23, remembering that the word heresies in this passage denotes sects, the meaning of which word may easily be understood by referring to Acts 5. 17; 15. 5; 24. 5, 14; 26. 5; 28. 22, even as God's disapproval of that which it denotes is seen in 1 Cor. 11. 19; Gal. 5. 20, and 2 Peter 2. 1. The English word 'heresies' is a transliteration of the Greek word, not a translation, it does not express the sense correctly.[1]

Every individual in an assembly ought to be in character like the godly man of whom the first Psalm speaks. It is the spiritual character of each individual in it which makes the spiritual assembly. No member can afford to be indifferent, however young, however seemingly unimportant. There is stimulating encouragement in the words, 'But, beloved, we are persuaded better things of you, and things that accompany salvation' (Heb. 6. 9).

An assembly is also GOD'S BUILDING (1 Cor. 3. 9). Under this heading, it is viewed in two ways, as an edifice already in existence and also as being built up in a spiritual way (that is to say edified). Both these thoughts are in the Greek word here rendered 'building.' In Matthew 24. 1, for example, it means a building, while in Rom. 14. 19, 1 Cor. 14. 3, and other places, it has the sense of edification. Everyone in an assembly should realize from Ezra 7. 10 that God's order is, first heart preparation, then the learning of God's mind, next putting it into practice, and finally teaching. The foundation of all this is 'Jesus the Christ' (1 Cor. 3. 11). Appreciate Christ as the God-man, foretold in the Old Testament, revealed in the Gospels. Feed your soul on His life on earth, His Cross work, His place in resurrection, His present exaltation, His awaited return.

We should understand that the primary application of 1 Cor. 3. 11 to 15 is to teachers of the Word.

Realizing that in spiritual things we are either going forward or backward, we may remember for our encouragement the words of the poet:

> Build thee more stately mansions, O my soul,
> As the swift seasons roll.

In the ninth verse the careful reader notices the change in pronouns, 'we . . . ye . . .'. The context shows that 'we' are Paul and Apollos, both of whom had been at Corinth in the Lord's work, Paul first, Apollos later. 'Ye' is plural in form, signifying the

1 See Note 11, p. 218.

Christians in the assembly at Corinth to whom the letter was addressed. Husbandry on the other hand, is a singular noun. The significance is that the Christians in the assembly, though many, constituted one cultivated field, one building (in verse 16) one temple, and (in 1 Cor. 12. 27) one body. It will be noted that the application of these terms is not to any mission or sect or inter-denominational combination or fellowship, but to assemblies of the New Testament character only.

In 1 Cor. 3. 16 an assembly is also called a TEMPLE OF GOD. The word used is that for the inner building in the temple, not that used for the whole temple, including courts and porches. It is instructive to notice two other references to what is called a temple (an inner temple, as above). They are 1 Cor. 6. 19 and Eph. 2. 21. In the former of these the body of the individual believer is said to be a temple of the Holy Spirit. In the latter the subject is not a local assembly of the saints, but the whole Church mentioned in Eph. 1. 19, 21, consisting of all believers from Pentecost till the Rapture of the saints, believers some of whom are now on earth and some with Christ, which when complete will be 'a holy temple in the Lord.' (This is never, in Scripture, called the Church of God). But 1 Cor. 3. 16 contemplates the believers in a local church, 'ye' (compare 1 Cor. 3. 9) constituting, not many temples, but a temple. To realize what we are meant to learn from this, it is helpful to remember that frequently in the Old Testament the temple at Jerusalem is called the Lord's house (as in 1 Chron. 22. 1, 2, 5; 2 Chron. 2. 1, 5, and other places). It was a magnificent structure with which all the life of Israel was connected. It was God's earthly dwelling-place, associated with thoughts of public religious service, of holiness, of witness. Carry these thoughts from the Old Testament temple to the New Testament assembly in contemplating the latter as God's temple. He does not want it spoiled (1 Cor. 3. 17). Beware of the introduction of anything into the assembly which is not in keeping with its temple character. Do not think that because people who know nothing of God's thoughts about a local assembly approve of a proceeding therefore it must be right for your assembly.

The Corinthian congregation was also called a BODY OF CHRIST (1 Cor. 12. 27). Each of its members is likened to a part of the human body, which for purposes of comparison and instruction is described extensively and in detail in verses 14 to 26. Has each member of the human body—the eye, the ear, the hand—its own work which no other organ can perform? So each brother and sister in an assembly has his or her own work to do. Is the human body one body? So is a local assembly one body, composed of different members of course, but all these combined as one. Just here, in each of the churches of the saints, is the appropriate place for the display of unity. God looks for Christian unity in operation, not merely in profession, in each such assembly. It is quite futile to seek to produce it elsewhere. Has God so fitted together all the parts of the human body that there is no schism in it? (That means, no cleavage, rent or split—see 1 Cor. 12. 25). So in an assembly there are not meant to be cliques, cleavages or rents. The Christian love of each is meant to embrace all, in good will, kindness, consideration, help. We may recognize, therefore, that under the designation of a body a local assembly is intended to manifest unity, diversity, and mutual inter-dependence of its members. By the sharing of such fellowship with each other, it is the will of God to dispel all confusion from each assembly and establish peace in it, even as the Lord Jesus had bidden the disciples to have peace among themselves (1 Cor. 14. 33; Mark 9. 50).

As a guide to the character of the unity which subjection to the Holy Spirit will produce, the passage Eph. 4. 4-6 is given. It reads: 'There is one body, and one Spirit, even as ye are called in one hope of your calling; one Lord, one faith, one baptism, one God and Father of all, who is above all, and through all, and in you all.' It is noteworthy that Christian baptism is included in this enumeration, that is, the baptism in water of a believer on credible profession of his faith in Christ. In this passage the word *one* in each of its occurrences has the force of *one and one only*, as it has also in 1 Cor. 8. 6 and 1 Tim. 2. 5. Unity which is based on the violation of any of these seven onenesses is not to be regarded as pleasing to God.

In close connection with this way of looking at a local church it is instructive to study the thirteenth chapter of 1 Corinthians. It is seldom realized that this chapter has an assembly background. It has primary reference to the activities of the

4

members of a church. It is precisely in this connection that love should be in evidence in every activity and in every person, not bent on claiming rights but on serving others. Practising love to each other is what will make people recognize that we are real disciples of Christ (John 13. 35). Follow after love (1 Cor. 14. 1), not to get it, but to give it, for love in operation binds us together while it testifies to others what we are.

In 2 Cor. 11. 2, of the Corinthian congregation Paul writes: 'I have espoused you to one husband, that I may present you as A CHASTE VIRGIN TO CHRIST.' He does not say they were a company of chaste virgins. The individual saint is likened to a faithful virgin in Rev. 14. 4, but in 2 Cor. 11. 2, it is the collective body which is before us. The company itself is likened to a young woman awaiting marriage. While so waiting she is expected to be true and faithful to her future husband. Similarly the Corinthian assembly was expected to be true and faithful to an absent Christ. It is thus that love to Him is shown.

Paul's last epistles were 1 Timothy, Titus, and 2 Timothy. Having written long before, to the Corinthian assembly, Paul now writes to Timothy in order that people should know how it is necessary to behave in an assembly. This is the force of the statement of 1 Timothy 3. 15. A local assembly is here called A HOUSE OF GOD, A CHURCH OF A GOD WHO IS LIVING, A PILLAR AND SUPPORT OF THE TRUTH.

Timothy was then at Ephesus (1 Tim. 1. 3), a large and important city, the chief of the Roman province of Asia. It was from Ephesus that Paul had written his first epistle to the Corinthian assembly (1 Cor. 16. 8). Later, from his prison at Rome he had written to the Ephesians (Acts 28. 30, 31).

At Ephesus there was a very well-known heathen temple. It was regarded as one of the seven great wonders of the world. Its length was about 425 feet, its width about 220 feet. It had 127 marble pillars each 65 feet high. An inner portion of the temple was the house of a wooden image of the goddess called in Acts 19. 34, 'Diana of the Ephesians.' This figure was supposed to have fallen from heaven. The silversmiths of Ephesus made much money by the manufacture and sale of models of this inner shrine of the goddess (Acts 19. 27).

What kind of behaviour was associated with this house of Diana?

We are assured that it was of a wicked, licentious character on the part of the temple-priests, of the women who were kept at the temple and of others. Debasing immoralities are always associated with idolatry. But, as a contrast to the behaviour that obtained in connection with the house of this goddess, the epistle tells how it is necessary to behave in a house of God. 'First of all' (1 Tim. 2. 1) note the place given to the assembly prayers, then the different instructions to the men (verse 8) and the women (verse 9), and the subsequent teaching of chapter 3. Note also, in 1 Tim. 4. 16, the beneficial results of continuance in these things—one is thus able to save himself and to be a saviour of others.

Then, after using the expression, a house of God, he says that an assembly is a church of God Who is living, not dead as was the Ephesian goddess. It is interesting at this stage briefly to consider the Greek word (*ekklesia*) which is, both in 1 Tim. 3. 15 and elsewhere, as a rule, translated church. It occurs in the narrative of the disturbance at Ephesus in Acts 19. 32, translated 'assembly.' Here it is applied to the unruly mob, as it is also in verse 41. But in verse 39 the same Greek word is used of a company of citizens in lawful convention for the conduct of public business. In contrast with these secular usages the Apostle says that the Christians at Ephesus form an *ekklesia*. It is an assembly of a God Who lives. But he extends his description, saying that it is a pillar and support of the truth. (The word which is rendered ground in the Authorized Version might also be rendered support, or stay, or bulwark). The pillars of the great Ephesian temple were not, of course, part of the foundation, but they were a stay of the building, a buttress for it. In the same way, the assembly at Ephesus was not the foundation of the truth—that would be far too much to claim— but it was a support for it, maintaining it, that is, accepting and honouring and practising the doctrines of the faith, based as they are on the mystery of godliness which is described in 1 Tim. 3. 16. And as the pillars of the Ephesian temple were for display, so is the assembly's witness to the truth to be manifest. Thus a local church is a pillar and stay of the truth. It does not teach; it is taught by. those fitted of God to do so. It is a public testimony for the truth, however, in its godly order and in the work of the Lord with which it is identified.

An assembly is also referred to in the New Testament as a LITTLE FLOCK. The true reading of well-known words in John 10. 16 is, 'there shall be one flock, one shepherd.' It is a diminutive of the Greek word for flock which is used as a designation of an assembly. Consider, for example, Acts 20. 28. Here the elders of the church at Ephesus, addressed by Paul on his return from the third missionary journey, are charged to take heed to themselves and also to the little flock in which they were. They were enjoined to feed the Christians. The word means to tend, after the manner in which literal shepherds care for their flocks. The tending not only covers the function of providing food, but the other exercises of guarding them from dangers, guiding them in right paths and keeping them together for protection and safety. If it be remembered that Eastern shepherds do not drive their sheep but lead them, it will be appreciated that these elders of the church at Ephesus were expected to tread in right paths themselves as they sought to tend the sheep. Otherwise they would lead them astray. Recognize in your assembly those who both know the right way to walk and walk in it. Pray for them, esteem them very highly in love for their work's sake, follow their faith (1 Thess. 5. 12, 13; Heb. 13. 7, 17).

In 1 Peter 5. 2 is a similar charge, 'feed the flock of God which is among you.' It is a good exercise to think how much time, money and energy are spent on believers in an assembly by those who seek to guide them according to this passage. Teachers and pastors often spend themselves for the benefit of believers to their own personal loss and disadvantage. While it is true that they cannot get their full reward by anything their fellow-saints do, yet they are helped and encouraged as they see such results among the little flock as are mentioned in 1 Cor. 16. 15-18. It is instructive to read John 21. 15-17, where are found three injunctions to Peter, of which his injunctions just mentioned are an echo, impressed on him by the Lord Himself. They are, 'feed My lambs,' 'tend My sheep,' 'feed My sheep.' Tending is more than feeding. It includes feeding and folding, guiding and guarding.

In Eastern homes in apostolic days the lampstand was a very important piece of furniture. Made of wood, on a kind of tripod, it stood about three feet high. On it was placed the lamp. The

Lord's words, given in Matt. 5. 15 are, 'Neither do men light a lamp, and put it under the bushel, but on the stand; and it shineth unto all that are in the house' (R.V.). This shows the use of the stand. It is a light-bearer.

In Rev. 1. 12, 20; 2. 1, the word candlestick is really lampstand. The seven assemblies of Rev. 1. 11 are likened to seven STANDS ON WHICH LAMPS ARE PLACED. This would teach us that each assembly exists as a stand from which light is meant to shine forth. Welcoming God's light, a church should radiate it, the assembly exists for this purpose. The congregation will do this as the individual saints in it shine as light-bearers (Phil. 2. 15). God's unit of individual witness is, of course, the individual Christian. His unit of collective witness on earth is the local congregation in each place.

These lampstands of Revelation are to be distinguished from the golden lampstand of the twenty-fifth chapter of the book of Exodus. For though the latter had seven branches and the whole was beaten out of the one piece of gold, each stand of Revelation, on the contrary, was an entity in itself. It was not a branch of anything. There was no Asian Church of which each of the seven assemblies in Asia might be thought to be a constituent part, even as there was no such association of assemblies as the Galatian Church composed of the churches of Galatia (1 Cor. 16. 1), no union of the churches of Macedonia (2 Cor. 8. 1) into any so-called Macedonian Church, no joining together of the churches of Judæa (Gal. 1. 22) to form a Judæan Church. An assembly is not represented in Scripture as part of any larger body.[1] The assemblies were not related to each other in such a way as to form a widely spread fellowship. Scripture does not teach that the churches are grouped together in anything that might be regarded as the Church of God on earth. But one assembly is not meant to be callous or indifferent to the welfare of the others, for the message to each of the seven embodies these words, 'He that hath an ear, let him hear what the Spirit saith to the churches' (Rev. 2. 7, 11, 17, 29; 3. 6, 13, 22). And the fact that the lampstands of Revelation were of gold reminds us that they are of God, for the symbolic significance of gold in Scripture is that it speaks of Deity.

In conclusion we recapitulate and note the main thoughts

[1] See Note 3, p. 211.

associated with the various ways in which assemblies of the saints are described in the New Testament. A local church is regarded as

1 An assembly of the saints—sanctification and coming together.
2 A church of God—provision, responsibility.
3 A church of Christ—purchase, subjection.
4 God's cultivated field—fruit-bearing, blessing.
5 God's building—instruction, edification.
6 A temple of God—holiness, worship.
7 A body of Christ—unity, diversity, interdependence.
8 A chaste virgin espoused—true-heartedness, love.
9 A little flock—feeding, guiding, guarding.
10 A house of God—behaviour, rule.
11 A pillar and ground of the truth—order, loyalty.
12 A lampstand—light-bearing, witness.

CHAPTER III

CHURCH LIFE AND FELLOWSHIP

J. R. ROLLO

NINETEEN centuries ago there stood on the river Orontes and some fifteen miles from the sea at the Eastern end of the Mediterranean the city of Antioch. It was a splendid city, the metropolis of Syria, with a reputation for learning and culture, and a mixed population of Jews, Greeks, Syrians, and Romans totalling some two hundred thousand souls. There must have been many visitors to the famous city who would note its commercial prosperity, and who, on closer acquaintance, would sense its vice and licentiousness, only to conclude that its practices followed the pattern of any other heathen centre, where ease and sin turn men's minds from serious thought.

About 42 A.D. an unusual visitor with an unusual quest arrived in Antioch. His name was Barnabas, and he had been sent by the church in Jerusalem to confirm a report of a new wonder in the Syrian capital. And wonder it was! What he encountered caused him to rejoice, and what he saw he epitomized in the phrase 'the grace of God.' This he saw operative in a group of persons, unrelated by any other tie of kinship. We are not told they had common race, common social status, common culture or common political creed. What we do know is that their manner of life marked them out as distinctive in this cosmopolitan centre of conflicting interests. We learn from a writing to one of them-selves (for Titus was of Antioch) the tremulous secret of this new experience. Paul writes, 'The grace of God that bringeth salvation hath appeared to all men, teaching us that, denying ungodliness and worldly lusts, we should live soberly, righteously and godly in this present world' (Titus 2. 11, 12).

That this was a reality is echoed in the fact that the disciples were first called Christians there. It was a nickname, a term of obloquy, yet soon to become a badge of honour. They were disciples first and Christians afterwards, and herein lay the strength of their kinship. The New Testament speaks elsewhere of those who are sanctified in Christ Jesus (1 Cor. 1. 2) and called into the fellowship of the Son (v. 9). Their fellowship is with the Father (1 John 1. 3) and they enjoy the communion of the Holy Spirit (2 Cor. 13. 14). All this reverses the condition of things brought about by wilful disobedience and the choice of self-will in Eden's garden. It does more of course. The prodigal son was not brought back to the garden but to the table, where he was made to sit in suitability to the father, feasting on that which delighted the father. This is the work of sovereign grace. If Moses, the representative of the law must take off his shoes in the presence of Jehovah, grace provides shoes for the returning feet of the prodigal. This triumph of mercy institutes a fellowship which is divine in character and eternal in nature. As such, therefore, it is inviolable, though the enjoyment of it is dependent upon the condition of the spirit of the believer.

Is it any wonder then that the heathen people of Antioch were made to see something radically different about the disciples of Christ? They themselves were dead to God, unresponsive to His character and claims, while the Christians were alive to God, indwelt by the Holy Spirit and endowed with a new life which separated them from the world, and at the same time drew them irresistibly together into holy fellowship.

When Barnabas had continued here some time, beholding the grace of God, he reported back to the church at Jerusalem, whose leaders quickly realized that here was a spontaneous growth, a miniature of the invisible and indivisible church of which the risen Christ is the head. In the intervening centuries, history is not silent upon the existence of many such companies, whose members have found spiritual unity in acknowledging the lordship of Christ, the presidency of the Holy Spirit, the inerrancy and ultimate authority of the Holy Scriptures. Such companies are not created by synod or council; still less are they disrupted by encyclical or act of parliament. Their allegiance is neither to an organization nor an earthly delegate, but to the ascended Lord.

We may pause here to note that the unhindered power of the Holy Spirit guided and controlled those who were saved at Pentecost to be baptized and to continue steadfastly in the apostles' doctrine and in holy fellowship, observing the breaking of bread and prayers. They were joined in spirit as they worshipped; they were sensitive in care for each other, especially for those in trying circumstances, and they maintained united witness of the wonderful works of God to those in darkness around them. The enriching ministry of Paul as he laboured in Antioch would lead them into deeper enjoyment of their partnership with God, and into more fervent love for each other. When they learned of impending famine in Judæa, they were quickly alert to the needs of their brethren in the stricken area, and hastened to express their love in a practical way. The very word 'fellowship' is translated 'contribution' (Rom. 15. 26; 2 Cor. 9. 13).

Another day in the life of the church at Antioch is pictured for us in the thirteenth chapter of Acts, when the call to special service was heard. Just as the New Testament knows nothing of spiritual tramps, floating units who own no spiritual home, so there is nothing to endorse the attitude of the free-lance who seeks to carve out for himself a path of service independent of his brethren. In the case before us, the divine call is echoed in the appreciative fellowship of the saints in the church, who are eager to identify themselves with Barnabas and Paul. Let there be no misapprehension as to the essential nature of this link with the chosen ones. It was forged in the fires of prayer and fasting, and as they laid hands on them and sent them away, there was no idea of a partnership made fragile by distance. That it was not so is proved by the fact that when these same servants had prospered in their mission they returned again to Antioch, and when they were come and had gathered the church together they rehearsed all things that God had done with them (Acts 14. 27).

Before leaving Antioch we may permit ourselves a glance at another aspect of its fellowship, that is, its relationship with the neighbouring church at Jerusalem. It is clear from the circumstances of its origin that the assembly at Antioch was independent, yet the problem of the place of circumcision in the gospel of free grace gave rise to the situation depicted in Galatians 2. 11. While it is true that the matter was referred to the church leaders in Jerusalem, there is no idea of their legislating and imposing their decisions on the provincial assembly. The courteous and guarded terms of the letter suggest on the contrary that their moral influence was relied upon to guide the younger body in a path that would not be too burdensome. That it was received in this spirit may be inferred from the phrase in Acts 15. 31, 'they rejoiced for the consolation.' On this point Hort says: 'The authority of the apostles was moral rather than formal; a claim to deference rather than a right to be obeyed.'

The principles so delineated in the corporate life of the saints at Antioch are a pattern of a New Testament church, and we depart from their simplicity at our peril. Superficially, conditions have altered, and in the light of the epistolary writings of Paul more detail has been filled into the skeleton picture; nevertheless broad principles consistent with the whole tenor of the revealed will of God emerge for those who will to know His doctrine.

Enough has been said to emphasize the essential unity of fellowship. Language is ransacked to provide metaphors to illustrate this vital truth, prophesied by Caiaphas when he said Christ should gather in one the children of God (John 11. 52), and so deeply desired by our Lord in John 17, when He envisaged the standard of unity (v. 11), the achievement of unity (v. 21), and the result of unity (v. 23). We are sons of one family with the same Father, and hence are knit together in love. We are members of one body having the same Head, and hence are joined together. We are priests in one priesthood with the same High Priest, and hence are gathered together. We are stones in one temple, indwelt by the same Holy Spirit, and hence are framed together. 'There is one body and one Spirit, even as ye are called in one hope of your calling; one Lord, one faith, one baptism, one God and Father of all, who is above all, and through all, and in you all' (Eph. 4. 4-6). Each is the fellow of the other, a companion without whom the other is incomplete. This is beautifully underlined in the fact that the usual Greek word for fellowship is used outside the New Testament of the marriage relationship.

All this is of primary importance. The concept of fellowship always carries with it the idea of mutuality. There can be no one-sided fellowship; it pertains to both parties, to the one as truly as to the other. The Word of God strains at the fetters of language to present graphically the greatness of the truth. The crowning figure used in Ephesians 5 is pertinent and beautiful. It has been said that this very passage is enough to stamp the New Testament as an inspired book, because at the time Paul wrote there was not a woman or man who had ever dreamt of cherishing and nourishing as the proper attitude of husband to wife.

Such is the ideal church fellowship as presented in the Scripture, though Christendom furnishes a picture vastly different. True believers are found in various associations, and the enquiring soul is met with a babel of conflicting voices. Ecclesiastical Rome loudly asserts her sole supremacy and excommunicates all who reject her authority. On the other hand Protestantism has broken up into various denominations, each hedged around by man-made requirements. The pity of it is that many of these proclaim their loyalty to truth and bolster up their claims by reference to Scripture. In this, as in other connections, let us remind ourselves of the word from God: 'Let him that thinketh he standeth take heed lest he fall' (1 Cor. 10. 12).

Much has been written and spoken about the focal point of fellowship as seen in the Lord's Supper. 'The cup of blessing which we bless, is it not the communion of the blood of Christ? The bread which we break, is it not the communion of the body of Christ? For we being many are one bread, and one body; for we are all partakers of that one bread' (1 Cor. 10. 16-17). Linked with this is the ordinance of baptism, which expresses in an unmistakable way the association of the believer with his Lord in His death, burial and resurrection. The early church knew no other practice than that converts from heathen creeds should bear witness to their faith in Christ by observing this ordinance.

No greater mistake can be made, however, than to regard fellowship in these ordinances as something distinct from its true nature as outlined above. To recognize this fact would save us from many a misconception and malpractice as to the oft-repeated phrase—'receiving into fellowship.'

By this phrase we can only mean the outward acknowledgment of something which is spiritual and already existing between an individual and God. A 'letter of commendation' is not creative of this, but is merely an endorsement from those who have intimate

acquaintance of the person concerned. Probably the chief value
of such a document is the guidance it furnishes to those who are
stewards of the Lord's Table. They exercise a double function:
first, of welcoming the true child of God; but second, of seeing to
it that such a one is free from fundamental doctrinal error or moral
inconsistency. When anything else is lauded as a test of 'receiving,'
there lies the blight of sectarianism and ecclesiastical arrogance.
It is no exaggeration to say that loyal adherence to the simplicity
here portrayed is that which will save from degenerating into a
sect. The character of the feast determines the spirit in which it
must be kept, and the twin evils of unwarranted exclusion and
internal cliquism are to be scrupulously guarded against.

It is the firm belief of the writer that many of the troublesome
questions relevant to this topic would solve themselves if the
assembly concerned were in a healthy condition before God. To
adorn the doctrine of Christ, which includes His heart's desire
for the unity of those who profess His Name, is to hold by the
power of attraction. The thing called 'occasional fellowship' will
readily blossom into something richer and deeper where the tone
and atmosphere of the company are genuinely indicative of the
divine presence. When Solomon was engaged in building the
temple of the Lord, he took into association with him in this great
work, Hiram, King of Tyre, who was a Gentile but ever a lover
of David. He was enlisted to do the artistic work, providing
cedar trees from Lebanon from which was made ornament of
design and strength. A greater than Solomon has taken into
partnership in the upbuilding of His church those whose love has
been won. They cannot save, but just as the cedar's smell was
easily recognized, they may exude the fragrance of holy endeavour,
and, as the king of trees was cut down to be of use, so they may
know surrender and the spirit of sacrifice. In this way they will
attract to the Saviour. Further, it will be noised abroad that Christ
is in the house, and the local church will exhibit the features of a
home, as distinct from a stopping place for a passing visit.

This leads us to an examination of the realistic conditions
which obtain in the normal congregation, where there must
inevitably be the interplay of differing personalities, each emerging
with varied gift, training, and temperament. We have only to

think of those chosen by the Lord to be His disciples to learn that God is not a God of mass production or of drab uniformity. What astounding contrasts, how different they were from each other— Peter from John, Philip from Thomas, Matthew from Simon, no two of them alike. But Christ took them all and incorporated them into one holy fellowship, welded together in a common faith, in a common love, under a common leadership.

Again, Christ never interfered with their individuality. So to-day He takes these things that men bring Him and multiplies them. James and John were enriched with conspicuous gifts, and were raised to conspicuous positions but of some of the twelve we hardly hear again. Their service was a hidden work, un-applauded; they went on living righteous, holy lives in obscurity, answering to the divine will for them. But it is equally instructive to note that those of the twelve who were closest in intimacy with Christ were subsequently most prominent in service. This was no arbitrary choice.

So in the church of to-day. We are members of one another, 'fitly framed and knit together through that which every joint supplieth, according to the working in due measure of each several part, making the increase of the body unto the building up of itself in love' (Eph. 4. 16, R.V.). There is a richness in variety, the contri-butory elements yielding a product of singular strength. But the governing condition of all this is fellowship. The man in the street has oriented his mind in recent years to the idea of one-man leadership. Business combines, political trends, military strategy, all echo the same lesson. Wherever this spirit enters into the church, and one who loves pre-eminence lords it over God's heritage, the real spirit of fellowship is nullified and development in the highest sense ceases. Leadership is needed to-day more than ever, yet such leadership must be based upon the willing and loyal co-operation of all.

Fellowship, then, is a glorious privilege but also a challenging responsibility. Each member of the assembly has a part to play in the activities of the church, even though it may only be obedience to those who exercise the stewardship of rule. This last named grace of obedience may play a greater part in the harmony of the community than the exercise of a teaching ministry. Thus far it is to the glory of God. A sense of responsibility ought to permeate all fellowship. There should be no sleeping partners. To show passive unconcern is to ignore the claims of God, and yet is it not true that in every church there are the strenuous and the spectators, the labourers and the lookers-on? It is pertinent to remember that lukewarmness is nauseous to God.

Having received the weak according to the injunction of Romans 14, we are not without guidance as to how we should treat such in the everyday life of the assembly. The church is a nursery for young babes, and the greatness of Paul is seen equally in his wisdom as a father in exhortation and comfort, and in his gentleness as a nurse in cherishing. It is a matter of experience that some Christians will fall behind in their assimilation of doctrine, unable to pass from first principles. Some will find it difficult to withstand the wiles of Satan. Yet the Scripture teaches we are to bear the infirmities of the weak (Rom. 15. 1).

It is pitifully easy to be intolerant of another's infirmity, but nowhere in divine teaching is such an attitude condoned. After an eventful life not free from failure, David, in his hymn of testimony sang, 'Thy gentleness hath made me great' (2 Sam. 22. 36), and this has been echoed in the hearts of thousands since his day. Gentleness flows from long-suffering. This latter means having just cause for anger, yet not being angry, and is a state of the heart, whereas gentleness seems chiefly to be a fruit of the lips, ever checking the hasty word and substituting a soft one. No wonder it acts as one of the mightiest powers in the life of the Church.

Infirmity, of course, is not sin, though the two are often confused. If we are to be tolerant towards infirmity, we are likewise charged with maintaining the honour of God's house, and notice must be taken of any flagrant departure from righteousness. Fellowship is disrupted in such circumstances, and is not restored until the offence is brought to light and dealt with in a Scriptural manner. It is not a kindness to turn a blind eye to evil with a mistaken idea that unity is thereby preserved. Instead, irreparable harm may result if the conscience of the assembly be sinned against. The fellowship of the believers can easily be strained at such a crisis, particularly when natural ties of family or friendship are allowed to distort or destroy spiritual good sense in the matter of discipline.

The value of a united front among those who rule cannot be over-estimated.

Sometimes the smooth flow and usefulness of the life of the church are disturbed by friction and quarrels. Jealousy rears its ugly head, envy and malice echo in evil speaking, and grief and barrenness are the terrible results. To sow discord among brethren is to do the Devil's work. Paul wrote to Euodias and Syntyche at Philippi beseeching them to be in harmony, and in this connection he stated a general principle: 'Let your moderation be known to all men. The Lord is at hand' (ch. 4. 5). This word moderation has given the translators much trouble, a fact which is reflected in the variety of words used to express the original. Trench gives it 'yieldingness'; Alford translates 'reasonableness of dealing'; Way says, 'unselfishness as your distinguishing character'. A multitude of situations arise in church life which call aloud for this very virtue, which is verily twice blest. 'It blesseth him that gives and him that takes.' Moderation is that capacity of spirit which considers the rights of others, and while being conscious of one's own rights, waives them, thus rectifying the injustice of justice. We may not, like Shylock, take a rigid stand upon the bond, but hearken to the plea of Portia that 'earthly power doth then show likest God's when mercy seasons justice.' If we find it difficult, let us ever remember that God has not rewarded us according to our iniquities. As the heaven is high above the earth, so great is His mercy towards them that fear Him. The man of the world is careful to defend his dignity and his rights ; the Lord's man is careful to guard the honour of his Master of Whom it is written, 'even Christ pleased not Himself' (Rom. 15. 3).

The church is a school for character and the emergence of testing situations is a means of grace. It has always been a hard thing to recognize one's own limitations and not beat against them, and there is a glory attached to the man of the two talents and to the man of the one talent, which is absent from the man with five talents. It may be easy to go on when a man is always first in prominence, but in a church the majority must take second place, and do it graciously. Aaron, Barnabas, and Silas were all men who were overshadowed by a contemporary, yet each discharged a valuable work. The reward is to faithfulness and not

brilliance. The second place in the service of God is a greater
honour than the first in the service of the world, and the first place
by the Saviour's side in glory will be the portion of the second
place man who has been faithful down here.

But the life of the church must not be a pool whose
waters revolve in eddies of self-complacency or of tranquil, passive
unconcern. It is recorded in Mark 3. 14 that our Lord ordained
twelve for a twofold purpose. First, that they should be with
Him; but second, that He should send them forth. He admitted
them to a sacred fellowship and intimacy in order to equip them
to be His representatives. 'Christ has no body now on earth, but
ours are the eyes, the hands, the feet with which He is still to go
about doing good' (Teresa). The result of our fellowship is that
we are empowered to touch poor, leprous souls with healing power,
and to speak the word of life in living echoes of His tones. There is
a vital relationship between experiences of fellowship and service
which cannot be violated without incalculable loss. The church
has forfeited its throbbing power when it is content to luxuriate
in its privileges and position of favour, regardless of the implicates
of such fellowship in the face of the clamant needs of a bankrupt
civilization and a bruised and bleeding world at her gates. Communion which does not lead to service is mere selfishness, and service
which is not inspired by constant fellowship is nothing but the whirr
of religious machinery.

'Now unto Him that is able to guard you from stumbling, and
to set you before the presence of His glory without blemish in
exceeding joy, to the only God our Saviour, through Jesus Christ
our Lord, be glory, majesty, dominion and power, before all time,
and now, and for evermore. Amen' (Jude vv. 24, 25, R.V.).

CHAPTER IV

BAPTISM

H. LACEY

THE FIRST PRACTICE OF THE ORDINANCE

THE coming of Messiah had been long foretold. From the day of the Fall, the light of its hope increasingly illumined each succeeding phase of history, until in the days of Isaiah it became clear that He would be preceded by a forerunner so that the people might be prepared for His advent. In due course that forerunner appeared in John, the son of Zacharias and Elisabeth, who came preaching 'the baptism of repentance' (Mark 1. 4). Those awakened by his searching ministry were immersed by him in the river Jordan (Matt. 3. 6). In this way they gave public evidence of their repentance and of their expectation of the immediate appearing of the One Who was to lighten the Gentiles and be the glory of the people, Israel.

The forerunner thus prepared Messiah's way, and by his practice of baptism earned the title of 'John the Baptist.' The people, Herod, the disciples, and even Jesus Himself likewise spoke of him thus. All the Gospels describe his ministry, and the Acts mentions it six times. We learn that John's baptism was:

(a) National: it was to all the people of Israel (Acts 13. 24);

(b) Local: it took place at Bethabara (John 1. 28); Ænon (John 3. 23); and at Jordan (Matt. 3. 6).

(c) Temporary: eventually it was superseded (Acts 19. 3-4);

(d) Elementary: those developments indicated later were clearly presupposed (Acts 18. 25).

THE ORIGIN OF THE ORDINANCE

Prior to John's ministry the ordinance of the baptism of persons by immersion is not specifically mentioned, but after it, the ordinance is spoken of almost a hundred times and there is much development of doctrine. John's own words: 'He that sent me to baptize' (John

1. 33), seem to indicate a unique commission, and the words of the Lord's challenge to the Pharisees, 'whence was it? from heaven or of men?' (Matt. 21. 25), give a hint of direct revelation.[1]

The plural 'baptisms' (Heb. 6. 2, translated 'washings,' 9. 10), is used in a wider sense of all purifications by water made under the Jewish economy, such as of the high priest's flesh, the priest's hands and persons ceremonially unclean. Utensils also are said to have been baptized (Greek, Mark 7. 4). The Pharisees washed (Luke 11. 38, Greek, baptized) their hands on coming from the market-place before taking a meal, lest any defilement enter their bodies. Without such washing their hands were regarded as 'common' (Greek, Mark 7. 4).

The idea of sanctification was implicit in these washings and especially so in the ceremonial washing which took place when the priests of Israel were set apart for their ministry. By the application of public immersion to the people in a general way their setting apart to receive and serve the coming Messiah, Whose advent John heralded, seems to have been indicated.

Though the ideas inherent in the manifold washings and that implicit in the ordinance are naturally related, it is necessary to differentiate between the traditional customs and the divine appointment of John. It is necessary, also, to distinguish between the words used to designate each. The washings are called *baptismos*, whereas the ordinance of immersion is called *baptisma*. This usage is faithfully adhered to, and even Col. 2. 12 is no exception since the later texts give the word as *baptisma*.

THE WORD 'BAPTIZE' IN THE SEPTUAGINT

The Septuagint has *baptizo* twice: 'So Naaman . . . dipped himself . . . in Jordan' (2 Kings 5. 14); and, 'transgression overwhelms me' (Isa. 21. 4). In the first instance it renders *tabhal* which means 'to dip' (as Lev. 4. 6, 17; 9. 9; 1 Sam. 14. 27; Job 9.

[1] John the Baptist seems to indicate that his baptism was intended to be the means of introducing Christ to Israel as the true Messiah (John 1. 31). At this baptism the identity of Jesus was established by the opened heavens, the audible voice and the descent of the Spirit as a dove upon Him (John 1. 32-34). Christ stated that the true Shepherd entered by a limited and prescribed way—a door (John 10. 1-3 and 8). When, after the rise of the Gnostics, John the evangelist wrote to confirm believers in their faith that Jesus was indeed the Messiah and the Son of God he seems to allude to the baptism in evidence by saying 'This is He that came by water' (1 John 5. 6). He seems also to allude to the Cross by the further words, 'and blood.' No other claimant to Messiahship ever came by either means and certainly none by both.

31, etc.), and in the second, *ba'ath*, which conveys the idea of being overcome with fear, of being terrified. Belshazzar's iniquities returned to overwhelm him in fear and judgment. It is evident that the Septuagint translators understood *baptizo* to mean to dip, to plunge, or to overwhelm.

THE MINISTRY ACCOMPANYING JOHN'S BAPTISM

In the days of John the Baptist, as ever, the tendency to emphasise a ceremony at the expense of the real sanctification implied in it was all too evident. The adherents to the washings remained oblivious to their own unwashed moral state (Mark 7. 1-23). Therefore, though little is said about the ordinance itself, John's awakening ministry that accompanied it is described. He denounced the tendency to find rest of conscience in a religious extraction and excuse for moral lethargy in a privileged lineage. He called for fruit worthy of repentance. From the people he required that they should share raiment and food with the needy; upon the tax-gatherers he urged righteousness in business; and the soldiers he charged to refrain from violence, to use justly their power and to be content with their wages (Luke 3. 3-14).

THE BAPTISM OF JESUS BY JOHN

As others were baptized by John confessing their sins, Jesus was baptized praying. With characteristic grace and faithfulness He insisted on fulfilling all righteousness. The Father chose that hour as one of the occasions to proclaim His pleasure in His sinless, beloved Son.

THE PREPARATION OF MESSIAH'S WAY

Although confession of sins was made, the remission of sins was not present in John's ordinance. It was prospective and in anticipation of the One through Whom remission should come. In this way it played a vital part in the preparation for Messiah, as is seen in the fact that those who had been baptized of John justified God when they heard Jesus, but the Pharisees, having refused his baptism and the repentance and confession implicit in it, rejected the counsel of God manifest in Christ (Luke 7. 29-30).

THE BAPTISM OF THE DISCIPLES OF JESUS

John the evangelist, characteristically informing us of matters unmentioned elsewhere, records a part of the Baptist's ministry which scintillates with figures of Christ (John 3. 22-30 or to 36). In it he reveals another baptism by showing that the ministry of Christ and His forerunner overlapped. Before John was imprisoned, while he was baptizing in Ænon, Jesus came there also making and baptizing disciples.

The new implications, which now attached to the ordinance, made it as distinct from that of John as was the ministry of the Bridegroom from His mourning and fasting forerunner. The ordinance formerly anticipated Messiah's advent, but now it expressed its fulfilment and confessed the Nazarene to be the Messiah of Israel. To it the former gave place as naturally as spring does to summer, and as the forerunner himself did to the One he heralded.

John's baptism was practised for little more than months. Of longer duration was the practice of the baptism of the disciples of Jesus. However, this, too, was superseded by the baptism of Christian believers, which was authorized after the Cross and which continues throughout the present age. The words of Paul to the twelve men at Ephesus (Acts 19. 1-6) make a sharp distinction between John's baptism and its significance and the baptism of Christian believers and its implications. The men to whom he spoke had been immersed by John, yet they were baptized again in the name of the Lord Jesus.

THE PASSION—A BAPTISM

The Lord Jesus called His Passion a baptism (Luke 12. 50), and until it was fulfilled the Cross ever cast its shadow over His path. At the threshold of His ministry His announcement as 'the Lamb' anticipated this baptism; while at the first Passover He Himself referred to it cryptically (John 2. 19 and 3. 14). But after Peter's confession at Cæsarea Philippi, when His followers were assured of His Messiahship and convinced of His Deity, He spoke of it plainly. The metaphors: an hour, a cup, an exodus, and a baptism were used by Him. By 'a cup' he depicted the Father's will and His submission to it. 'An exodus' likened the Passion to a portal through which the Conqueror of sin, death, and Satan would pass to the throne of glory. But by 'a baptism' He impressed the dread nature of His immersion in shame, and agony, and death for us. And the words, 'how am I straitened (pained) until it be accomplished' disclosed the feelings which ever moved in the breast of the Lover of Men.

In the face of so costly an immersion for us, how simple to draw the inference as to the mode of baptism pressed on us by His love!

THE BAPTISM IN THE HOLY GHOST

As he baptized with water, John foretold the advent of a mightier Baptizer and His baptism in the Holy Ghost. Jesus was identified as the sole Administrator of this unique baptism by the descent of the Holy Spirit upon Him (John 1. 33). Simultaneously His Deity was also indicated (John 1. 34).

The expressions 'with (or in) water,' and, 'with (or in) the Holy Ghost' which John used (Matt. 3. 11-12) indicate the contrast between the elements by means of which these differing baptisms were realized.

This baptism was 'the promise of the Father' (Luke 24. 49; Acts 1. 4). It had been foretold before John (Isa. 44. 3; Ez. 36. 26-27; Joel 2. 28). Jesus spoke of it during His ministry (Luke 11. 13; John 14. 16-17, 26; 15. 26; 16. 7), and after His resurrection specified the time, 'not many days' (Acts 1. 5), when it should be fulfilled and the new garment of power should fall upon them from on high and the investiture of the Church be realized. This must be regarded as being as signal an event in this age as the descent of Jehovah on Sinai in a past age and comparable with the dwelling of the glory in Israel's Tabernacle in the Wilderness.

Although Jesus confirmed John's prophecy He was as silent about the words, 'and in fire,' as He had been about the day of vengeance when He read the scroll of Isaiah in the synagogue (Luke 4. 16-22). These expressions are synonymous designations of a day when He Who inaugurated this age in the baptism of the Spirit and by this means gathers the wheat into His garner will wind it up in that baptism which will consume the chaff in unquenchable fire (Matt. 3. 11-12).

THE FULFILMENT

Peter declared that the effusion of the Day of Pentecost was such as Joel predicted (Acts 2. 15-21). He also declared it to be the fulfilment of the promise of the Father which the ascended Jesus had poured forth (Acts 2. 32-33). At a later date, having witnessed the incorporation of the Gentiles, he described it as the fulfilment of John's prophecy (Acts 11. 15-18).

THE EXPLANATION (1 Cor. 12. 12-13)

Two distinct expositions have been given of the reference to baptism in the twelfth chapter of 1st Corinthians. On the one hand it has been taken to refer to the baptism in the Spirit which John predicted; and on the other as a reference to baptism in water. Water baptism, and water baptism only, seems hardly an adequate exposition here because:

(a) it has nothing in the passage to suggest it beside the word baptize which is used in both senses elsewhere;

(b) it leaves us with neither explanation of, nor doctrinal reference to the baptism of the Spirit, whereas the passage provides just that explanation of the baptism of the Spirit for which it is natural to look;

(c) so conspicuously predicted and singularly fulfilled an event requires explanation;

(d) it involves a totally different exposition of the words, 'in one Spirit', than those words can possibly suffer in the immediate context;

(e) it is out of keeping with the argument of the passage in which the Holy Spirit is so conspicuous.

Against the background of the idea of the many idols and consequently the many demon spirits associated with them with which the Corinthians had been associated hitherto, and of their returning influence that was having a disintegrating effect upon the church at Corinth, the apostle asserts the exclusive source of the Christian ministry and the oneness and the sameness of the Holy Spirit as the means of its inspiration, seemly conduct and becoming harmony. The Holy Spirit was the mind and the power for the operation of all gifts. The Holy Spirit was the means of the incorporation of the body of Christ. In one Spirit had they all been baptized into one body. The Holy Spirit was the fountain of living water of which all alike had been made to drink, first for their own satisfaction and then for the inspiration which would issue in the profit of others.

As the baptism of the passage is said to result in the formation of the one body, and as the human body is used as a type of the body of Christ, it is natural for us to recall the formation of the original human body. That body of dust became instinct with life by the inspiration of God. He breathed into his nostrils the breath of life. The spiritual counterpart of this seems to be indicated by the symbolic action of Christ when He breathed on those He had gathered and said, 'Receive ye the Holy Ghost' (John 20. 22). In this way He seemed symbolically to anticipate the reality of Pentecost and the inauguration of that body, which like the body of the babe is complete, and yet which like the body of the child, the youth or the man is ever growing of itself. Its members are not incorporated by an external process, but as the healthy, natural body once existing and living builds cell upon cell and lays fibre to fibre, so the body of Christ once for all incorporated by that once for all baptism of the Holy Spirit is instinct with the eternal life of Christ its Head and maketh therefore increase of itself (Eph. 4. 16).

THE BAPTISM OF CHRISTIAN BELIEVERS

The Commission

It was on the evening of the day of the resurrection that the baptism of Christian believers was first mentioned. Mark, Luke, and John provide us with accounts of the revelation of the Risen Lord to those who were gathered in the room. Each shows how that the Lord commissioned His people with a universal evangelism.

John's account shows the character of that service. Its discharge in the power of the Spirit would mean either remission or retention of sins.

Luke's account shows the manner of its execution amongst all the nations. It was to be by the preaching of repentance and remission of sins in His Name.

Mark's record shows the extent of this evangelism and the results of the hearers' attitude towards it. The disciples were to go into all the world and to preach the Gospel to the entire creation.

Disbelief would result in complete condemnation, whereas belief in the message and submission to baptism would mean salvation (Mark 16. 15-16).

On the very day He emerged from the tomb the Lord spoke of baptism, and on the eve of His ascension He talked of it again. Though it was from one of the mountains of Jerusalem that He ascended to the Throne, it was on one of the mountains of Galilee that He met the disciples for the only time by appointment, and authorized them to baptize into the name of the Father, and of the Son and of the Holy Ghost (Matt. 28. 16-20).

The note struck by the solitary grandeur of the detached and unnamed mountain suits the strain of Matthew's music of Christ. The One in Whom is vested all authority disdained Jerusalem or any named earthly centre as the place from which to direct His servants and expressly chose this remote place which symbolizes His exalted seat from which to direct His servants and to indicate the manner of their work for Him.

The introduction to the commission is a statement of the limitless authority of the Risen Lord in heaven and upon the earth. The conclusion is an assurance of His royal presence with His obedient servants throughout every kind of day up to the consummation of the age.

The commission itself has three clear features: first, they were to make disciples or learners of all the nations; second, they were to baptize into the Name of the Father, and of the Son and of the Holy Ghost; and third, these baptized believers were to be taught to observe all that Jesus had commanded. The Father had been made known in the earth by the incarnation of the Son, and by it, too, the Spirit had been manifested as never before. Those learners were to be baptized into public association with the Name of the Triune God Who had thus been manifested. Ever afterwards they would be taught increasingly the behaviour suitable to the honour of that indivisibly one Godhead which hath but one Name and yet hath in the Father and the Son and the Holy Spirit, three ever-blessed distinguishable and co-equal persons.

To this commission, whether in part or the whole, no temporariness pertains. The promise conditional upon its fulfilment holds to the end of the age. The responsibility to make disciples, to baptize them, and to teach them can know no more interruption than can the sovereignty of Christ or the availability of His presence. The baptism of Christian believers is, therefore, as necessary a part of Christian service to-day as is the preaching of the Gospel and the teaching of believers.

THE FORMULÆ

That the formulæ of Acts vary from that of Matthew (if indeed they are formulæ) should cause no difficulty. For to be baptized 'into the name of the Lord Jesus' (Acts 8. 16; 19. 5), 'in the name of the Lord' (Acts 10. 48, A.V.) or 'in the name of Jesus Christ' (Acts 10. 48, R.V.) involved an understanding confession of the co-equality and oneness of His Deity with that of the Father, or else it were idolatrous of the subjects and unfaithful of the apostles. The Name is one, though special emphasis on certain aspects of it might be necessary to meet deficiencies in different classes of hearers.

THE PRACTICE OF BAPTISM IN THE ACTS

The history of the Acts shows that the early believers faithfully discharged their Master's commission. They made disciples. They baptized them. And they taught them assiduously the ways of Christ. Baptism was preached by Peter on the day of Pentecost, and those who believed were baptized (Acts 2. 38-41). When the Samaritans believed Philip's preaching they, too, were baptized (ch. 8. 12). The seeker from Ethiopia, having found the Saviour desired immersion, and Philip was not slow to grant a request so evident of the health of the new-born soul (ch. 8. 36-38).

When Saul of Tarsus was saved, Ananias was sent with the instruction, 'arise, and be baptized, and wash away thy sins' (ch. 22. 16). Thus was he urged to act for himself and to be baptized in such a way as to repudiate the sins of his past life which had already been cleansed by Christ. As there was no lack of evidence of a genuine work of God, and as there was no Scriptural objection, Peter commanded those of the house of Cornelius to be baptized, and they were baptized at once (Acts 10. 47-48). With Lydia and those who believed, and with the jailor and his household who heard the Word and believed it, it was not otherwise (ch. 16. 15

and 31-34); and 'many of the Corinthians hearing, believed and were baptized' (ch. 18. 8).

The twelve men at Ephesus although immersed by John, were baptized again after receiving Christ (ch. 19. 1-6). It is noteworthy that a baptism Scriptural in its day, but which took place prior to faith in Christ did not obviate the necessity for Christian believers' baptism. How much less can any practice before conversion of any form of baptism with less Scriptural warrant obviate the necessity at any subsequent time?

So faithfully did these believers obey their Master, that irrespective of sex, race, or colour, every convert was baptized. The New Testament Epistles take this for granted and never envisage an unbaptized believer.

Some have thought that there was some deviation from this on the part of Paul (1 Cor. 1. 13-17). But this is not really so. John's baptism, which began and ended with himself, was administered only by him, but when Jesus came baptizing He did not Himself perform the manual act (John 4. 1-2). This His disciples did that the validity of baptism might not depend upon the worth of the baptizer, but upon the appointment of God. Paul simply followed his Master's example.

Baptism in the Epistles
Romans 6. 1-11

The hortatory portion of the epistle to the Romans opens with a reference to baptism. This paragraph is an answer to an anticipated objection. The preceding chapters show that the ungodly are justified by faith, and close with the deduction that, 'where sin abounded, grace did abound more exceedingly' (Rom. 5. 20, R.V.). The unsanctified reasoning of Jewish factiousness and of Gentile lawlessness argued that such a doctrine favours sin on this ground, namely, the more sin, the more grace. The argument that meets this uses the death of the believer in the death of Christ as a fulcrum with baptism as a lever to remove the objection and to leave the believer with no logical course open but to reckon himself to be dead to sin and alive to God.

The death of the believer in the death of Christ is as definitely taught in the New Testament as is the death of Christ for the

believer's sins. This is stated clearly elsewhere in passages which
do not treat of baptism (2 Cor. 5. 14; 1 Peter 2. 24). It is the background of this passage in which reference to death in different
ways is made no less than fourteen times. However, emphasis is
laid not so much on the doctrine itself, which though recalled to
mind is largely taken for granted, but upon the expression of it in
the ordinance.

The argument proceeds to its climax in five stages:

(a) Being baptized into Christ involves being baptized into His
death. Therefore by means of baptism we are buried into
death. Consequently, as to sin, the baptized believer is in
a sphere of death (vv. 2-4).

(b) That this is designed, not merely that we should be dead,
but that a walk—a practical experience—beyond death, in
newness of life might result (v. 4).

(c) That this identification with Christ in death is as vital as
that of a graft in a tree. To be grown together (planted
together, A.V.) in the likeness of His death anticipates the
likeness of His resurrection (v. 5).

(d) That the nature of that death is crucifixion which is a legal
sentence that follows trial and condemnation. Our old man
has been dealt with in this way. Like Nebuchadnezzar,
though his existence was not terminated, his power was
completely broken, so the bondage to the old master is
broken, and no obligation to him remains (vv. 6-7).

(e) Yet is the believer not in a state dominated by death. Christ's
death led to resurrection, and that to a life lived to God, and
in that the believer partakes of this also, the only logical
issue of the position is that he reckons himself dead to sin on
the one hand, but living to God in Christ Jesus on the other
(vv. 8-11).

Baptism by immersion is the fit symbol in which all this is
expressed in an appropriate way.

In Paul's day the faith that accepted Christ showed its acceptance
in baptism as naturally as the faith of Noah in a coming flood built
an ark because of it (Heb. 11. 7). The water without the faith is
nothing. The faith without the water was never contemplated

in those days. That faith saw the man, not merely his sins, on the cross and in the tomb, and expressed itself in burial in the waters of baptism. It is evident therefore that in his baptism the believer virtually says: 'I make Christ's death to sin my death to sin.' Baptism is the symbolic expression of the response of the heart to the teaching that Christ's death is the believer's also.

Furthermore, that union with Christ which is contracted by faith and ratified in baptism involves more. Implicit in the ordinance is not only death and burial, but resurrection. For emersion appropriately illustrates the rising to walk in a new sphere of life by means of new principles.

Both aspects of truth are illustrated in the reference to the baptism of the fathers in the cloud and in the sea (1 Cor. 10. 1-11). As the sea closed behind them the domination of Pharaoh was effectively ended, and as the wilderness opened before them they embarked upon a new life with God under the guidance of the cloud and the new leadership of Moses.

Their inconsistency with their baptism is shown in the words which contain an undertone of horror and disgust which is the more evident when we see that the force of the words 'baptized unto Moses' really is 'they baptized themselves unto Moses,' and when we contrast them with the observation, 'Howbeit with most of them God was not well pleased: for they were overthrown in the wilderness' (v. 5, R.V.). Having pledged themselves to a new leadership in a new path they failed to go through with it. It is plainly said that these things are written for our admonition (v. 11).

WATER BAPTISM OR SPIRITUAL BAPTISM

There has been some material difference of judgment on the nature of baptism to which reference is made in Romans, Galatians, Ephesians, and Colossians. Some maintain a spiritual baptism to the exclusion of water baptism. Others assert water baptism to the exclusion of a spiritual sense. We shall be as ill-advised as the two knights in the following legend if we assert either negative. These two were approaching on either side of a hill a shield suspended at its summit. One asserted that the shield was made of gold and the other that it was of silver. A duel followed and unhorsed, injured, and prone after their controversy and conflict, looking up at that shield, each from the side opposite to his first approach, discovered the measure of his error and the degree of his accuracy, for the one side was silver and the other gold. The true gold of the antecedent spiritual fact of the death of the believer in the death of Christ, *and* also the counterpart silver of the mirror of this truth in a physical immersion in water constitute the matter of these passages.

If we assert a water baptism to the exclusion of a spiritual one, we shall err as much as if we assert a spiritual one to the exclusion of a water baptism, and, sidetracked from the balanced practical teaching involved in the inclusion of both, the worse of our folly, we may repent at length as did the knights of old.

'BAPTIZED FOR THE DEAD' (I Cor. 15. 29)

The reference to baptism in this verse is one of a series of inferences of a reduction to absurdity argument with which Paul met the propositions of error. Some among the Corinthians said that there is no resurrection. Contending for the resurrection the apostle argues: If there be no resurrection of the dead, then the logical inferences are:

(*a*) neither hath Christ been raised (v. 13);
(*b*) our preaching is vain (v. 14);
(*c*) your faith is vain (v. 14);
(*d*) we are found false witnesses (v. 15);
(*e*) ye are yet in your sins (v. 17);
(*f*) they . . . which are fallen asleep . . . are perished (v. 18);
(*g*) we are . . . most pitiable (v. 19).

After the parenthesis of verses 20 to 28 the verse in which we are specially interested resumes the argument. When it is punctuated as follows its sense is immediately evident: 'Else what shall they do that are baptized? It is for the dead, if the dead rise not at all. Why, then, are they baptized for them?' (v. 29). This provides the stepping stone to the climax of the argument: 'If the dead are not raised, let us eat and drink for tomorrow we die' (v. 32).

Thus he shows that the denial of resurrection blasphemes Christ, impugns apostles, robs believers, reduces baptism to a farce, since it is merely for the dead if there be no resurrection, and leaves us with only one logical course open—that of fatalistic Epicureanism.[1]

[1] The philosophy of Epicurus that the highest good was pleasure.

It is probable that failure to appreciate the nature of this argument in ancient days led to a custom of baptism by proxy which was unknown in apostolic times. The same failure in more recent times has led to the interpretation of the passage in the light of this unwarranted custom, instead of in the light of the general argument of the chapter.[1]

GALATIANS 3. 27

The fine figure of one who dons a beautiful robe describes the conception of baptism in this verse.

The servile minds of the Judaizers had not accepted the emancipation from the Law which had been effected by Messiah's becoming a curse upon a cross, and therefore they could not appreciate the Christian dispensation as the dispensation of the Spirit, neither could they rise to the liberty and dignity of sonship.

The apostle reduced their propositions to absurdity and exposed the blasphemy inferred in them (ch. 2. 17 and 21; 3. 10-11). He appealed to faith in Christ and baptism unto Him to help the Galatian believers to the enjoyment of true experience in Christ.

Law-keeping and observance of days were the sackcloth of slavery and circumcision was its brand mark. In their coming to Christ this had been exchanged for the fine silk of His beauty. Christ was to them the 'man's robe' (the *toga virilis* assumed by every Roman on reaching manhood). One man in Christ had they become. Religious, national, and social distinctions disappeared. As the result they were sons, true descendants of Abraham, not slaves.

Incorporation by baptism in the Holy Spirit into the body of Christ and the symbol of this in immersion in water should have made them conscious of their new robe, and should have forbidden turning back from the excellency and dignity of sonship to the rags of their erstwhile bondage to the Law.

EPHESIANS 4. 5

Embedded in the rich strata of the epistle to the Ephesians is the little gem of the barest mention of our subject. This lies at the beginning of the hortatory portion between the mention of a unity

[1] See Note 4, p. 212.

to be preserved and that of a unity to be attained. Having shown the nature of the believer's calling the writer encourages his readers to walk worthily of it by giving diligence to keep the unity of the Spirit by means of the manifestation of the graces of lowliness, meekness, longsuffering, and forbearance. Baptism is mentioned as one of the seven features which constitute this existing unity.

As there is one body of which all alike are members, as there is one Spirit by which all in common are sealed, as one hope gleams before all similarly, as one Lord has, in the same way, right of control over all, as only one body of truth exists for the belief and guidance of all alike, and, as there is one God to whom the worship of all ascends, so is there but one baptism to which all submit. There is not a Jewish baptism and a Gentile one. Nor are there variations of the ordinance to suit the tastes of these or any other classes. There is one baptism. There is not a baptism of pouring, a baptism of sprinkling and a baptism of immersion. Nor can there be a dedicatory rite administered to the as yet unconverted in prospect of their conversion and an illustrative ordinance which mirrors a salvation already real. There is one baptism, the baptism of Christian believers, as much in common to all genuine believers as that there is 'one Father of all, who is over all, and through all, and in all' (ch. 4. 6).

Each of these seven facts, and the one baptism amongst them, is part of a developing argument that leads on to the mention of a unity to be attained upon the basis of the recognition of this existing unity.

COLOSSIANS 2. 12

The dignity and sufficiency of Christ is stated in this epistle to show that the believer is complete in Him (ch. 2. 10). An assertion of a mystical Christian circumcision, together with reference to the believer's death and resurrection which is mirrored in his baptism show that he is cut off from all sources of proffered aid to holy living or to his approach to God (ch. 2. 12-3. 4).

In a kingdom where no rival may reign, under the sway of the Maker of angels, Who made His very Cross a triumphal car to bear His manhood to the throne, and in Whom the fulness of the Godhead dwells in bodily form, the soul has no need of angel mediatorship, requires no ordinances for spiritual advancement and can dispense with asceticism as a means of combating the tendencies of the lower nature.

By that mystical circumcision the whole man has been cut off, and by a divine operation he has been introduced into a sphere where Christ is all in all (ch. 3. 11).

As David used Goliath's sword to sever the head of the would-be tyrant, Paul uses the ordinance of baptism to make an end of all the ordinances which endeavour to enslave the redeemed man to anything less than Christ.

Their baptism was a copy of their deed of freedom. Why, then, should they allow human hands to bind on the shackles of profitless ordinances and fruitless prohibitions? (ch. 2. 20-23).

Their emergence from the baptismal waters was intended also to direct their minds to things far above ritualism and sanctimoniousness to where Christ is enthroned (ch. 3. 1-2). And when Christ is revealed, the true value of that hidden life, bereft of ordinances, will be properly seen and appreciated (ch. 3. 3-4).

THE FIRST EPISTLE OF PETER

When Peter mentioned baptism he associated it with salvation (ch. 3. 21). The Lord Himself did so in the words, 'He that believeth and is baptized shall be saved' (Mark 16. 16), which appear in Mark only. Peter's close association with Mark makes this interesting. At Pentecost Peter connected baptism with salvation by calling for repentance and baptism and saying, 'Save yourselves from this crooked generation' (Acts 2. 38-40).

When he writes this epistle he writes of salvation ready to be revealed unto which believers are kept by faith (ch. 1. 5), of salvation which his readers were receiving as the outcome of their faith (ch. 1. 9), of salvation unto which the born-again soul grows by the food of the Scriptures (ch. 2. 2, R.V.), and, finally he connects baptism with salvation and illustrates the sense he implies by using the Flood as a type (ch. 3. 21).

The passage repudiates the idea that baptism in any way contributes to salvation by way of cleansing (ch. 3. 21), but it shows that it does so by way of becoming the criterion of all subsequent conduct in a corrupt world.

From a manner of life as profitless as the slavery of Israel in Egypt the sacrifice of Christ had delivered them as the Passover had their fathers (ch. 1. 18-19). From an aimless existence those hitherto wandering sheep had returned to the Shepherd, and from the sins of that existence the sufferings of Christ had emancipated them, so that as the Bishop of souls He might superintend their lives that the purposed righteousness should be attained (ch. 2. 24-25). Now, having been introduced to God, with their consciences made good and seeking after Him, they were provided with a test of action, baptism, which Peter calls the answer (A.V.), or interrogation (R.V.), or demand of a good conscience.

As the waters of the Flood separated Noah from the generation of the ungodly, its associations and its doom, so the antitype (like figure (A.V.), true likeness (R.V.), antitype (Greek), the waters of baptism become to the believer an act of severance from a manner of life, vain, aimless, and sinful.

This consciousness of the nature of baptism is understood to be normally ever present to a good conscience and contributes to an experience of present salvation from the pollutions of the world by sharply dividing between the kind of things that belong to the old world of unregenerate experience on the past and death side of the ordinance and the kind of things that belong to an experience of the will of God and of communion with Him on the resurrection side of the ordinance.

The two and a half tribes of Israel who crossed Jordan leaving a witness of death to the old paths in its waters and one of resurrection on the Canaan bank, but who recrossed those waters and lived in a sphere which negatived the meaning of both, provide an illustration of a kind of experience which a proper understanding of baptism and right use of it by the conscience forbids.

6

CHAPTER V

THE LORD'S SUPPER

ANDREW BORLAND

THE Lord's Supper is a subject of perennial interest and of tremendous importance. As with all other matters that concern Christian belief and behaviour it must be held in proper balance; yet its frequent observance forces a recognition of its significance in the practice of the Christian Faith. To some students the seeming paucity of reference to the ordinance in the New Testament Scriptures relegates it to a place of secondary consideration. True it is that no hint of its observance is clearly given in most of the epistles, but the obvious reason for that is probably that it was so universally observed in the churches that there was little necessity to mention it specifically. Where it is mentioned, as in 1 Corinthians, the subject is introduced to teach important moral lessons which were being forgotten in the confused thinking and unseemly actions of the Christians in Corinth. The evils attendant upon the development of human tradition had not yet manifested themselves, so that occasion did not offer for repeated written ministry of a corrective nature on the subject.

But are the references so infrequent as to deny it the careful investigation of Christians exercised about knowing what the mind of the Lord is? Quite extensive sections of the New Testament are devoted to the subject directly or indirectly, and two passages are of prime moment in the application of the doctrines associated with its observance, namely, 1 Cor. 10 and 1 Cor. 11. Besides these two sections, it is definitely mentioned in the three synoptic Gospels, where its inauguration is recorded (Matt. 26. 26-30; Mark 14. 22-26; Luke 22. 14-20); also it is mentioned in Acts 2. 42, 46; 20. 7; in which passages it is learned that the churches in apostolic days kept the remembrance in accordance with the Lord's instructions. Some students of the subject would add to these the long section in John's Gospel which records the discourse on the Bread of Life (ch. 6. 29-63), a passage which commands the attention of all who desire to understand the secret of the growth of the spiritual life the Christian possesses. Add to these the discourse on the True Vine, recorded in the same Gospel, and delivered on the night when the Lord instituted the Supper for His remembrance (ch. 15. 1-11); for who can doubt that there still lingered with the disciples the recollection of the recent symbolical action of their Master as they surrounded the Paschal Table in the upper room? Moreover, one of the most beautiful post-resurrection incidents reaches its touching climax when the unrecognized Lord reveals Himself at the supper table in the home in Emmaus, when as He sat at meat . . . He took bread, and blessed it, and brake and gave to them. 'And their eyes were opened, and they knew Him' (Luke 24. 30-31). Delightful episode, with so many heart-moving lessons to those who love to sit round the table with the Heavenly Host, as week by week He communes with them and makes Himself known while they 'break bread.'

This breaking bread has formed part of the Christian witness during all the years of Church history. Almost every section of the Christian community practises the symbolic act in some form or other. In sub-apostolic, non-canonical literature there are references to its observance from the earliest years of the second century, and we may read in the annals of believers in all parts of the world with what joy devoted disciples have met together, oftentimes in most distressing circumstances, to carry out their Lord's request. Engraved on the rock-faces in the Catacombs of Rome are unmistakable evidences that there, during the early centuries of the Christian era, hidden from the prying eyes of their calumniators, Christians met to keep the ordinance. Amidst the ruins of the buildings of the 'vanished church of North Africa' can be found proofs that believers in that once most fruitful field for the Gospel, carried out both the ordinances of baptism by immersion and of 'breaking bread' in remembrance of their Lord. And who has not read, with a lump in the throat and a tear in the eye, of the Scottish Covenanters, meeting by their hundreds in places of appointment remote from the haunts of men, that, accompanied by the curlew's cries, they might sing their Redeemer's praises and keep their sacrament with Him? With pomp and pageantry the Lord's Supper has been celebrated for centuries in magnificent cathedral and awe-inspiring abbey; with simple severity the same Supper has been solemnized in churches whose services are modelled after the doctrines of the Reformation, while in upper rooms, in log-cabins, and primitive native buildings, with still less formality and ritual, unpretentious believers have met to obey their Lord's behest. Yet with such diversity, there is an observable fundamental similarity—bread and wine as symbols of the Lord's body given, and the Lord's blood shed.

Notwithstanding the solemnity of the facts—the Upper Room discourses, Gethsemane and Golgotha—with which the Lord's Supper is historically associated, no subject in the doctrine and practice of the Christian Church has been more fruitful of distressing controversy. Mainly the controversialists may be divided into two sections. The sacramentarians depend much upon the elaboration of a ritual to produce an impression on the senses. Usually—though not always, as, for example, in Presbyterian communions—the ceremony is of an ornate character, the grandeur of which robs the observance of its intrinsic signification. On the other hand commemorationists favour a simple service devoid of any sensuous appeal—a plain memorial gathering whose impressiveness is derived from the spiritual atmosphere provoked by the conscious nearness of the spiritual world.

Many Christian gatherings have gone back to the original sources of instruction, and, abandoning the traditions of men— for tradition has wrought irreparable havoc in the ranks of the Christian community—have attempted to carry out what is conceived to be the mind of the Lord.

One of the outstanding features of such companies of believers is that they celebrate the Lord's Supper every seven days on the first day of the week. For such procedure they have apostolic precedent, for that is the evident inference from the statement in Acts 20. 7: 'Upon the first day of the week . . . the disciples came together to break bread.' Although several illustrious Christian leaders were present in the company, and although amongst them was the Apostle Paul himself, yet the Christians did not assemble to be regaled by a magnificent display of Christian oratory; they came purposively to do what the first disciples in Jerusalem had done—to break bread.

At the beginning of the nineteenth century the situation was as follows. In Roman Catholic circles the Lord's Supper had developed into the highly elaborate rite of an idolatrous Mass. In a section of the Church of England, the Episcopalian celebration continued, despite the evangelical emphasis of the Book of Common Prayer, to follow closely the example of Rome, and consequently there had been a constant tendency for those who love the appeal of the sensuous, the appeal of the æsthetic, to hark back to Rome and to copy its unscriptural ways. In Presbyterian circles, the celebration of the Lord's Supper had become the quarterly or half-yearly sacrament, celebrated by all who are on the church roll, having, in many cases, little regard to their public confession of the Christian Faith. Amongst the Quakers the attitude adopted was that of complete disregard, the contention being that the observance of the Lord's Supper was unnecessary as an aid to true religion which is of the spirit. Ceremonies, they contend, like the scaffolding of an edifice, necessary at the commencement, can be dispensed with, for spiritual experience is above ritual observance. Thus, obviously moved by the Spirit of God, about 1830 a number of spiritually-minded Christians, after much concern stimulated by prayerful study of the relevant passages of the New Testament, left their ecclesiastical associations, and almost spontaneously, in various parts of the British Isles, and in remote parts of the world, the movement 'out' grew, until to-day, through an ever-increasing missionary enterprise there are numerous such gatherings in every continent, and on many of the islands of the Seven Seas.

One of the distinguishing features of these gatherings is the fact that they dispense with unnecessary ceremonial. The communion table is not railed off, nor elaborated to give it the semblance of an altar. No specially ordained minister is necessary before the elements can be dispensed. No president is acknowledged to conduct the service—the meeting, like that described in 1 Corinthians 14, is open when such as are exercised may have a psalm, a doctrine, etc. Nor are there any fixed rules of procedure such as are recognized in ecclesiastical circles, the only rule being that in the actual observance of the Lord's Supper, the sequence recorded in the Gospels and in 1 Corinthians 11 is followed.

The foregoing, which is more historical than doctrinal, may

have provoked the question: "But why do Christians deem it necessary to celebrate the Lord's Supper and meet to break bread?"

First, we follow divine instructions. On the night when He was betrayed, when He had met with His disciples, the appointed hour having come, and when, in the knowledge that He 'should depart out of this world unto the Father,' He had washed the disciples' feet, 'the Saviour of the world took bread,' and Himself instituted the Supper by which He desired His followers to remember Him. How beautifully the scene has been depicted in the thirty-fifth paraphrase appearing in the appendix of Bibles used in Scotland!

'Twas on that night when doomed to know
The eager rage of every foe;
That night in which He was betrayed,
The Saviour of the world took bread.

And after thanks and glory given
To Him who rules in earth and heaven,
That symbol of His flesh He broke,
And thus to all His followers spoke:

'My broken body thus I give,
For you, for all, take, eat and live;
And oft the sacred rite renew,
Which brings My wondrous love to view.'

Then in His hands the cup He raised,
And God anew He thanked and praised,
While kindness in His bosom glow'd,
And from His lips salvation flow'd.

'My blood I thus pour forth,' He cries,
'To cleanse the soul in sin that lies;
In this the covenant is sealed,
And Heaven's eternal love reveal'd.

With love to man this cup is fraught;
Let all partake the sacred draught;
Through latest ages let it pour
In mem'ry of My dying hour.'

We break bread because we love the Lord who requested us to do so, lest we should forget the meaning of His sacrifice.

Second, we follow the apostolic practice, the record of which has been preserved for us. Of the converts on and after the day of Pentecost, we read: 'They continued stedfastly in the apostles' teaching and fellowship, in the breaking of bread and the prayers' (Acts 2. 42, R.V.). That verse describes the fourfold purpose for which those early Christians assembled.

(a) They met to hear instruction from the apostles themselves. That instruction at first would, in all probability, take the form of narrating the stories of incidents in the life of our Lord, and of rehearsing discourses He had given. Obviously the events and words associated with the Upper Room would form an integral part of that 'doctrine.'

(b) They met to enjoy spiritual and material fellowship—an expression of a sense of their oneness in Christ, as they shared their experiences and their goods (when necessary).

(c) They met to 'break bread' and (d) to pray. No explanation is given of the term 'breaking of bread,' for inferentially the expression had, by the time when Luke wrote his account, become a technical phrase for the Lord's Supper, the name being derived from the first act in the celebrations.

We break bread, then, because it has been a feature of Christian practice to do so since the very beginnings of the Church era.

A supplementary question to the one we have been answering arises, namely, 'Why do we break bread every Lord's Day?' Again for answer we may call to witness apostolic and sub-apostolic testimony.

(a) Evidently at first every meal was a Eucharistic meal—a celebration of the Lord's Supper. In Acts 2. 46, it is recorded of the early Christians in Jerusalem that they, continuing daily . . . in the temple, and breaking bread at home (not 'from house to house') did eat their food with gladness and singleness of heart. 'The phrase 'at home' is to be understood as referring . . . to the united gatherings of the Christians held in each other's houses, or, perhaps, owing to the increase in the number of converts, in several houses at once.'[1]

(b) It formed an integral part of the early Church Agapé, or love-feast. References to these are to be found in Jude's Epistle, 'these are spots in your feasts of charity' (v. 12), and in 1 Corinthians 11, where the Lord's Supper is closely linked with such gatherings,

[1] Simpson, *The Communion of The Lord's Supper*, p. 32

and where the apostle takes opportunity to condemn the excesses to which some of those present permitted themselves to succumb. Christians evidently met to partake of a common meal. Rich and poor sat down together, master and slave ate together, but at Corinth the original idea had been forgotten, and a meal that was meant to encourage fellowship developed into an occasion for gross intemperance. Such was the condition of the participants that they did not really eat the Lord's Supper (v. 20), and did not discern the Lord's body (v. 29). They were eating and drinking unworthily, thus bringing divine judgment upon themselves. It would appear that, to avoid such unseemly behaviour, the celebration of the Lord's Supper was at an early date separated from the love-feast.

(c) As already mentioned, from Acts 20. 7 we gather that it was the custom of the Christians to meet on the first day of the week to break bread, and, as the apostle considered the celebration of such importance that he delayed his hurried return to Jerusalem for seven days, we may conclude that already the meeting on Lord's Day was acknowledged as the principal assemblage of the week. It may be inferred that instruction about the Lord's Supper was included in the regular teaching of the Apostle Paul, at Troas, and 'as in all the churches of the saints' (1 Cor. 14. 33).

(d) In the Didaché, described as *The Teaching of the Twelve Apostles* (written about 100 A.D.), the following reference, among others, is found: 'on the day of the Lord, come together and break bread and give thanks, having first confessed your transgressions.' That accords with what is found later, written by Justin: 'On the day which is called Sunday, there is an assembly in the same place of all who live in cities, or in country districts, and the records of the apostles or the writings of the prophets are read. . . . Then we all together rise and offer up our prayers, and . . . when we have concluded our prayer, bread is brought and wine and water, and the president . . . offers up prayers and thanksgivings with all his strength, and the people give their assent by saying Amen, and there is a distribution and a partaking by every one of the Eucharistic elements . . . Sunday is the day on which we all hold our common assembly . . . because Jesus Christ, our Saviour, on the same day rose from the dead.'

The latter passage is of great importance, not only because it is confirmatory of our contention that the Lord's Supper was celebrated weekly by second century Christians following apostolic precedent, but also because it intimates the beginnings of departure from simple New Testament teaching by the introduction of the president who soon developed into the official representative of the assembly, without whose presence the Supper could not be celebrated. That custom led to the recognition of ordained clergy who have arrogated to themselves the sole right to dispense the elements. Dr. Moule, an Episcopalian, describes its proper celebration as, 'through ordered human ministration,' while Professor Moffatt, writing on *The Presbyterian Churches* (p. 116), declares that 'any layman who is specially endowed with the gift, may on occasion teach and preach, yet the regular ministry of the Word and of the Sacraments is reserved by the Church for its ordained presbyters'; and the Confession of Faith asserts that neither Baptism nor the Lord's Supper 'may be dispensed by any but by a minister of the Word lawfully ordained.' In such ways a clerical class grew up, based on sub-apostolic practice, but without justification from the authoritative New Testament writings. The ordained cleric cannot but oppose a return to primitive methods.

From such early divergence, gradually and insidiously, further departure from the original intentions appeared, until in 831 Radbertus, a cleric in Picardy, wrote a book in which he affirmed that, 'at the instant of consecration, the elements are changed into that body which was born of the virgin: the outward appearance only remains as before.' Thus the Roman Church corrupted the commemorative aspect of the Lord's Supper into the celebration of the Mass. After consecration the Host, or Victim (i.e., the wafer) and the wine are elevated so that communicants can adore Christ as being actually present. The Mass is called the 'sacrifice of the Mass,' in the belief that in it 'there is offered to God a true, proper, and propitiatory sacrifice for the living *and the dead*.' Nothing could be further from the teaching of the New Testament. It strikes a blow at the sufficiency of the death of our Lord.

The Reformation in the sixteenth century was a vigorous protest against the palpable errors of Rome, but, while it destroyed much and recovered much, it did not break completely free from the ecclesiastical procedure which separated the congregations into clergy and laity. The quotations above from Moule and Moffatt are evidence thereof.

In 1825, J. G. Bellett, who had met Anthony Norris Groves in Dublin, wrote these memorable words of his friend: 'It appeared to him from Scripture that believers, meeting together as disciples of Christ, were free to break bread as their Lord had admonished them, and that in so far as the practice of the apostles could be a guide, every Lord's Day should be set apart for thus remembering the Lord's death and obeying His parting command.' To those who are accustomed now to meet in that simple, unpretentious way, such a discovery means nothing, but to men who were wedded to Church systems it was momentous, captivating.

This reversion to the Scriptures has had repercussions in the furthest corners of the world. Gatherings for the breaking of bread are now an integral part of that witness which derives its virility from its simplicity. The Scriptures are recognized as sufficient to guide and instruct in all doctrine and practice. It is accepted that it is the prerogative of the Holy Spirit to call a man to the service of Christ without ecclesiastical ordination, and, consequently, the Lord's Supper came to be celebrated without the presence of some clerical dignitary. The oneness of the Body of Christ (i.e., the Church) is recognized, irrespective of the denominational names by which believers may be designated, and opportunity to display that oneness is given in the weekly gathering to break bread.

This breaking of bread is, then, an act which has divine authentication, can be traced to an historical inauguration, and has been proved to have apostolic corroboration. It is an act of *communal commemoration*. Ringing down through the intervening centuries there come to us moving words from the Saviour's lips, uttered in the Upper Room: 'This do in remembrance of Me' (Luke 22. 19). Who would not put that act of remembrance first before every other consideration, leaving the service where man's voice is heard to express love and devotion to One who died for us and rose again? Sweet are those seasons when, musing upon Himself, we realize how near He is, in fulfilment of His own blessed promise, 'where two or three are gathered together in My Name, there am

I in the midst of them' (Matt. 18. 20). No matter how grand is the function, honoured by dignitaries and officials, performed with splendour and awe-inspiring ceremony, if He is not present there is no real remembrance. Yet, despite the absence of such human trappings if the hearts of the believers are set upon Himself, if their love is sincere, and their devotion void of pretence, He will not deny to them a most hallowed realization of His nearness, not in the elements, but by spiritual apprehension.

Moreover, it is an act of *triumphant celebration*. The keeping of the Lord's Supper has been made possible, not only because our Lord died for us, but also because He brought life and incorruptibility to light through the Gospel. It is not a memorial to the dead; such an act would put Him in the same category as the heroes and martyrs of the past. But, no! He lives in glorious triumph. It is that fact that gives significance to His death. It was that fact that thrilled Cleopas and the other disciple as, with the alacrity of an overwhelming discovery, they hastened back from Emmaus to Jerusalem to inform the disciples that they had seen the risen Lord. It is because He is such a One, alive, omnipresent, everliving, that He can now in spirit draw near, go with us 'by the way' as we remember Him, and make 'Himself known in the breaking of bread' (Luke 24. 35). The Supper is His. He invites. He acts as Host. We are His honoured guests as by faith we meet with Him at His trysting-place. How true are the words of Bonar's hymn:

> Here, O my Lord! I see Thee face to face;
> Here would I touch and handle things unseen;
> Here grasp with firmer hand th' eternal grace,
> And all my weariness upon Thee lean!

Further, it is an act of *individual participation*. The apostolic description of the action is expressed in these words, 'The bread which we break' (1 Cor. 10. 16). That is an individual act. Four imperatives associated with the Supper impress that fact upon us: Take, eat, drink, do. 'Take', that means individual appropriation; 'eat', that suggests individual participation; 'drink', that implies symbolical individual assimilation; 'this do', conveys the idea of individual activity in a community of believers. The breaking of the bread does not have reference to the action of any one individual at the table. That breaking has no symbolic significance. 'To make any particular person, or an act not prescribed in Scripture essential to the right observance of the ordinance, is to move on the way that lies through ritualism to clerisy and priestcraft.'[1]

As we break the bread, that is, as we each individually take our share of the loaf, there is symbolized, among other facts, these two, first, that no one has spiritual life who has not received Christ by faith into the heart (John 1. 12), and, second, that that life is sustained only as by faith we each feed upon the Living Bread, the glorified Lord Himself.

This act, too, is one of *personal identification*. The participant is said to be a partaker of the Lord's table (1 Cor. 10. 21). Although the expression 'the Lord's table' has a connotation wider in application than the expression 'the Lord's Supper,' it is closely related thereto in meaning and intention. It stands for the idea of fellowship in all the provision which the Lord has made for His people, and part of that provision is symbolized in the acts at the breaking-of-bread gathering. In participating in the Lord's Supper the participant acknowledges in the presence of others who are sharing with him in the experience that he is identifying himself with the Lord who is Host at the table, and in so doing declares that all his spiritual strength is derived from fellowship with that risen Lord. The worldling has his own sphere of fellowship. He partakes with those like-minded at the provision spread on another table —the table provided by the god of this age, a provision as real as was that associated in ancient Corinth with the table of demons. Between the two tables there can be no compromise—no yoking of believer with unbeliever, no fellowship between righteousness and unrighteousness, no communion between light and darkness, no concord between Christ and Belial. The ethical significance is obvious. The person who partakes of the Lord's Supper is expected to sit continually at the Lord's table, associating himself with all that the divine Provider stands for in righteousness, hatred of sin, separation from evil, and devotedness to God. Viewed in that light, it becomes impossible not to think of the Lord's Supper as a serious matter, not only as a privilege to be enjoyed, but as a fellowship with the Lord in His opposition to evil of every kind

[1] C. F. Hogg, *What Saith the Scripture?* (p. 160)

in the world that makes provision for its own. How searching the act! How solemn the responsibility!

That leads to a most important consideration in connection with the Lord's Supper, a consideration all too easily overlooked. The ostensible celebration of the Supper may be for some an act of *possible condemnation*. It is most thought-provoking to read in 1 Corinthians 11. 29: 'For he that eateth and drinketh unworthily, eateth and drinketh judgment to himself, not discerning the Lord's Body.' The selfish debauchery at the love-feast in Corinth had occasioned more than the apostle's strictures; it had brought down the severest judgment of the Lord, for they were considered 'guilty of the body and blood of the Lord' (v. 27), and as a consequence many of them were weak and ill, and some had even died (v. 30). Now that the meeting for breaking bread has been separated from such social gatherings as were common in apostolic days, there is no possibility of a repetition of the same evil, but it is still possible to meet in such a perfunctory fashion and participate in such an unsympathetic manner, that the remembrance of the Lord is reduced to a mere formality without meaning and without effect upon the behaviour thereafter. Can the Lord be pleased with such conduct? Does a heartless participation not grieve Him now? Is it not probable that much of our spiritual weakness can be traced to a familiarity that robs the Lord's Supper of its solemnity and induces a contempt for that conduct which befits those who profess to be the Lord's? New communicants should always be reminded of the obligations devolving upon those who remember the Lord, that the act is not merely a privilege to be enjoyed, but also an occasion for pressing consciously upon all the duty of acknowledging in all things the Lordship of Him whose Supper it is. There are ethical implicates which no intelligent participator can avoid discovering and which no sincere Christian dare minimize.

The method suggested for escape from such a contingency as is here stated to be possible is quite simple. 'Let a man examine himself, and so let him eat and drink' (v. 28). The context explains the meaning. The Christian coming to the Lord's Supper should come with a reverent exercise to 'discern the Lord's body', that is, he should be putting himself constantly through a process of examination, making personal investigation as to what the bread and wine stand for, so that he will eat and drink worthily. Such examination is a healthy exercise and indicates a seriousness of attitude produced because one realizes the gravity of unthoughtful participation in the Supper. It is true that the believer will never stand in the same utter condemnation as the world, but he may so act at the Lord's Supper as to come under divine chastisement such as a father gives to an erring son (v. 32). Better by far is it for each one, duly concerned, to come with a discerning heart, so that the assembling to remember the Lord will be for spiritual good and not for possible condemnation.

Nor should it be forgotten that the celebration of the Lord's Supper is an *act of Gospel proclamation*. 'As often as ye eat this bread and drink this cup, ye do show (proclaim, announce) the Lord's death' (v. 26). Some maintain that the Lord's death is visibly set forth in the breaking of the loaf and in the pouring out of the wine into the cup, and that the crucial moment of the gathering is reached when some one, after the giving of thanks, proceeds to the table, breaks the loaf, and thereby 'shews' the Lord's death. Several reasons can be adduced for believing that that is not the meaning of the phrase.

(*a*) The actual words of Scripture are, 'as often as ye *eat* this bread and *drink* this cup, ye do shew.' It is not in the breaking of the bread as maintained by the above interpretation, but in the actual eating and drinking that the declaration is made. Eating and drinking are individual acts, and in the dual act, considered as one, the believer proclaims the Lord's death. That truth is set forth in the words of the hymn:

> Meeting in the Saviour's Name,
> Breaking bread by His command,
> To the world we thus proclaim
> On what ground we hope to stand,
> When the Lord shall come with clouds
> Joined by Heaven's exulting crowds.

(*b*) The term breaking bread does not refer to such symbolical breaking as has been mentioned. To break bread has a semi-technical meaning in the New Testament. It connoted the participating in a common meal. The record in Acts 20. 7, that the disciples came together to break bread, indicates that the action was communal and not representative. It describes what the *disciples* did; they shared the common meal by which they brought to remembrance their Lord and His death.

(*c*) The verb used never has the signification of setting forth visibly. It invariably connotes oral declaration. That fact may be verified from any reliable concordance. C. F. Hogg in *What Saith the Scripture?* writes: '*Katangello* always refers to speech, never in any place does it mean to show in the sense of exhibit or present. The passages in the Epistles are Rom. 1. 8; 1 Cor. 2. 1; 9. 14; 11. 26; Phil. 1. 17, 18; Col. 1. 28. Let the reader compare them and judge for himself' (page 157). Under PROCLAIM, W. E. Vine in his *Expository Dictionary of New Testament Words*, states: '1 Cor. 11. 26, where the verb makes clear that the partaking of the elements at the Lord's Supper is a proclamation (an evangel) of the Lord's Death.' Discussing the same passage Dr. Moule in *Outlines of Christian Doctrine* (p. 265), writes: 'The verb . . . is frequent in the New Testament, and invariably elsewhere in it bears the common meaning of telling news to human hearers.'

(*d*) Our Lord's body was not broken, it was given. Of what, then, is that representative breaking symbolical? Can it have any significance at all? There is not the slightest hint in any of the relevant passages in the New Testament that such a procedure had apostolic example or instruction to encourage it. It is unwise to build any ritual breaking upon the clause, 'which is broken for you' in 1 Cor. 11. 24, for, as is commonly accepted, there is very doubtful manuscript authority for the word 'broken.'

(*e*) The death of our Lord is already visibly set forth in the separation of the wine from the bread. That separation symbolizes a violent death. The bread represents the Body or entire personality, while the wine, already poured out into the cup, symbolizes the yielding of that entire personality in vicarious sacrifice. Thus the Lord's death is before the communicants during the whole service and its individual application is acknowledged in the personal appropriation symbolized in the breaking and the supping.

(*f*) The phrase in 1 Cor. 10. 16, 'the bread which we break,' cannot have any reference to a representative act at the table symbolizing the breaking of the Lord's Body. The breaking is intimately related to the partaking in verse 17, and is the preliminary individual act in a communal meal in which all present participate. Nor does it suggest that each is breaking the body of our Lord, but, amongst other truths, teaches, as already indicated, that as the physical body is sustained by eating (i.e. breaking and partaking) material bread, so is the spiritual life of the believer sustained through feeding by faith on the living Bread.

Further, the celebration of the Lord's Supper is an act of *affecting anticipation*. Its duration is circumscribed by the words, 'till He come.' What soul-stirring historical facts move the intelligent and sensitive believer as He views the symbols on the table! His Lord has already been here, and he looks back to see the burden He bore. His Lord is now absent and during His absence the believer looks up and appreciates the fact that the Sacrifice of Calvary has been enthroned at the right hand of the Majesty on high—a Mediator, a High Priest, an Advocate with the Father. In thought which traverses space and time, Golgotha and the Throne are linked, and the remembrance of that death is sweeter because of the triumph which followed. But the instructed believer looks beyond. The Supper then becomes to him prophetical in character. It has an eschatological reference, for did not our Lord, when He celebrated the Last Passover with His disciples declare: 'I will not any more eat thereof, *until* it be fulfilled in the kingdom of God'? (Luke 22. 16). '*Till* He come' remarks Paul in 1 Cor. 11. 26. '*Until* the kingdom of God shall come,' intimates the Lord as recorded in Luke 22. 18. Without discussing the recognizable distinction in the two intimations, it is to be observed that both look forward to a consummation devoutly to be wished. The same sentiment is expressed in the words of Bonar's hymn:

> Feast after feast thus comes and passes by,
>   Yet, passing, points to the glad feast above,
> Giving sweet foretaste of the festal joy,
>   The Lamb's great bridal feast of bliss and love.

Numerous other matters might have extended discussion in relation to the Lord's Supper, but our intention has been briefly to remind ourselves that celebration thereof is Scriptural in authority, simple in character, and spiritual in significance. Man adds his ritual acts, some unadorned (and probably harmless), others so ornate and involved that they obscure the meaning, and convert what was originally a plain meal into a performance, the nature of which is far removed from that of its original intention. To those who endeavour to keep close to the Scriptural pattern its very simplicity is an eloquent appeal for personal dedication of all the potentialities of our redeemed beings in response to the love of that Blessed Lord who gave Himself that He might redeem us unto Himself as a people whom He might possess for His own, and whom He might set free from lawlessness to live for His glory and honour.

If the Apostle Paul were writing to us to-day he would declare as he did to the Corinthians: 'For as often as ye eat this bread, and drink this cup, ye do shew (proclaim) the Lord's death, till He come' (ch. 11. 26), and our absent Lord, anticipating His own glorious and personal triumph would exhort, as He did on the night on which He was betrayed: 'This is My Body, which is given for you; this do in remembrance of Me' (Luke 22. 19). The safest way to preserve the commemorative act is to preserve it in its Scriptural simplicity, adding no formalities of any kind, lest the slightest ritualistic performance detract the heart from the Lord Himself, in whose name such gatherings are convened by the Holy Spirit to the glory of God.

CHAPTER VI

GOVERNMENT IN THE CHURCHES

W. R. LEWIS

IN every sphere, whether national, ecclesiastical, or domestic, there can be no peace or prosperity without rule according to God, for He is not the Author of confusion but of peace (1 Cor. 14. 33). It is an appalling description that is given us, in the closing chapters of the book of Judges, of the violence and corruption that were rife in the days 'when there was no king in Israel' (Judges 19. 1). Though in contrast to the Law, with its liturgy, the New Testament leaves much to the enlightened judgment of the believer in regard to assembly worship and government, the Spirit of God must be in control if what is done is to be worthy of God (1 Cor. 12. 4-9; Phil. 3. 3, R.V.). Few specific regulations are laid down regarding these functions, but this does not mean that it is of little consequence what we do, or that we may now do that which is right in our own eyes. What is required is an exercise of heart and a discipline of a higher order of spiritual intelligence than when these details of human action were prescribed in the rudiments of the Law. The Spirit of sonship has been given to us and it is assumed that, with the New Testament before us we can gather what is the mind of God even where there may be no prescribed rules of conduct.

It is evidence, not of spiritual development, but of spiritual decline where there is a turning again and a being in bondage to weak and beggarly rudiments with their forms and ceremonies (Gal. 4. 9). Rule in an assembly is a spiritual matter and it is the spiritual who will own in heart and conscience those whom God has set in their midst to do a shepherd's part. They can soon recognize those who care for their souls and labour amongst them as constrained by the love of Christ. How great is the departure from the will of God in Christendom is seen in national systems of religion where rulers in the professing church are appointed by a Pope, or by a king on the advice of the political head of the government for the time being, and in the case of the lower ranks of clergy, at the request of the patron of a living, who may or may not be a child of God! The Anglican bishop, unlike an elder of the New Testament, takes the oversight of a large number of churches in his diocese and exercises authority over its clergy. His is an office that is nowhere contemplated in the Scriptures, for its elders are responsible to the Chief Shepherd alone and they have a strictly local charge. Even in Non-conformity, departure from the Scriptures is evinced where pastors are imported from outside the congregation, as a result, perhaps, of a trial sermon and in response to the suffrages of the congregation. It is not the function of a flock to choose its shepherd. That is the prerogative, alone, of the Owner of the flock.

THE NECESSITY FOR OVERSEERS

In the recoil from traditional episcopacy there is a danger of overlooking the gracious provision of pastors or elders which the Holy Spirit still continues to make for the well-being of the saints. It is evidently the will of God that there should be rule in each assembly and, where the Spirit of God and His prerogatives are honoured, leaders, sooner or later, will be raised up within it.[1] It is noteworthy, however, that the authority He now bestows is moral rather than official. Office, apart from the power and unction of the Spirit of God, is unknown in this era. It is not a sacerdotal caste or priestly order, differing from the rank and file, that is to be recognized, but a God-ordained administration by those whose life and conduct are to be worthy of all honour amongst their fellow saints. The word translated 'rule' in the A.V. is really 'stand before,' or 'take the lead.' To serve, then, not to rule, must be their object. The shepherd in Scripture never drives the sheep; he goes before them. So it is with spiritual shepherds. They have authority, but it is an authority conferred, not by official appointment, but by way of example. Happy is that assembly where the

[1] In a newly-planted assembly there are usually found one or more brethren who take the lead by entertaining visiting brethren, in seeking to reach the unsaved, and in visiting the sick and sorrow-stricken. As others from time to time manifest such care and concern they are consulted in the various details that affect the welfare of the assembly and without any formal recognition, they are, by their work and loving concern, marked out and acknowledged as obviously taking the lead.

holy life of its leaders can be pointed to and where their manifest faith is such as can be imitated (Heb. 13. 7, 17).

THEIR APPOINTMENT

In the early days of the history of the Church it was the apostles or their delegates (like Titus) who appointed elders (Acts 14. 23; Titus 1. 5), but there was no handing on of this authority to succeeding generations. It is clear from the context that the injunction in 2 Tim. 2. 2, 'The things that thou hast heard of Me among many witnesses, the same commit thou to faithful men, who shall be able to teach others also,' refers to the impartation of instruction, not to the conferring of office or of gift. It is teaching that is to be handed on, not ordination. Those who claim the powers of the apostles should show their warrant from the Scriptures. Evangelists and teachers cannot be appointed by men; it is their possession of a gift from God that constitutes their authority to use it. So with elders, where such a gift is manifestly possessed they should be recognized and their ministry be thankfully accepted and their co-operation be sought by their fellow-elders. If the spiritual gift is lacking no human ordination can supply it and no lack of human ordination can destroy the responsibility for the exercise of such gift or for its recognition by others in whomsoever it may be found.

It is an unspeakable honour to be set as an overseer by the Holy Spirit in (not over) the church of God (i.e., the local assembly) 'which He hath purchased with His own blood' (Acts 20. 28). It is the Good Shepherd Himself who puts into the hearts of His servants an earnest care for the welfare of His people (2 Cor. 8. 16). This desire is of divine implanting and can never be derived from man's appointment. In every scripturally gathered assembly, however small, God can be counted upon to raise up those who will take the lead, for He knows how much the well-being of an assembly depends upon their fostering care. It is clear from Acts 20. 17, 28; Eph. 4. 11, and 1 Peter 5. 1, 2, that elders, overseers (or bishops) and pastors are synonymous terms and that plurality of elders in each assembly is the will of God (Acts 14. 23; 20. 17; Phil. 1. 1; Tit. 1. 5), the word 'elders' referring, no doubt, to their spiritual experience and maturity, and the word 'overseers,' or 'pastors,' denoting the work they are called upon to do.

THEIR WORK

It will be in the cloudy and dark day, yet to come, that Jehovah will manifest His shepherd care towards His people Israel. He will search for and seek out His sheep; He will deliver the scattered flock and feed them with good pasture; He will make them lie down in a good fold; He will seek that which was lost and will bring again that which was driven away; He will bind up that which was broken and strengthen that which was sick (Ezek. 34. 11-16). It is in similar conditions that He deals thus with His other sheep to-day, and it is in like circumstances that His under-shepherds manifest that they have been truly made such by the Holy Spirit. Shepherd work is a work eagerly to be desired, for it is Christlike work (1 Tim. 3. 1).

They are to feed (tend) the flock (Acts 20. 28). This involves more than finding pasture. They are to guard the flock, for grievous wolves are ever seeking to enter in, while within, there will arise men who will endeavour to draw away disciples after them. All this requires sleepless vigilance (Titus 1. 9, 10). They are to guide or lead the way as examples to the flock (Heb. 13. 7; 1 Peter 5. 3). They are to instruct, reprove, rebuke, exhort those committed to their care, admonishing the disorderly, encouraging the fainthearted, supporting the feeble, that is the hindmost, who by lack of spiritual stamina are liable to be cut off by the foe. There should be no spiritually feeble saints at all (Psa. 105. 37), and the fact that there are such speaks of decline and of the neglect of the spiritual manna and water which would have imparted to them energy to keep step with the rest (Deut. 25. 18; Gal. 5. 25). In the case of physical sickness the elders are to be called together for prayer (Jas. 5. 14). They are to be long-suffering toward all. This is a godlike characteristic. How easily can patience, with us, become exhausted, whereas love suffers long and is kindly disposed however much it is provoked. They are to restore in a spirit of meekness those who are overtaken in a fault (Gal. 6. 1). For the delicate discernment this demands, the spirit of self-judgment is essential, for in proportion as we become acquainted with ourselves shall we deal tenderly (not weakly) with others. It requires clear sight and a delicate touch to extract the mote from a brother's eye (Matt. 7. 4); it needs great skill and careful handling to set a broken limb, to mend the rent that sin has made. In cases of discipline they must investigate the matter judicially and, if necessary, inform the church. Such cases are to be judged in the light of divine revelation after thorough enquiry and the clearest evidence (Deut. 17. 2-4).

THEIR QUALIFICATIONS

There are no apostles or their delegates now to point such leaders out, but the Holy Spirit, who appoints them, has done this for us very clearly.[1] The work they are called to do is a good (or beautiful, noble, honourable) work and it requires beautiful or honourable characters. The degree of their influence will depend upon their spirituality. As they prosper in their own souls in a holy and righteous walk and in close communion with God, so will be the measure of their influence and usefulness in the assemblies of the saints. The features of a God-given overseer as given in 1 Tim. 3. 1-7 and Titus 1. 6-9, R.V., are manifold so that the flock need be in no doubt as to the persons to be recognized. It is noticeable that personal and relative moral qualities rather than exceptional gifts are necessary.

An overseer, then, must be holy, that is, holy in conduct and character, not merely as set apart for sacred use. A holy life is the outcome of acquaintance with God and His Word in reverent obedience without reserve. There is nothing austere about this holiness; it is akin to graciousness (Psa. 145. 17, R.V.). Only as he himself is under authority can he expect to have authority over others. He must be just. 'He that ruleth over men must be just, ruling in the fear of God' (2 Sam. 23. 3, 4). Lovingkindness and righteousness are characteristic of divine government. To do right without fear or favour is the requisite of all righteous rule. The sun rules the day but it also serves the tiniest as well as the greatest of terrestrial creatures. Those who rule in the Church

[1] In a newly-planted assembly the evangelist or missionary who has been used of God in its formation will be on the look-out to discern those whom the Spirit of God is qualifying to take the lead and will seek to impress upon such their responsibility to fulfil their ministry and upon the gathering the necessity of recognizing those who give evidence of the Scriptural qualifications. Possibly it may be thought well for the assembly to be called together to commend such leaders to the Lord, so that the assembly may fulfil its responsibility to know and esteem them for their works' sake. At all events teaching should be given from time to time as to the raising up and the recognition of overseeing brethren,

of God must know no distinction between small and great, rich and poor, for He knows none. It is so natural for us to be swayed by prejudice or partiality, all unconsciously to ourselves, and only the fear of God can overcome this tendency in those whom He calls to rule amongst His people.

He must be without reproach. There must be nothing in the past or present of his Christian life that could be laid hold of as inconsistent with the position of a spiritual guide to others. He must be blameless as a steward of God, for he has the direction and administration of a household of God. In an age when polygamy was prevalent he must be the husband of *one* (not *a*) wife. Any laxity in marriage relationship or lightness with the opposite sex would bring havoc into the assembly and would totally debar him from the work of oversight. He must be temperate or sober. His spirit will affect others far more than his advice. There must be self-restraint, not only in bodily but also in spiritual impulses, no running to extremes, but walking in the midst of the paths of judgment (Prov. 8. 20). He must be sober-minded, sane, sensible, of sound discretion and judgment. Cheerfulness of spirit is, indeed, a blessing, but lightness of spirit is the reverse; the gravity called for must be natural and simple. He must be orderly (courteous, modest, or mannerly), for roughness or uncouthness are nowhere countenanced in Scripture; not self-willed (that is, arrogant, taking no account of the feeling or judgment of others; bent on having one's own way), which betokens a refusal of the yoke of Christ; not soon angry (passionate, irascible). He may have overcome the love of the world and yet manifest, at times, an evil temper, a proud and stubborn will. It is these things that bring disorders in their train.

He must be given to hospitality, in no wise 'forgetful to show love to strangers (those away from home), for thereby some have entertained angels unawares' (Heb. 13. 2). If it is one of Christ's little ones, he entertains Christ Himself. He must be a lover of goodness whenever found and hold to the faithful Word which is according to the (apostolic) teaching, that he may be able both to exhort in the sound teaching and to convict the gainsayers. He must be apt to teach—he may not have the public gift of labouring in word and doctrine, but, at least, he must be able to impart instruction in private through his knowledge of God and His Word. He ought to know how and when to give milk to babes and strong meat to those who need it. He must not be given to wine and no striker (or brawler). In those first days the most elementary virtues had to be insisted upon, but we have not got beyond the need of warning against self-indulgence and the combativeness of a passionate temperament. We may not strike with our fists, but it is easily possible to wound more deeply with our lips. On the other hand he must be gentle, reasonable, considerate of the feelings of others, fair and forbearing, and slow to take offence. Someone once said that an overseer needed 'the wisdom of a father, the affection of a mother and the skin of a rhinoceros'. He must not be contentious, quarrelsome, aggressive, disputatious. As far as possible he is to avoid controversy, like his Master (Matt. 12. 19). 'The Lord's servant must not strive' (2 Tim. 2. 24). When we can pray for those who oppose us the strife is ended and the war of words is closed (Job 42. 10).

The apostle could say to the elders at Ephesus: 'These hands have ministered unto my necessities, and to them that were with me. In all things I gave you an example, how that so labouring ye ought to help the weak and to remember the words of the Lord Jesus, how He Himself said, 'It is more blessed to give than to receive' (Acts 20. 34, 35, R.V.). An overseer, therefore, save in exceptional circumstances (such as when engaged in whole-time labour in Word and doctrine) should earn his own living in order to be able to afford material as well as spiritual support to those who need it. He must be no lover of money, but generous and large-hearted; one that ruleth well his own house, having children in subjection with all gravity (propriety of demeanour), for 'if a man knoweth not how to rule his own house, how shall he take care of the Church of God?' It is possible to be a coward in his family while heroic enough in public. As head of his household he is responsible for the conduct, dress, and manners of his wife and children as well as his own. His family is to be a picture of what he wishes other families to be. The character of his family, then, may be either a great help or a grave impediment to his exercise of oversight. If his wife cannot keep his counsel, if his home becomes a place where the failures of saints are discussed, who is likely to confide in him for help and comfort when experiencing secret trials?

He must not be a novice, or recent convert, 'lest being puffed up he fall into the condemnation of the devil.' A novice cannot occupy the delicate position of an overseer. He must have a good testimony from them that are without, 'lest he fall into reproach and the snare of the devil.' Men of the world have a shrewd judgment of what we ought to be. What a disgrace for an assembly if an elder becomes discredited in their eyes by falling into debt or by slackness in business methods or if he cannot be relied upon in word or work!

Such a standard of practical godliness can never be too high for the qualifications requisite from those who lead, tend to raise the standard of life in those who are led. It is given not to depress us but to stimulate our earnest desire for such spiritual attributes. We need prayerfully to study our own characters, to look at the blacks as well as the whites, at the weak points as well as the strong, and as the Spirit of God writes the truth of His Word on our hearts, He will enable us to delineate by lip and life the same to others. If we do not care to look things in the face, and would rather limit our vision so far as we ourselves are concerned, let us pray for the courage of introspection, for the sincerity which sees things as they really are and for the faith which looks away to the All-sufficient One who knows us altogether and can provide for all our need. If we watch ourselves narrowly we shall not be able to pay ourselves many compliments. Perfection is beyond us here below but with our eye upon Christ there will be the steady aim to fulfil these qualifications on the part of all who aspire to exercise oversight. These marks are given not that we may criticise one another, but for self-examination, and it would be well if those of us who attend what are called oversight meetings were to read these verses more often than we do. It might help us to ascertain from the Lord Himself our true place in His assembly and save us from trying to occupy a position for which we are manifestly unfitted. If we prayerfully ponder them we shall have little cause to boast of the scripturalness of our conduct; we shall be occupied not so much with the obvious errors of Christendom, as with our own shortcomings, and if an assembly lacks those who aspire and earnestly strive, with God's help, to fulfil these conditions, let them cry to Him to provide such guides. Yet how seldom do we hear a prayer for pastors!

OVERSIGHT MEETINGS

The chief part of real oversight is carried on altogether outside the oversight meeting, which often might, more suitably, bear the name of a business meeting. Nevertheless the fact that Scripture always assumes a plurality of elders necessitates their meeting together for prayer and deliberation on all matters relating to the welfare of those who compose the church. It is all-important that they should be united in their judgment, for a divided oversight means a divided fellowship. Any undue individuality of action, regardless of the fellowship of the other elders, will lead to the spirit of Diotrephes (3 John 9). Such meetings should consist of overseers alone, of those who are in the fullest confidence of each other, and of the assembly (Acts 15. 6; 21. 18). In Acts 20. 17 it was the elders alone who were sent for and addressed by Paul.

A meeting of all the brethren in an assembly for this particular object has no divine sanction.[1] To suggest that the teaching of the Acts and Epistles relating to elders is of no permanent application is a dangerous principle and would provide ground for abandoning other assembly truths. It is only those who are doing the work that are to be recognized. Their steps will be marked as they walk before the saints; their voice will be listened to with respect by the godly. The position can never become a sinecure, and while they do the work those who needlessly oppose them rebel against the Lord.

In days of persecution it was a post of physical danger, but it is at all times one of temptation and great responsibility, calling for sobriety and faithfulness, by constant taking heed, first of all, to themselves, and then, to all the flock, every member of which is equally precious to Christ. The true overseer cannot walk light-heartedly in such a path; it leads to the Judgment Seat of Christ. There each day and hour will be brought under the survey of the

---

[1] There are often matters of a private and confidential character that need prayerful consideration by those of mature experience, who have the confidence of the saints and can be depended upon for wise counsel and who will refrain from speaking of such matters outside such private meetings.

Lord to whom account will have to be given by those whom He has charged to watch (lit. to be sleepless) on behalf of souls. It is of their own conduct, not that of others, they must then give account (Heb. 13. 17). The Chief Shepherd will require His sheep at their hand if they neglect their charge.

THE RECOGNITION OF ELDERS

Whenever the divinely-given qualifications are discerned as possessed in any measure, the saints are responsible to recognize those who labour amongst them and to esteem them very highly in love for their work's sake (1 Thess. 5. 12, 13). They are to be in subjection to those who thus addict themselves for service of this kind (1 Cor. 16. 15, 16). They are to be obeyed, for they watch for souls as those that must give account, that they may do this with joy and not with grief (Heb. 13. 17). In view of their responsibility before the Lord how much they need the prayers of those committed to their charge! Needless criticism must be displeasing to the Lord for it lessens their authority and leaves nothing in its place. They are not to be rebuked but are to be entreated as a father (1 Tim. 5. 1), and no accusation is to be received against them but before two or three witnesses (1 Tim. 5. 19).

THEIR REWARD

The Apostle John, himself an elder, wrote: 'Look to yourselves, that we lose not those things which we have wrought, but that we receive a full reward' (2 John 8). Can our conduct, then, conduce to the shame of those who watch for our souls; can it involve their losing something of their reward? If it does, how unprofitable for us at the Judgment Seat of Christ! It was the provocation of the people that caused Moses to speak unadvisedly with those lips of his which should always have spoken for God, and thereby to forfeit his entrance into the promised land (Psa. 106. 33). It is solemn to lose one's own full reward; doubly solemn to be the cause also of another losing his. On the other hand, unlike earthly success, the best way to help another to get his heavenly reward is so to act that I may obtain my own.

A company of God's people largely answers to those who seek to guide it. In the Seven Letters to the Churches, the angels addressed seem to stand for the responsible element of the respective assemblies, for they are addressed as morally identified with the characteristics of each assembly. If this is how God looks at those who represent the gathering what a responsibility is theirs who seek in any measure to care for those entrusted to them!

When the work of oversight is truly performed it is an arduous and humbling task and often a thankless one. There is no earthly inducement or way of gain or worldly distinction attaching to such labour in the Lord. But when the Chief Shepherd shall be manifested there is 'a crown of glory that fadeth not away' to be bestowed on those who have taken up the work, 'not of constraint, but willingly, according unto God; nor yet for filthy lucre, but of a ready mind; neither as lording it over the charge allotted to them, but making themselves ENSAMPLES TO THE FLOCK' (1 Peter 5. 1-4, R.V.).

CHAPTER VII

PRIESTHOOD AND WORSHIP

FREDK. A. TATFORD

WITH man's expulsion from Eden, the personal intimacy which he had enjoyed with his Creator was brought to an abrupt conclusion, and the necessity immediately arose of finding some means for the re-establishment of communion with God. It was out of this need that the sacerdotal function really originated, since access into the divine presence became possible only by way of sacrifice and the latter quite clearly necessitated a priesthood. As Prof. Plumptre says: 'The idea of a priesthood connects itself . . . with the consciousness, more or less distinct, of sin. Men feel that they have broken a law. The power above them is holier than they are, and they dare not approach it. They crave for the intervention of someone of whom they can think as likely to be more acceptable than themselves. He must offer up their prayers, thanksgivings, sacrifices. He becomes their representative in things pertaining to God.'

Bahr connects the Hebrew word *cohen* (priest) with an Arabic root meaning *to draw near*, and this aptly expresses the true work of the priest. His primary function was to act as a mediator between God and man: on the one hand, to propitiate God and to present the worship due to Him; on the other, to afford the worshipper the assurance of forgiveness and absolution.

THE FAMILY PRIEST

In patriarchal times, the head of each family was the household priest. Abraham, Isaac, and Jacob, for example, built altars and offered sacrifices to Jehovah; after the Flood, Noah offered representatively on behalf of those who were saved in the ark (Gen. 8. 20). Job offered sacrifices regularly for his sons (Job 1. 5). Later, in Egypt (Gen. 41. 45), Midian (Exodus 2. 16), and Canaan (Gen. 14. 18), spiritual leaders were consecrated and set apart to superintend national devotions. After Israel's exodus from Egypt, that people followed a similar path and priestly authority and functions were centralized in the person of one man, Moses. The hereditary priesthood of the heads of the families was not abolished but, at the request of the people—and with the divine approval— their duties were transferred to Moses (Exodus 20. 19; 24. 6).

It was clearly impossible for one individual to discharge the sacerdotal functions on behalf of a whole nation and when the Sinaitic covenant had been completed he was allowed to divest himself of the responsibilities and to transfer them to his brother, Aaron, and his descendants. The hereditary priesthood accordingly then became vested in the Levitical tribe.

At the very time at which the people voluntarily divested themselves of their privilege, however, Jehovah had indicated His intention of making the whole nation a priesthood—a purpose which will ultimately be realized during the millennial age (Isa. 61. 6). As Edersheim remarks: 'When, on Mount Sinai, Moses was directed to set apart his brother Aaron and his sons for the priestly office, there was a peculiar significance in the institution at that time and to that people. For God had just vouchsafed a revelation of Himself to Israel, which would distinguish that nation to all ages from every other one, and which had brought the Jews into a relationship with God such as had never been enjoyed since the Fall. Israel was now to become to God "a kingdom of priests, and an holy nation" (Exodus 19. 4-6). If Israel but obeyed God's voice, and kept His covenant, there would have been no need of a priesthood. Yet, though this obedience was set before Israel as a possible frame of mind, it never became a real one.'

The Aaronic Priesthood

In the pagan religions the priesthood became the sole depository of the truth and of the sacred mysteries of which the common worshipper was completely ignorant. The priests of Israel, on the contrary, were representative men, separated and consecrated to represent their fellows in the presence of God and to impart the knowledge of divine truth to the nation.

The details (Exod. 29) of the consecration of the Levitical

priesthood are most interesting and are not entirely irrelevant to the priesthood of a later day. Aaron and his sons were first of all completely bathed with water—the expressive symbol of regeneration (John 13. 8-10). The Apocalyptic seer heard the cry from the churches that Christ 'loved us and washed us from our sins in His own blood, and hath made us kings and priests.' The full cleansing of regeneration is an essential prerequisite to priesthood. After the clothing of the priest he was next anointed with the holy oil, in token of his spiritual sanctification, and the blood of the ram of consecration was then applied to his right ear, hand, and foot—the reminder of the purging by blood of hearing, service, and walk. Finally, his 'hands were filled' with portions of the sacrifices to be offered to the Lord as a wave offering—the typical presentation in worship of the merits of Christ. It is impossible not to be impressed with the relevance of every detail to the Christian priest of the present age, but the significance is too patent to require comment.

The sanctity of the sacerdotal office is markedly emphasized in connection with the Aaronic priests. It was with bared feet and reverent step that the Jewish priest moved about his appointed tasks. Frequent lustrations, abstinence from wine and strong drink, abstention from mourning, and separation from every defiling thing were imperative requirements (Lev. 10. 9; 21. 1-6). External ablutions were merely indicative of the absolute holiness required of those who served God in His earthly dwelling-place. The priest was to be physically, as well as liturgically, perfect. Physical deformity disqualified him from the service of God (Lev. 21. 17-23). He was to handle holy things. The lesson is one which might well be copied by all who are engaged in spiritual service to-day. The things of God are not to be lightly handled and holiness of life and character is still required of the priest of this age.

Dr. Driver defines the functions of the Old Testament priest as follows: 'to give *torah*; to bear the ark; to stand before Jehovah to minister unto Him, i.e., to serve God in particular by offering sacrifice; to burn incense; to bear the ephod; to bless in Jehovah's Name' (Deut. 10. 8; 17. 10, 12; 18. 5; 21. 5; 24. 8; 31. 9; 33. 10; 1 Sam. 2. 28).

IMPERFECTION OF THE OLD ORDER

However meticulous the performance of the ritual and ceremony of the Mosaic law, however completely the sacrificial requirements were observed, the service of the Levitical priesthood never attained perfection. It was never complete or final. It was characterized by the necessity for continual repetition. The same sacrifices were presented repeatedly, but the offerings of those priests could never permanently free the worshipper from sin nor purge the conscience from dead works (Heb. 10. 1, 2). The ministry of the Aaronic priests was ever tinged by frailty and human failure. As Dr. Kurtz says: 'From the very nature of such a mediatorial office, two things were essential to its true and perfect performance; and these the Aaronic priest no more possessed than anyone else in the nation which stood in need of mediation. The first and immediate demand for a perfect priesthood, appointed to mediate between the holy God and the sinful nation, would be perfect sinlessness; but how little did the family of Aaron, involved as it was in the general sinfulness, answer to this demand. Secondly, true and all-sufficient mediation required that the mediator himself should possess a doublesidedness; and in this the Aaronic priest was quite as deficient as in the first thing demanded, namely, perfect sinlessness. To represent the people in the presence of Jehovah, and Jehovah in the presence of the people, and to be able to set forth in his own person the mediation between the two, he ought to stand in essential union on the one hand with the people, and on the other with God; and in order fully to satisfy this demand, he ought to be as much divine as human. But the Aaronic priesthood partook of human nature only, and not at all of divine!'

The very imperfections of the Levitical priesthood and the characteristic lack of finality about its work, patently indicated the need for a better and more perfect priesthood, and this need was ultimately met and satisfied in the priesthood of Christ.

Long before the institution of the Levitical priesthood, the king-priest, Melchizedek, appeared upon the pages of history as a type of an undying priesthood (Gen. 14. 18; Heb. 7. 3). No record was given of his birth or of his death; no mention was made of his genealogy. He flashed across the path of Abraham for a few fleeting moments, wearing all the typical guise of an eternal being. After the fashion of this regal priest, after the order of Melchizedek, God later declared, through the Psalmist, an unending priesthood should come forth (Psa. 110. 4)—a prophecy to be realized and fulfilled in the person of God's own Son.

THE GREAT HIGH PRIEST

'It is very difficult,' writes Dr. Alexander Maclaren, 'for us to realize what an extraordinary anomaly the Christian faith presented at its origin, surrounded by religions which had nothing to do with morality, conduct, or spiritual life, but were purely ritualistic. And here, in the midst of them, started up a religion bare and bald, and with no appeal to sense, no temple, no altar, no sacrifice. But the apostles with one accord declare that they had all these things in far higher form than those faiths possessed them, which had only the outward appearance.'

The external ritual of the Old Testament has disappeared, its rites and ceremonies, its sacrifices and offerings, its festivals and fasts, completely superseded by the abiding reality of which they were but the dim shadows and types. No white-robed priests minister to-day in an earthly temple; no smoke arises from the burning holocaust upon the altar; no fragrant perfume beclouds the holiest of a temporal sanctuary. But the spiritual antitype is no less real and true. In a heavenly sphere, to which flesh finds no access, sits the Great High Priest of a different order, and there minister before Him in that celestial scene the consecrated priests of a different age.

Specific qualifications were laid down by the writer of the Hebrews epistle as essentials for every holder of the sacerdotal office. In the first place, the priest must be capable of sympathizing with others in their infirmities; secondly, he must be called of God and not self-appointed; and thirdly, he must naturally have something to offer (Heb. 4. 15; 5. 2, 4; 8. 3).

Aaron perfectly satisfied these conditions. As man, he was cognisant of the problems of humanity and could feel with his fellows in their trials and difficulties. It is quite clear, moreover, that his high priestly appointment was not the result of self-seeking but was by the explicit will of God. Whilst on the third count, the Levitical offerings were plainly prescribed and the Aaronic

8

priest was always in a position to present to Jehovah that which He had required.

In an even fuller measure does our Lord Jesus Christ satisfy the requirements of the Hebrews letter. In order that He might 'be made like unto His brethren,' He became incarnate. As man, He was tested and tried in all respects as we are (apart from the experiences of, and those resulting from, sin), and is consequently able to sympathize with His people in their infirmities. He is indeed qualified to be 'a merciful and faithful high priest in things pertaining to God' (Heb. 2. 17)

Nor was Christ a self-appointed priest. He 'glorified not Himself to be made an high priest; but He that said unto Him . . . Thou art a priest for ever after the order of Melchizedek' (Heb. 5. 5).

Moreover, this Great High Priest of a new order was not without something to offer, and the merit of the Priest adds infinite value to the gifts and sacrifices which He presents. The fragrance of His own glories and the worth of His own Person are the constant delight of the Father's heart, but the value of His sacrificial work brings rest, joy, and satisfaction to the Eternal God.

The superiority of the priesthood of Christ over that of Aaron's line is strongly emphasized in the Epistle to the Hebrews. The contrast is indicated at the very outset by the fact that the very order of His priesthood was not Aaronic but related to an earlier priesthood altogether. He came after the order of Melchizedek, so that the latter himself must have been personally superior to the Levitical priests who followed him.

To this royal priest, Melchizedek, Abraham, 'the father of the faithful,' gave a tenth of his spoils, and thereby plainly acknowledged the supremacy of Melchizedek's priesthood. Virtually, the yet unborn Levi and his descendants (the future priests of Israel, to whom the tribes of Israel paid tithes in obedience to the law) representatively in the person of their ancestor paid tithes to Melchizedek. It is perfectly clear, therefore, that they were of an inferior order to him (Heb. 7. 4-11).

Again, it is obvious that the lesser is always blessed of the greater and not the reverse. It is extremely significant, therefore, that it was not Abraham who blessed Melchizedek, but the latter who blessed Abraham (Heb. 7. 6).

Thirdly, from a typical point of view (since there was no record in Scripture of his parents, or genealogy, nor of his birth or death), Melchizedek's priesthood was eternal and permanent, whereas that of Aaron was patently only temporary and transient (Heb. 7. 3).

Not only is the order of Christ's priesthood superior to the Aaronic order, but He is personally superior to all the priests of the earthly sanctuary. The Levitical high priests were necessarily many, by reason of their mortality, but since Christ continues for ever, He has an unchangeable priesthood. The high priests of that earlier day passed, sooner or later into the arms of death, but Christ ever liveth (Heb. 7. 24, 25). They were ever standing, since their work was ever incomplete, but He, having completely finished His work has 'sat down on the right hand of God' (ch. 10. 12). His priesthood was founded upon the immutable oath of God, whereas 'those priests were made without an oath' (ch. 7. 21). Since they were sinful by nature, the earthly priests had 'to offer up sacrifice, first for their own sins, and then for the people's' (ch. 7. 27). But Christ offered Himself once, and then, not for Himself, but for the sins of His people. The Jewish high priest entered the holiest of the tabernacle (and later the temple) only once a year (on the day of atonement), but Christ has 'entered in once for all into the holy place.' Only into an earthly sanctuary could they enter, but He has entered into heaven itself. The Levitical high priest was compelled to repeat this annually, but Christ has entered once and for ever. Whereas the earthly priest entered with the blood of bulls and goats, Christ has entered by His own blood (Heb. 9. 12-26). Their offerings could never permanently free from guilt, but He has offered one sacrifice for sins for ever and has made complete purgation for sin (Heb. 1. 3; 10. 10, 12). Shadow and transience characterize the earlier priesthood; permanence and abiding character are impressed upon the latter.

Since the Church is a heavenly—and not an earthly—body, it is in consonance that the priesthood of Christ should be heavenly and not earthly. Indeed, the New Testament plainly states that if He were upon earth, He would not be a priest, since He came, not of the priestly tribe of Levi, but of the royal tribe of Judah, 'of which tribe Moses spoke nothing concerning priesthood' and of which no member gave attendance at the altar (Heb. 7. 13,

14; 8. 4). He is the High Priest of a heavenly priesthood, exercising His sacerdotal ministry in a heavenly sphere on behalf of a heavenly people. He is 'a minister of the sanctuary and of the true tabernacle, which the Lord pitched, and not man' (Heb. 8. 2).

CHRIST'S MINISTRY

Prof. Kurtz says of the Levitical priesthood that its design and purpose 'was mediatorial communion with God, mediation between the holy God and His chosen people, who had drawn back, in the consciousness of their sinfulness, from direct communion with God.' He rightly remarks that 'like all communion, this was reciprocal. Priestly approach to God involved both bringing to God and taking from God. The priests brought into the presence of God the sacrifices and gifts of the people, and took from God His gifts for the people, namely, reconciliation and blessing.

The high priesthood of Christ is similarly connected very intimately with the establishment and maintenance of communion between God and His people of the present age. In fact, the Church is dependent for its communion with God upon the efficacy of the priestly work of its Lord. It is through Him that the believer has access into the presence of God; none may stand before the Eternal save in the merit of the glorious Lord. He not only frees the sinner from the guilt and defilement of sin, but also leads the now purged worshipper into the holiest of all, where, unashamed and unafraid, he may pour out his worship before a Father God. Yet even that worship would be unacceptable but for the fact that Christ adds His perfume to the worshipper's censer (Rev. 8. 3). It is equally true that all the blessings of the heavenlies become the Christian's portion only in the Person of his Lord (Eph. 1. 3).

In a very practical sense, He maintains His people in fellowship with the Father. In every circumstance, He meets their need. His blood has atoned for their sin and their sins. Constant cleansing He affords for the contaminations of life's road, in the 'washing of water by the Word' (Eph. 5. 26).

The Lord Jesus Christ is the permanent Mediator for every member of the Church. 'He ever liveth to make intercession for them,' and 'is able also to save them to the uttermost that come unto God by Him' (Heb. 7. 25). His unceasing and unwearying care is devoted to those who belong to Him and, in the heavenly sanctuary their case is constantly presented by the great Mediator and Intercessor. Never are they out of His thoughts; in His perfect priestly ministry, He makes it His permanent charge to bear them up in the presence of God.

Moreover, He sympathises with His brethren in their infirmities. By reason of a personal knowledge of human life, with all its trials and difficulties, problems and perplexities, sorrows, and sufferings, He 'can have compassion on the ignorant and on them that are out of the way' (Heb. 5. 2). His is no mere academic omniscience, but a compassionate understanding, born out of the wealth of an experimental knowledge of the path of humanity. As Perfect Man He fully understands life's burdens and tribulations, and His ready sympathy is extended to His own in every circumstance.

He sustains and strengthens His people through all the rigours of life. No cry of need falls unheeded upon the ear of that Great High Priest; succour and maintenance are supplied in every difficulty. He is ever ready to furnish 'grace to help in time of need' (Heb. 4. 16). It is His sacerdotal responsibility to ensure, not merely that restoration to communion is available to the one who has fallen, but also that preservation from failure is possible in the very nick of time, and all His sufficiency is made accessible to the needy soul.

Well might the writer to the Hebrews term Him 'a merciful and faithful high priest.' His compassions are unfailing and His faithfulness, like His mercies, is freshly proved each waking day.

CHRISTIAN PRIESTHOOD

In the Mosaic economy, priesthood was restricted to descendants of the tribe of Levi. Every Aaronite of that line, unless deformed or disfigured, was a priest by virtue of his birth into the tribe. The priestly class was quite distinct from the remainder of Israel: its members alone could draw near to God, and no other Israelite had such a privileged position.

All such distinctions have now been removed and all believers of this dispensation have an equal right and privilege to draw near to God in and through the Lord Jesus Christ. Christianity recognizes no special, distinctive priesthood: all Christians are alike priests. 'In removing that which separated man *from God*, in communicating to all the same fellowship *with God*, Christ also removed the barrier which had hitherto divided men *from one another*. Christ, the Prophet and High Priest for entire humanity, was the end of the prophetic office and the priesthood. There was now the same High Priest and Mediator for all, through whom all men, being once reconciled and united with God, are themselves made a priestly and spiritual race. Since free access to God and to heaven had by the one High Priest been opened once for all to believers, they had, by virtue of their union to Him, become themselves a spiritual people, consecrated to God; their calling being none other than to dedicate their entire life to God as a thank-offering, to make their life one continual priesthood, one spiritual worship' (Neander). The divine purpose for Israel was that the whole nation should be a kingdom of priests. The purpose of God for the church is that every member should be a priest. 'Ye are a chosen generation, a royal priesthood, a holy nation, a peculiar people,' wrote Peter (1 Peter 2. 9), and the seer of the Apocalypse declared that believers had been made 'kings and priests unto God' (Rev. 1. 6; 5. 10; 20. 6).

It was generally acknowledged by the Fathers that all Christians are priests of the present dispensation. Justin Martyr, for example, refers to all believers as 'the high priestly race of God,' and Irenæus declares that 'every just man is of the priestly order.' Tertullian asked: 'Are not we laymen also priests?' and again maintained elsewhere that 'the laity also have a right to administer the sacraments and to teach in the church. The Word of God and the sacraments were by God's grace communicated to all, and may, therefore, be communicated by all Christians as instruments of God's grace.' The Middle Ages confirmed the testimony of the Fathers. St. Thomas Aquinas, for instance, says that 'the righteous layman is united to Christ in a spiritual union by faith and love, and therefore hath a spiritual priesthood for the offering of spiritual sacrifices.' In more modern days, Bishop Lightfoot contends that all Christians 'may practise the continual priesthood,' and Canon Bernard says that all Christ's 'people have in Him that right of immediate access to God which is characteristic of priesthood.'

The New Testament knows nothing of a special sacerdotal caste distinguished from the laity (indeed, the word *laos* is used of all the people of God, and *kleros*, not of an official body, but of the special charge allocated to a particular worker). By the end of the second century, however, distinctions had arisen—possibly through the influence of some Jewish element—and, as Neander writes, 'The universal priesthood, grounded on the common and immediate relation in which all believers stood to Christ as the source of divine life was repressed by the spread of the idea that there is a special mediatory priesthood attached to a distinct order.' It was not long before the ministerial or clerical class who assumed this distinctive position felt it incumbent upon them also to separate themselves from secular employment, thereby virtually ignoring the injunction laid upon all Christians of a priestly consecration of the whole life. Once spiritual and secular things were separated and a closer relation to God envisaged in the former than in the latter, the conclusion of separation from secular things for a privileged few was inevitable.

It is argued by some that priesthood pertains to the Church as such and not to the individual believer. Dr. Moberley, for example, states that 'the ministerial organs are not priestly in detachment from, or antithesis against, the body, but because the body is priestly, they are the organs of its priestliness.' In *England and the Russian Church*, Khomiokoff takes a very similar view. 'The seven sacraments,' he says, 'are in reality not accomplished by any single individual who is worthy of the mercy of God, but by the whole church in the person of an individual.' But, as Fairbairn says: 'Paul never predicates priesthood of the body, and though he enumerates its organs, he never attributes to them the priestly office.' Priesthood is clearly the responsibility and privilege of the individual believer and its functions must be exercised personally.

It is sometimes suggested that, even if there is no distinct sacerdotal caste, it is a convenience if the priestly functions are delegated to the clergy. This would involve, however, an inevitably complete surrender. If functions were delegated, they would obviously never be exercised by those who thus delegated them, and the layman, although still a priest *de jure*, would effectively cease to be one *de facto*. His prerogative of drawing near to God and presenting his spiritual sacrifices would have been voluntarily forfeited: it is impossible for such exercises to be carried out by proxy. The Christian's priesthood is derived from his relationship to Christ, and is incapable of transmission to another. Every child of God (irrespective of sex), by virtue of sonship, is a priest of the present dispensation.

FUNCTIONS OF CHRISTIAN PRIESTHOOD

The first and highest employment of the Christian priest is to draw near to God. Because he has a High Priest over the house of God and since his sins have been purged and his life cleansed and sanctified, he is entitled—and even enjoined—to draw near into the Father's presence (Heb. 7. 19; 10. 21, 22). Access to God is not based upon the merit of the priest nor upon the value of his own work, but is made possible only by the supreme merit of the High Priest Himself. It is through Him that the way into the holiest has been made, and His death was necessary that the sacred veil might provide an entry and not prove a barrier (Heb. 10. 20). In the Levitical economy, access into the Holy of Holies was restricted to the high priest and even he might enter only once a year (Lev. 16), but the Christian priest has the right of entry at all times into the immediate presence of the Almighty God.

In all religions, priesthood is intimately connected with sacrifice, and the two were clearly correlative terms in the Levitical era. In this dispensation, however, the priesthood is a spiritual one and it is a natural corollary that the sacrifices offered are spiritual, too. Peter specifically details the work of the holy priesthood of this day as the offering up of 'spiritual sacrifices, acceptable to God by Jesus Christ' (1 Peter 2. 5). The expiatory offering of Christ was complete and perfect, so that no question arises—as the Romanists suggest—of a fresh sacrifice of Christ.

The first and most essential sacrifice required of the Christian priest is his whole being. 'I beseech you, therefore, brethren,' wrote the Apostle Paul, 'that ye *present* (a technical word for a priestly act) your bodies a living sacrifice, holy, acceptable unto God' (Rom. 12. 1). Here is not the slaying of the body but its hallowing. The one who stands before God as priest to-day must be prepared for the supreme act of worship, a complete self-immolation. The whole life is to be consecrated in a heartfelt devotion to the Eternal One. As Sanday puts it: 'The best gift man can offer is the moral discipline of self.' There cannot, in fact, be full worship unless the whole being is offered to God.

Praise and thanksgiving are also among the sacrifices to be presented. 'By Him, therefore, let us offer the sacrifice of praise to God continually,' said the inspired writer to the Hebrews, 'that is, the fruit (or *calves*), of our lips giving thanks to His Name' (Heb. 13. 15). Just as the earthly priest offered burnt and gift offerings to Jehovah on behalf of the Jewish worshipper, so the heavenly priest pours out his offering of praise to his God. The sacrifice he brings is not the lowing calf of an earlier dispensation, but the adoring and grateful thanksgiving of his lips. 'Offer unto God thanksgiving,' said the Psalmist. 'Whoso offereth praise glorifieth Me' (Psa. 50. 14, 23).

Quoting the Psalmist's words, 'Let my prayer be set forth before Thee as incense; and the lifting up of my hands as the evening sacrifice' (Psa. 141. 2), Archbishop Leighton declared that prayer itself was a spiritual sacrifice to be offered in this day. He writes: 'It is not the composition of prayer, or the eloquence of expression, that is the sweetness of it in God's account and makes it a sacrifice of a pleasing smell or sweet odour to Him, but the breathing forth of the desire of the heart; that is what makes it a spiritual sacrifice, otherwise it is carnal, and dead, and worthless in God's account. Incense can neither smell nor ascend without fire; no more doth prayer, unless it arise from a bent of spiritual affection.' Even if the analogy between prayer and sacrifice is of somewhat doubtful legitimacy, it is quite patent that prayer is one of the principal media by which priestly communion is maintained. It is pertinent, too, that the priest is consistently regarded as acting in a mediatorial capacity: it is his responsibility to intercede on behalf of his fellows. He bears them up before God and presents their cases in the presence of the Almighty. What means can he employ other than prayer? Nor is this priestly function limited to the needs of the household of faith; the priest's responsibility is to lift up hands of prayer on behalf of all men everywhere (1 Tim. 2. 1).

The Apostle Paul touches upon another side of the sacerdotal ministry when he describes the love-gift sent to him by the Philippian church as 'an odour of a sweet smell, a sacrifice acceptable, well pleasing to God' (Phil. 4. 18), and the same thought is continued in the exhortation to the Hebrews 'to do good and to communicate forget not: for with such sacrifices God is well pleased' (Heb. 13. 16). It was a characteristic of the early church that the needs of the poor were never overlooked, but the apostolic assessment of almsgiving as a priestly sacrifice sets the whole matter in an entirely different light. The practical fellowship, which springs from a spirit of love and sympathy, is so highly esteemed by the Lord that He regards it as comparable with the offerings consumed upon the altar, the odours from which ascended to satisfy the divine heart. This takes Christian giving out of the realm of eleemosynary charity and places it on the highest possible plane: it is a sacerdotal function of the Christian priest.

It is a function of our Great High Priest to sympathize with His brethren in their infirmities, and a similar ministry is committed to every member of the royal priesthood. The church is suffering to-day from the lack of this ministry. The compassion of God's people should flow out to those in difficulty and trial, to the perplexed and burdened, to the sorrowing and suffering. In all the tribulations of life, the weary one should ever be able to turn to his brethren for help and understanding. The competence and adequacy of such ministry are, of course, dependent upon the personal experience of the priest, and sympathy and comfort can be ministered only if the priest himself has practical knowledge of the particular trial. Each member of the church is fitted for the work allocated to him, and the very experiences that so fit him also equip him for the sympathetic understanding of others in similar experiences.

If, in the fullest possible measure, the Great High Priest furnishes the grace to help in time of need, every priest is under an obligation to fulfil the same function. The priestly heart discerns the first signs of slipping or backsliding in a fellow-believer and, at the very moment of need the hand is reached out to help and to hold back. Deep trouble may disturb the soul of a saint: the true priest sees beneath the calm exterior and grace to help is furnished in the nick of time.

'The priest's lips should keep knowledge,' says Malachi, 'and they should seek the law at his mouth; for he is the messenger of

Jehovah of hosts' (Mal. 2. 7). It may be deduced, therefore, that the ministry of teaching is also committed to the priest. As the messenger of God, he is responsible to impart the divine message to those in need. Such instruction is obviously not limited to the church itself; rather is the responsibility upon the members of the church to teach those who are without knowledge. It should be possible for saint and sinner to seek—and find—help from every Christian priest.

THE GLORIOUS FUTURE

The end of the priestly story is not told in this dispensation. During the glorious millennial age, the prophet foretells that Christ will sit upon the throne of Israel as King and Priest (Zech. 6. 13), the perfect Antitype of the king-priest Melchizedek.

In that day the purposes of God for His earthly people will be realized, and Israel 'shall be named the priests of the Lord,' and men shall call them 'the ministers of our God' (Isa. 61. 6).

The priests of this Church age will be associated with Christ in His glory—'they shall be priests of God and of Christ, and shall reign with Him' (Rev. 20. 6). The experiences of the present are equipping for the future.

So that the whole universe will be bound together by golden sacerdotal chains; on earth, the priests of Israel—a whole priestly nation functioning for others; over earth, the priests of this age, reigning with their Lord in glory; and supreme above all, the Sovereign Priest after the order of Melchizedek.

CHAPTER VIII

THE CHRISTIAN MINISTRY

G. C. D. HOWLEY

THE first days of Christianity were days of great expansion. The tiny beginnings of a few disciples gathered in an upper room in Jerusalem gave place, no more than a generation afterwards, to a situation when the Gospel had been preached 'in all creation under heaven,' i.e., throughout the whole civilized world. The outpouring of the Holy Spirit at Pentecost had empowered the disciples and they had gone forth everywhere with the saving word of the Gospel. The results of their itinerant evangelism were speedily evidenced in the growth of the number of communities of disciples. These churches of the saints, in their turn, spread the Gospel still further afield so that the circle of disciples was steadily widening. This story of early expansion and consequent need for the establishment of the infant churches provides the historical basis for a ministry to meet those needs.

It is, however, necessary for us to define our terms because of the extent to which, sometimes, popular usage has moved from the original Biblical usage of certain words and doctrines. It would be easy, in a consideration of the Christian Ministry, to embrace as evidence towards a conclusion, the post-apostolic writings or practices, but that at once raises certain difficulties. It is true that many scholars have worked along the above lines in drawing conclusions on this theme, but we are entitled to enquire, to what extent we have any right to add to the teachings of the apostles as found in the New Testament. A doctrine of development is agreeable only so long as the developments in question are consistent with what is found in the Scriptures. Developments that appear to run counter to apostolic teaching and practice introduce confusion, in that they not only support wrong deductions but also obscure what the apostolic writings really do teach. While admitting that within the compass of the New Testament there is a simple form of development in teaching, we affirm that herein there is no contradiction. This chapter, for the above reasons, will confine itself to the Biblical writings as providing for us the only sure guide as to the nature and the expression of the Christian Ministry.

The popular use of the term 'minister' is a development from its simple and unofficial New Testament usage. The apostolic conception is broader and the word *diakonos*[1] means, in general, a servant, attendant, minister, whether as doing servile work, or as an attendant rendering free service. The word has probably a connection with the idea of hasting, pursuing to do one's master's bidding.[2] It can at once be seen that to limit the meaning of the word to a separate ministerial order as has so often been done in the course of Church history, does some despite to its essential meaning. Ministry in its various forms and expressions is that to which all are called, it is not the prerogative of a few but the portion and privilege of the many. It is not dependent upon mere human ordination but upon the 'ordination of the pierced hands,' by the imparting of spiritual gift from above.

During the earthly ministry of the Lord Jesus Christ, He constantly made claim upon the service of His disciples and much of His time with them was given over to instructing them so that they might effectually serve Him. Later, in apostolic times, the normal development of the Christian life is seen to be closely associated with service for Christ and the very ideas characteristic of the training of the disciples by the Lord are extended into the sphere of church life. The church at Corinth, for example, was early marked by signs of an ample provision for its growth and maintenance, and Paul gives thanks to God 'for the grace of God which was given you in Christ Jesus; that in everything ye were enriched in Him, in all utterance and all knowledge; even as the testimony of Christ was confirmed in you; so that ye come behind in no gift; waiting for the revelation of our Lord Jesus Christ' (I Cor. I. 4-7, R.V.). In the gift of the Holy Spirit lies the secret of the consolidation of these primitive communities, leading afterwards to their further expansion. Leaving, therefore, the historical and

[1] See Note 6
[2] See Abbott-Smith, *Manual Greek Lexicon*, page 108, and W. E. Vine, *Expository Dictionary of New Testament Words*, under Deacon. (Volume I).

theological explanation of our subject, let us examine its abiding values for church life to-day. We shall consider, firstly, the New Testament teaching on the ministry; secondly, the power for its exercise; and finally, glance at certain practical matters arising from such considerations.

THE DOCTRINE OF THE MINISTRY IN THE NEW TESTAMENT

The divine plan was, and is, that there should arise, from the midst of the churches of the saints, those gifted of God to provide for their spiritual needs. Behind all thought of spiritual ministry lies the truth of the glory of the risen, exalted Christ. His ascension is likened to a triumphal procession in which He proclaims His victory at Calvary, and freely distributes His bounty to men. Against this background of thought the Apostle Paul works out his teaching in the Ephesian letter, which teaching embraces the whole Body of Christ, and reveals what Christ has done for His people on earth. He has given gifts and each gift is a token of His triumph! The conception in Ephesians (ch. 4. 7-16, R.V.) is of the risen Lord giving gifts, which are men, for the benefit of the Body of Christ as a whole. 'And He gave some to be apostles; and some, prophets; and some, evangelists; and some, pastors and teachers,' and Hort aptly sums these up as 'the two types of exceptional and temporary functions' (apostle and prophet); and 'two corresponding types of ordinary and permanent functions' (evangelist, pastor and teacher).[1]

The exaltation of Christ, and the gift of the Spirit, means that our Lord still has work to do in the world, and that this has become possible through the formation of His mystical Body, the Church. The imagery used of a body and its head suggests, not only organic union with Christ but the functioning of His members as the purpose behind this union.

The gifts the Lord has bestowed as enumerated in this passage in Ephesians are all of them major gifts, indispensable for the welfare of the Body of Christ. He firstly gave them apostles, His band of immediate followers. A little later, with the spread of the Gospel He gave men who functioned as prophets, declaring

[1] F. J. A. Hort, Sermon Preached in Westminster Abbey, page 284, of *The Christian Ecclesia*.

the mind of the Lord to His people, by direct word from heaven. During the days in which the New Testament writings were being produced, and thus before any clearly defined collection of books could be authoritative, the ministry of prophets contributed to the supply of the needs of the Lord's people. But in the nature of the case such a ministry was temporary in character, and with the gradual recognition of the newer writings as possessing divine authority the gift of prophecy passed from the Church. Apostles and prophets, therefore, were exceptional and temporary functions. But to meet the permanent needs of the Body, Christ also gave two other gifts, those of evangelist, and pastor and teacher. The evangelist, the bearer of good tidings, went forth everywhere to proclaim the message of the Gospel and bring men and women to the knowledge of Christ. The work of the pastor and teacher— and note that the one person has a two-fold function—was to shepherd and feed the converts, instructing them and nourishing them in divine things.

But behind the giving of these major gifts is a purpose so important that we must give special consideration to it. Note the wording of the passage (v. 12) in the R.V.: 'for the perfecting of the saints, unto the work of ministering, unto the building up of the Body of Christ.' The bestowal of the prominent gifts by the risen Lord was not to give a monopoly to a comparatively small number of persons, but that the exercise of these gifts might, in turn, train and develop (perfect) the members of Christ so that all would be fulfilling their individual ministry. The final words in the passage (vv. 15, 16) reveal the consequence of the functioning of all the members in the binding together, nourishment, and growth of the Body. And this is what we find at Corinth, the result of the work of such gifts, a church 'enriched in Him' and 'coming behind in no gift' but showing many expressions of the endowment of the Spirit.

While the Ephesian passage expounds the universal truth affecting the Body as a whole, the teaching to the Corinthians deals specifically with a local expression of it evidenced in that particular community of believers. In every Christian church there should be found some evidence of a working of the Holy Spirit, in His sovereign distribution of gift. The stirrings of spiritual gift in a believer come, not from himself but from the Spirit of God. In the section in his letter to Corinth specially devoted to this theme (1 Cor. 12-14) Paul enumerates some of the particular gifts and here we notice a slight difference of standpoint. In Ephesians the Giver is the Lord Jesus risen and glorified, while in Corinthians the Holy Spirit is the One who sovereignly acts. In Ephesians the gifts are men bestowed on the Body for its benefit; in Corinthians the gifts are imparted as various manifestations of the Spirit in different individuals. Spiritual endowment is marked by great diversity, for God is not limited in His distribution or ways of working; He has room for all, and something for each to do in the Body.

We need to observe the enumeration of gifts in this section (ch. 12), for there are some gifts that were passing, while others were permanent. Though some of the gifts of a more spectacular nature were destined to pass away with the development of the churches, certain others would always be necessary for the fulfilment of the normal function of a church. The Holy Spirit divides to each member according to His pleasure (v. 11), for while there are many gifts and ministries, there is but one great end in view in all their exercise, the glory of Christ (v. 3). This will explain the manner in which the most dissimilar spiritual gifts are yet all traceable to the same divine Source, making, with all the variety, no jarring note, no disharmony, but rather a complementary contribution to the life of the church. Note further, that the apostle stresses that, in all the diversity in these gifts, there is an all-embracing unity of purpose; each member is necessary to the other, and to the whole organism, for the balance and oneness of the whole. In this way the needs of all believers are supplied and ample scope is found for expressing devotion to Christ in service in the Church. Each Christian is a member of the Body, with responsibility resting upon him in some particular way (1 Cor. 12. 27). The teaching concerning spiritual gifts gives place to Paul's famous poem of love (ch. 13) in which he indicates the true spirit of service, which in turn leads on to the practica injunctions of chapter 14, giving, so to speak, a working model of the principles already laid down.

It is apparent from this passage that the Corinthians were coming together for their gatherings for edification, 'an earnest company of men and women full of restrained enthusiasm, which might soon become unrestrained.'[1] There was a tendency at Corinth for a certain looseness in the exercise of gift, so that the believers tended to make a display of themselves in the church. The apostle gives them, therefore, a general framework, within which they were to regulate the exercise of their gifts. In the first place he compares the relative values of certain gifts, contrasting ecstatic ministries with those for edification (ch. 14. 1-19), following this by indicating the primary purpose in the use of these gifts and the possible issues from a right or wrong use of gift in the church (vv. 20-25). Then follows definite guidance to the brethren in the gatherings (vv. 26-33), and the women also (vv. 34-36), with a final word suggesting that a test of true spirituality is our measure of obedience to the apostolic injunctions as being the Lord's own command (vv. 37-40).

Both Paul and Peter speak of the Christian Ministry elsewhere, Paul as he writes to the Romans (ch. 12) and Peter in his first epistle (ch. 4. 7-11). Taking these two further passages, Paul urges the necessity for giving oneself to one's service, whatsoever it may be, so that it may be fulfilled and one's contribution to the life of the Body be made. Peter indicates that every gift or ministry is a stewardship from God, an expression of His grace to His people, and it is 'as good stewards of the manifold grace of God' that we are to serve, ministering 'as of the strength which God supplieth'; so that God will in all things be glorified.

In all this teaching scope is given to both men and women to fulfil a ministry in the church. In his famous letter to the Emperor Trajan, Pliny speaks of examining Christians in Bithynia, among whom were 'two slave women called ministers,' a passage which at once reminds us of the commendation of Phoebe, 'a servant of the church that is at Cenchreæ' (Rom. 16. 1). While it is true that the apostle shows the place of the women in the public gatherings of the church to be one of quietness, leadership being given unto the men on such occasions, it is also true that there is ample scope for women in their own sphere, for the New Testament writings give us glimpses—little more than glimpses, yet sufficiently embedded in the apostolic tradition—of women at work. As we

[1] *The Church and the Ministry in the Early Centuries*, by T. M. Lindsay, page 44.

9

saw earlier, ministry is but service, and all Christians are called to the service of Christ, so that even within the sphere of church life, other than the actual gatherings of an assembly of believers, there is much that women may do, both in regard to the Christian circle, and amongst other women in the work of witnessing.[1]

Whatever the manifestation of the Spirit in any individual it is not for his own benefit but for the benefit of all (1 Cor. 12. 7). Those gifts that are most profitably exercised in private will not be allowed to obtrude into the gatherings of the church, while those intended for the edification of the church should be so used. T. M. Lindsay truly remarks: 'We hear of no officials appointed to conduct the services,'[2] of the church at Corinth, yet the gracious restraint of the apostle is seen in his injunction: 'But let all things be done decently and in order' (1 Cor. 14. 40, R.V.). We have seen the way in which local churches in apostolic times made room for any gift of the Spirit that might be manifested as bestowed upon any of their members, and all encouragement was given for the development of such gift unto full maturity.

To sum up, the risen Lord has given gifts to men in the form of persons endowed with special ministries of permanent value in the Body and with a view to the setting in motion of great spiritual forces as all the members of His Body function in their places. These ministries are to be exercised in the local congregations of believers, always with the instruction and edification of the saints as a goal and with the end in view of magnifying the Lord Jesus Christ. Scope is given to both men and women in church life in their respective spheres.

These considerations lead us naturally to enquire as to the power available for the fulfilment of ministry in any aspect, and we shall next consider,

THE POWER FOR MINISTRY

The promise of Christ to His disciples was that they would be 'clothed with power from on high' (Luke 24. 49, R.V.) and this promise was fulfilled at Pentecost in the coming of the Holy Spirit. He is the power for all Christian ministry and by His aid alone may we

[1] See Note 7, p. 213.   [2] *The Church and the Ministry in the Early Centuries*, page 44.

engage in service. We speak frequently of the leading of the Spirit in relation to church life, and yet this is a much misunderstood subject. Many minds are in complete confusion as to the precise meaning of the term and still more as to the recognition of His leading when the church is met together. How are we to discern His leading? How do we differentiate between our own desires and the promptings of the Holy Spirit? Is any person who so wishes at liberty to participate in ministering in the church?

The clue is to be found when we observe, firstly, that the Holy Spirit is not once mentioned in the whole chapter dealing with the gathered church (1 Cor. 14). He has been spoken of earlier as the One who has been behind the distribution of spiritual gifts, but here, when it comes to the actual exercise of gift, prominence is given rather to the personal responsibility of the brethren. With primary reference to praying or singing (v. 15), the principle is shown by the words 'with the spirit,' and 'with the understanding also.' Spirit allied to understanding (or intelligence) is our guide here. The believer who habitually walks in the Holy Spirit's power will be brought under His influence almost unconsciously when in the church. There is to be the use of the reasoning faculty, the intellect, when gathered together, as to the fitness and general suitability of any part that might be taken in the meeting. To hear a hymn quoted is not sufficient reason, of necessity, to announce it to be sung by all; at all times we should use spiritual judgment as to our participation before hastily making any contribution. This will ensure that decency and order will distinguish all the proceedings of the church though there be no presiding personage. The open meeting is not for an any-man ministry, but is subject to godly order at all times.

It may be said that the glimpse given us of the church at Corinth in assembly indicates a temporary condition not necessarily obligatory upon any other church, even in those days, much less so for to-day. Yet there are many indications that the teaching of 1 Corinthians was not intended only for that church but also for the churches generally (cf. 1. 2, 9; 4. 14-17; 7. 17; 11. 16; 14. 33-36; 16. 1), and it is in the very chapter dealing most with the subject that certain details are accompanied by the comment 'as in all the churches of the saints' (ch. 14. 33). The one essential is that

believers should be under the influence and power of the Holy
Spirit in their meetings.   A Spirit-controlled gathering becomes its
own evidence of the presence of the Lord and onlookers will
confess 'that God is among you indeed' (ch. 14. 25, R.V.).

The foregoing matters lead inevitably to the raising of many
practical questions, so that we must devote some time to

SOME PRACTICAL CONSIDERATIONS

We have seen that all believers are considered in the New
Testament as being included in the Christian Ministry, but that
they occupy different places and serve in different capacities and
spheres.   Added to this we face the solemn fact that each servant
of God has a personal responsibility to discharge, for 'ye are the
Body of Christ, and severally members thereof' (1 Cor. 12. 27,
R.V.).   The well-being of the Body depends, in the final analysis,
upon the proper functioning of each several member.   Failure to
serve may seriously hinder the life and testimony of one's particular
assembly.   The finest service is that which builds up the Body of
Christ as expressed in the life of a Christian congregation.

Whilst recognizing the due distinction between different forms
of service, the early believers give no hint of any separate class of
ministers whose special privilege it was to administer the sacraments.
This is a notable feature which has been glossed over, as being at
variance with the age-old tradition of Christendom, yet, when we
consider the vital difference between ministry in the Old Testament
(the priesthood), and the service of New Testament times, we
cannot but conclude that much confusion of thought has succeeded
in incorporating elements of Judaistic religionism with the simpler
ecclesiastical polity of the New Testament.

Is there, then, no place for the full-time ministry of the Word?
The answer is, of course, that the New Testament both recognizes
and encourages the labours of brethren called to give their lives
to the service of the Word of God, and makes clear the responsibility of the saints to support in temporal things all who worthily
fulfil their ministry.   Touching the labours of brethren engaged
locally in such work, Paul points out the obligation of the believers
to render double honour especially to those labouring in the Word
and teaching, the context showing that honour here includes the

meaning of honorarium (1 Tim. 5. 17, 18).[1] With reference to those labouring in the Gospel he says: 'Know ye not that they which minister about sacred things eat of the things of the temple, and they which wait upon the altar have their portion with the altar? Even so did the Lord ordain that they which proclaim the Gospel should live of the Gospel' (1 Cor. 9. 13, 14, R.V.). And as concerning the work of the teacher (though the above words cover such work also), he says: 'Let him that is taught in the word communicate unto him that teacheth in all good things' (Gal. 6. 6). The New Testament reveals that provision is made for brethren so called of God to move amongst the churches engaging in the ministry of the Word of God, whether particularly labouring in the Gospel or in teaching the Lord's people.

Yet let it be very clear that whether we serve in relation to the church by giving our whole time, or while we also follow some secular occupation, the vital point is to have the call of God to our ministry. The releasing of a relatively small number of the Lord's servants to full-time ministry should not obscure from us the fact that the very large majority of His ministers fulfil their service whilst engaged in some trade or profession.

How, then shall we know our gift from God, that we may fulfil it? To this three simple suggestions may be applied: firstly, a strong inward desire to labour along certain lines; secondly, an ability manifesting itself to serve in that particular manner; and, thirdly, some measure of blessing in engaging in such work—these three things, when together, would suggest the call of God towards some specific service. The blessing of God will show itself in some result from our labours, and also in the Lord's servant feeling at home in the work he is doing. It is frequently the case that our gift turns out to be the work towards which we have a natural inclination and this might manifest itself in distinct ability in work amongst the young, the work of the Gospel at home or abroad, in visitation, in hospitality, in teaching or in some other of the manifold ways of serving.

In a healthy Christian assembly scope will be found for the development of the gifts of the Spirit, so that there will arise from the midst of the church those qualified of God to meet the needs

[1] See W. E. Vine, *Expository Dictionary of New Testament Words*, under Honour. (Vol. II).

of the saints. And ample encouragement is given for seeking the increase of gift, as when we notice, no less than three times in the section devoted to this subject in the letter to Corinth, an exhortation summed up in the words: 'Desire earnestly the greater gifts' (greater, in the sense of greater usefulness to serve others); 'spiritual gifts'; 'to prophesy' (I Cor. 12. 31; 14. 1, 39, R.V.)—prophecy in these passages being understood for to-day in the general sense of a desire to become the Lord's mouthpiece and messenger to His people, that they may be edified.

For all our service the finest training-ground is the life of a Christian church, sharing the fulness of church life and fellowship, pursuing personal communion with God by prayer and Bible study, responding to openings that come our way in which we may develop our ability in spiritual ministry, yet always being careful to see God's hand at work through others, and in other modes of service than our own. The touch of God's hand, an inward consciousness of spiritual vocation, with the fellowship of one's brethren in Christ, all these prepare the man of God for his life service; and the man or woman with such an experience will so labour, whatever his or her ministry, that Christ will be magnified and His people built up in holy things.

CHAPTER IX

DISCIPLINE IN THE CHURCH

W. E. VINE

THE subject of church discipline is to be considered first in regard to that which is directly exercised by God in the assemblies of His people. Any human exercise of it which is according to the divine will and counsel is that which is mediately carried out by the human instruments of His own appointment.

The word *paideia* primarily had the broad significance of training, whether by instruction or correction, that is to say, discipline in the wider sense of the term. It is rendered 'chastening' everywhere in the New Testament, except in 2 Tim. 3. 16, where it signifies 'instruction.' The more limited sense of chastening is that which occupies us in this chapter in regard to church discipline as exercised by God. And inasmuch as an assembly consists of individual members, the circumstances of each of whom affects the spiritual condition of the whole, we must consider, within the limits of this chapter, what Scripture says about the Lord's dealings with the individual believer by way of chastisement.

The natural and despairing mind may be tempted to regard the disciplinary hand of God as leading further away from Him. Viewed in the light of His Word it is an incentive to adjustment of the heart to Himself and to a deeper devotion to Christ. The Lord's exhortation concerning His chastening is, 'My Son, regard not lightly the chastening of the Lord, nor faint when thou art reproved of Him; for whom the Lord loveth He chasteneth, and scourgeth every son whom He receiveth' (Heb. 12. 5, 6, R.V.). Those addressed thus had forgotten the teaching of Scripture as to the nature and purpose of such discipline, and therefore were in danger of becoming weary, and fainting in their souls (v. 3).

No true believer is without experience of chastening; it is a seal of sonship, and a proof of the love and favour of his heavenly Father (vv. 6 and 8). Hence our attention is drawn to His purposes for us in such dealings: (*a*) by our subjection to Him as 'the Father of spirits' (the highest part of our redeemed being) we 'live'; that is to say, we realize the value, power, and joy of spiritual life (v. 9); (*b*) His chastening is 'for our profit'; He designs our true advantage and our utmost interest; (*c*) and this in order that 'we may be partakers of His holiness' (v. 10). His holiness is the perfect accordance of His mind and will with truth, righteousness and purity, and hence His essential and absolute freedom from everything to the contrary. His love acts in conjunction with His holiness. And since our highest welfare and joy consist in having a mind and will in complete conformity with His mind and will, His corrective dealings with us, which have this in view, are exercised in love; (*d*) accordingly He wills thereby to produce in us the peaceable fruit of righteousness, not the effect produced by righteousness, but righteousness as the fruit of chastening, and that in the enjoyment of peace with God and the peace of God.

The statement in verse 7 (R.V.), 'It is for chastening that ye endure,' signifies surely that our Heavenly Father's purpose in the chastening is to give us the disciplinary dealings of His love, and our enduring it in the right spirit gives us the true appreciation of His purpose.

Unless we realize all these purposes we are sure to fail to understand and to value chastening; it is essentially different from the judgments inflicted by God's displeasure and anger. Chastening is that kindly and tender discipline, exercised in perfect love, which trains us into true fellowship with God.

Yet the chastening itself 'seemeth for the present to be not joyous, but grievous' (v. 11), not that the pain and grief of affliction are merely apparent; on the contrary they are actually experienced and there is a gracious purpose in them.

This is fulfilled in the case of those who 'have been exercised thereby.' The word is taken from the training of the gymnast. Those who were preparing themselves for such scenes as the Olympic Games went through a variety of hardships and self-discipline in view of the stern conflicts ahead. The believer who is trained in the school of affliction, and is duly exercised by it, gains a deeper knowledge of sin and is strengthened to get the victory over hidden sin and transgressions. His testimony and service become more effective, and his filial response to the testing of his faith will be 'found unto praise and glory and honour at the revelation of Jesus Christ' (1 Peter 1. 7). This compensates now, and will more than compensate hereafter, for all that which is grievous in the times of testing.

We are apt to forget that 'many are the afflictions of the righteous'; it does not say 'many are the afflictions of the disobedient and hardened.' Theirs is another kind of experience. There is no peaceable fruit of righteousness in such cases.

Paul had his thorn in the flesh; John, the beloved, experienced the loneliness of Patmos. The time would fail to tell of Joseph, David, Job, Jeremiah, and others, for each of whom the Lord had His loving purposes.

Those who would encourage a Stoical attitude of mind, as if courage demanded an effort to banish the sense of sorrow or grief, are blind to the very character of God and ignorant of His gracious purposes. Nor is such an attitude and effort natural; affliction is grievous. The Stoical certainly are not spiritual; we are called upon to humble ourselves under the mighty hand of God, that He may exalt us in due time.

We have neither to despise the chastening, whether through Stoical endurance or wilful hardness of heart; nor, on the contrary, have we to faint when we are rebuked of Him. His dealings call for contrition, for that deep exercise of soul that calls us to His feet with a humble and earnest desire to understand His doings and to respond to the love that prompts them.

The Stoical spirit is not the spirit of a son of God; he does not regard sorrow and suffering as a dire necessity to be endured with resolute calmness; he refrains from thus despising the chastening. The Holy Spirit's gracious work is to convict us of sins and failings, that they may be confessed, forgiven and abandoned. He thus renews within our hearts the great, the paramount desire, that we may 'gain Christ and be found in Him,' that 'we may know Him, and the power of His resurrection, and the fellowship of His sufferings, becoming conformed unto His death' (Phil. 3. 10, R.V.).

DIVINE DISCIPLINE OF AN ASSEMBLY

We have mentioned that the manner of life of the individual

believer affects, for good or for ill, the condition of the local church of which he is a member. This principle is exemplified in the case of the church at Corinth, in 1 Cor. 11, in relation to the spiritual state requisite for partaking of the Lord's Supper. Irregularities in this respect brought the chastening hand of the Lord upon the whole company.

It is significant that the subject of the Lord's Supper and the symbolic emblems appointed for partaking of it, is preceded in chapter 10 by an admonitory reminder of the effects which the sins of certain Israelites had upon the whole nation. All the people experienced the privileges of the delivering power of God in bringing them out of Egypt, and of the supernatural provision made for them in their subsequent journeying. 'Howbeit with most of them (R.V.) God was not well pleased; for they were overthrown in the wilderness. Now these things were our examples,' or rather, 'in these things they became examples of (i.e., for) us,' 'to the intent that we should not lust after evil things, as they also lusted' (10. 1-6).

After recounting further evils of which they were guilty, and warning us against doing the like, the Apostle says again: 'Now these things happened unto them by way of example; and they were written for our admonition, upon whom the ends of the ages are come. Wherefore let him that thinketh he standeth take heed lest he fall' (vv. 11, 12, R.V.). From this he leads, by certain stages, to the danger of the general detriment of the assembly caused by certain members of it.

An outstanding instance of this principle is the sin of Achan (Josh. 7), to which we must refer when speaking presently of the necessity for church discipline by its own members. But the great lesson from the record of Achan's transgression is its consequences for the entire community. In this respect God's people are regarded corporately. If there is a sin in the midst, all suffer as a result. And the reason is this, that God is in the midst; everything depends upon Him, His protection, His leading, His power. They have no strength of their own. 'He is of purer eyes than to behold iniquity.' He cannot associate Himself with sin. He would compromise His essential holiness if He tolerated anything contrary to it. They must get right with God, or, He says, 'I will not be

with you any more' (v. 12). Instead of 'No man shall be able to
stand before thee,' now it was, 'the children of Israel cannot stand
before their enemies' (vv. 12, 13). Where holiness is lacking
weakness is exposed.

We are again reminded that individual members are not isolated
units, they form part of an organic whole, and constitute a moral
unity. The condition of things at Corinth in connection with the
Lord's Supper was such that many were weak and sickly among
them, and not a few were falling asleep, the reference being not
to a spiritual state but to physical conditions, to ill health and
death (ch. 11. 30). Not that all who suffered or were removed were
necessarily themselves guilty and suffering for their own misdeeds.
The guilt of actual offenders affected the whole assembly, which
became the subject of chastisement.

The evil in this respect lay in an unworthy partaking of the
bread and the cup. There were divisions among them, a fact
which meant that their coming together was not for the better
but for the worse. Some were indulging in luxury, putting the
poor to shame and despising God's assembly. When, therefore,
they assembled together it was not possible to eat the Lord's
Supper (v. 20, R.V.).

In partaking of the emblems we 'proclaim the Lord's death'
(v. 26). We are not said to show His death, as if we were exhibiting
it. Nor are we said to show it forth, as if we were representing
it. The verb is *katangellō*, which is used of preaching in ch. 9. 14
and seven other places in the New Testament (R.V., 'proclaim' in
each case). The acts of breaking the bread and drinking the cup
constitute a silent proclamation of the fact, significance and efficacy
of the Lord's death.

'Wherefore' (i.e., on account of this), says the Apostle, 'whoso-
ever shall eat the bread or drink the cup of the Lord unworthily,
shall be guilty of the body and the blood of the Lord' (v. 27). To
regard the bread and the cup as if they had no significance, that is
to say, without contemplation of the death of Christ as set forth
in the elements on the table, or to partake in a manner inconsistent
with the character of the ordinance, or again, to partake while in
an unspiritual state, or while indulging in sin in the private life,
or while entertaining bitterness of spirit against a fellow-believer

instead of living in brotherly love, is to partake unworthily.

The word *enochos*, guilty, means liable to the penal effect of (a deed); here it marks the guilt as being in respect of the body and blood of the Lord, that is, of being involved in the guilt of His death. It shows the solemnity of improperly regarding the privilege of partaking of the Lord's Supper, inasmuch as we thereby mar the character of that which gives proof of the absolute holiness of God.

Hence each believer is to prove himself, and so eat of the bread and drink of the cup (v. 28), each testing himself as to whether he or she is in a right state of soul or not for partaking worthily. If not, let him confess to the Lord what is wrong (1 John 1. 9), and if there is alienation between himself and a fellow-believer, let him be reconciled to him without delay (Matt. 5. 23, 24); he can thus renew fellowship with the Lord. 'For he that eateth and drinketh, eateth and drinketh judgment unto himself, if he discern not the body' (v. 29, R.V.). The body is not the local church, nor the whole Church the Body of Christ, but the Lord's body, as in verses 24 and 27. The judgment is that which brings about the disciplinary chastening by the Lord, for 'when we are judged we are chastened of the Lord, that we should not be condemned with the world' (v. 32).

No believer is without chastening; all are partakers of it; otherwise they are bastards and not sons (Heb. 12. 8). Therefore no believer will suffer the condemnation of the world hereafter. If a believer acts as if he were of the world he draws down upon himself the disciplinary chastening of the Lord, and so God's purpose is fulfilled.

Since, therefore, as we have seen from verse 30, the conduct of actual offenders affects the assembly as a whole, every individual member should experience deep exercise of heart, so that each one may live in holiness before the Lord. An unworthy walk involves an unworthy partaking of the Lord's Supper. To absent oneself only makes matters worse. The only course to take is self-judgment, repentance, and a return to the right ways of the Lord.

This is what the Lord enjoined upon the assembly at Laodicea, and still enjoins upon any company that is in a Laodicean condition. He says, 'As many as I love, I reprove and chasten: be zealous, therefore, and repent' (Rev. 3. 19, R.V.). That assembly had become self-satisfied, proud and luxurious. It gloried in maintaining that it was rich, and had gotten riches, and had need of nothing; all vain self-deception! for in reality it was 'the wretched one and miserable and poor and blind and naked' (v. 17, R.V.). No doubt its members had become possessed of considerable natural acquirements and material wealth, and all this at the cost of that spiritual vitality which evinces loving, loyal devotion to Christ. In their pitiable state they were destitute of the true riches, blind to their actual condition, and denuded of the garments of righteousness.

But it was their relation and attitude to the Lord Himself that grieved Him most. 'I know thy works,' He says, 'that thou art neither cold nor hot. . . . So because thou art lukewarm, and neither hot nor cold, I will spew thee out of My mouth' (v. 16). Lukewarmness is taken by some to signify half-heartedness. The more likely significance is the state produced by a mixture of worldliness and religion, just as lukewarm water is the result of mingling hot and cold. Lukewarm water acts as an emetic. Hence the Lord's metaphorical expression of loathing. The disciplinary act of spewing them out of His mouth indicates a complete rejection as a testimony.

The grace that counsels them (instead of commanding) to purchase from Himself the gold, the garments, the eye-salve (the riches of glory, divine righteousness through testing, the ways of practical righteousness, and the enlightenment given by the Holy Spirit), finds its confirmation in the climax of His appeal, 'As many as I love, I reprove and chasten.' There is very marked emphasis upon the second 'I'; it begins the statement in the original. Striking, too, is the fact that the word for love is *phileō*, the love of tender affection.

The absolute unity of the Father and the Son in the discipline exercised by each is seen in the parallel statement in Heb. 12. 6, already referred to, 'whom the Lord loveth He chasteneth.' Unitedly they operate, in their disciplinary dealings, for the real and lasting profit and welfare of each believer and each church.

DISCIPLINE BY THE ASSEMBLY

We must now consider the subject of the discipline necessary to be exercised in the local assembly by the assembly itself. God is holy and a God of order, and His very presence in an assembly by the indwelling Holy Spirit demands holiness and godly order. For an assembly is a temple of the Holy Spirit (1 Cor. 3. 16), a house of God.

In writing the first Epistle to Timothy the Apostle mentions as the great purpose therein that Timothy may know 'how men (i.e., believers, lit., 'how it is necessary') ought to behave themselves in the house of God, which is the church of the living God' (1 Tim. 3. 15); he is not giving Timothy instruction as to how he himself should behave; the preceding and succeeding contexts confirm the R.V. rendering.

Where, then, such conduct exists as contravenes the character of the house of God as such, discipline is necessary. Otherwise lawlessness will take the place of godliness, and it will be true as is recorded of Israel twice in the book of the Judges, 'every man did that which was right in his own eyes.'

Christ 'gave Himself for us that He might redeem us from all iniquity (lawlessness) and purify unto Himself a people for His own possession, zealous of good works' (Titus 2. 14, R.V.). Conduct contrary to this has to be dealt with. In the private life of the believer, as that which is known and seen by God alone, sin confessed is sin forgiven, and he who lives in the fear of the Lord learns to reckon himself 'to be dead to sin and to be alive unto God in Christ Jesus' (Rom. 6. 11, R.V.). There is another side to his life, however, as manifested to fellow-believers and to the world. Public sins dishonour the Lord and mar assembly testimony, and these call for public discipline.

The assembly at Corinth had lapsed into such carelessness and neglect in this respect that they ignored a known case of gross fornication, 'And ye are puffed up,' says the Apostle, 'and did not rather mourn, that he that had done this deed might be taken away from among you' (1 Cor. 5. 2, R.V.). They were commanded to put away the wicked man from among themselves (v. 13). Similar discipline was to be exercised towards anyone (besides a fornicator) who is named a brother, that is, one who professes to be born of God and thus is related to other believers, and yet by the character of his life disqualifies himself from being so regarded, by being 'covetous, or an idolater, or a reviler, or a drunkard, or an extortioner' (v. 11).

With such, those who constitute an assembly are 'not to eat,' a phrase particularizing the command not to keep company. The injunction involves an abstention from inviting such to one's house or accepting his invitations. Such an intercourse would not only be a practical recognition of his mere profession and a condonation of his evil, it would be a virtual identification with it. This abstention involves exclusion from the Lord's Table, though that is not the point of the injunction.

The assembly is to maintain a God-pleasing testimony to the world. We are to have 'a good report of them that are without.' The standard of morality must never be allowed to fall below even that of the world.

Again, the fact that a believer has had to be removed from fellowship should never become the subject of gossip, whether among the members of the assembly themselves or by any of them in conversation with those outside. What is necessary to clear the assembly in the eyes of the world and to justify the action is quite another matter, but evil reports spread fast enough without our taking part in fostering them.

Another matter to be avoided is the possible feeling of satisfaction that one who was not very helpful in the gathering has been got rid of. The question of personal dislike should not arise. There should ever be deep sorrow on the part of all that such a course was necessary. The paramount attitude should be that of regard for the Lord's honour, and tender-hearted concern for the erring ones.

To excommunicate from an assembly is to put the offender into the sphere of the world, where God's authority is disowned, and where accordingly Satan holds sway as 'the god of this world' (cp. 1 John 5. 19, R.V.). And though the authority of the apostle was in exercise in delivering the offender in Corinth unto Satan, and it may not be given to an assembly formally to do so, yet the principle of the act holds good.

For a believer to disregard God's claims and commandments is to give Satan the opportunity of fulfilling his malign purposes. He ever seeks to turn children of God from the right ways of the Lord, and is occupied in laying snares for them so as to make them his captives. Where, through self-will, this becomes true of believers, it will be the part of a true servant of God to correct such in meekness 'if peradventure God may give them repentance unto the knowledge of the truth' (2 Tim. 2. 25); the rendering of the next verse should be, 'that they may recover themselves (lit., return to soberness) out of the snare of the Devil—having been made captive by him (i.e., Satan, not the Lord's servant, as is inserted in the R.V.)—unto the will of God' (not 'at his will,' A.V.).

The evil effects upon a gathering where there is sin in the midst is illustrated by the case of Achan, and the serious consequences of his sin upon Israel as a whole. Deeply significant is the opening statement in Josh. 7 concerning this, that 'the children of Israel committed a trespass.' Achan's sin in taking of the devoted thing brought, not simply trouble and defeat, but guilt upon the whole people, and God said to Joshua 'Israel hath sinned; yea, they have even transgressed My covenant which I commanded them; yea, they (not one of their number) have even taken of the devoted thing; and have stolen, and dissembled also' (v. 11). Accordingly the people had to sanctify themselves, and execute judgment upon the guilty one and upon all that appertained to him (vv. 15, 25), the intimation being that his family was involved in the guilt.

It was because there was sin in the midst that Israel could not stand before their enemies. So in the spiritual realm. 'Our wrestling is not against flesh and blood, but against the principalities, against the powers, against the world-rulers of this darkness, against the spiritual hosts of wickedness in the heavenly places' (Eph. 6. 12, R.V.). If there is unjudged sin in the assembly the power of the gathering becomes weakened and room is made for the influence of the world. There may be the usual round of meetings, but little apprehension of true devotion to Christ and little real spiritual blessing. As all Israel had to deal with Achan, so an assembly as a whole must put away evil from the midst.

There was iniquity in the assembly at Pergamos. They had some that held the teaching of Balaam, and some that held the teaching of the Nicolaitans. The Lord therefore called upon the assembly there to repent; 'or else,' He says, 'I come to thee quickly, and I will make war against them with the sword of My mouth' (Rev. 2. 16).

In Israel no one was put to death save at the mouth of two or three witnesses (Deut. 17. 6), indicating the exercise of the most careful scrutiny into the circumstances. The same care is necessary in an assembly. Further, since the erring believer is still a child of God and is, therefore, in inseparable relationship with the Lord, discipline is to be exercised only with a view to restoration to fellowship. Meanwhile deep humiliation is called for on the part of the whole assembly, for 'a little leaven leaveneth the whole lump.' Such an attitude will be accompanied by prayer and intercession for the one who has become the subject of discipline.

To restore a brother to fellowship does not involve his taking part in oral ministry in the meetings again. The fact of the discipline exercised, and the cause of it, are sufficient to render it only consistent with the public testimony of the assembly that, while enjoying renewed fellowship, he should refrain from taking part in the way mentioned.

The assembly at Corinth had responded to the Apostle's instruction and injunction in his first Epistle. The disciplinary measure had been taken by the many (lit., the more). They had grieved greatly and their sorrow was shared by Paul. Moreover the offender had been genuinely and deeply sorry for his sin and had manifested a spirit of true repentance. So much so that there was now a danger of his being 'swallowed up with his overmuch sorrow' (2 Cor. 2. 7, R.V.). Accordingly there was a need of full and immediate restoration. They were to forgive him for all he had caused (for God had forgiven him his transgression), and to comfort or 'encourage' him, assuring him of their love (v. 8).

This was not mere emotion; the forgiveness, encouragement and love (happy the renewal of fellowship in this manner!) were to have as their further motive and aim to prevent Satan from gaining an advantage (v. 11). It follows, therefore, that he gains an advantage by undue delay in restoring the repentant. If the advantage be secured by ensnaring the evildoer, let the assembly guard against his gaining an advantage in this other way. We are to guard against laxity on the one hand and rigidity on the other. Love that delights to restore triumphs over the devices of the evil one.

There are other measures of discipline in an assembly than that

10

of excommunication. The church at Thessalonica was exhorted to admonish the disorderly (1 Thess. 5. 14, R.V.); the word signifies insubordinate, and this spirit manifests itself in different ways; idleness and officiousness (busybodies) are mentioned (2 Thess. 3. 11). Again, refusal to submit to rule (an evidence of weakness, not of strength), is a transgression of the direct command of God to 'be in subjection . . . to every one that helpeth in the work and laboureth' (1 Cor. 16. 16, R.V.). Admonition must be in the power of the Holy Spirit and be given with the fellowship of the assembly, to the profit of all concerned.

The members of an assembly are commanded to 'withdraw' themselves 'from every brother who walks disorderly' (2 Thess. 3. 6, R.V.). The word is used metaphorically, of shrinking from a person. A stronger form of the verb is used of Peter's attitude in separating himself from those from whom he should not have separated (Gal. 2. 12). The injunction certainly involves abstention from keeping company with the disorderly. How the withdrawal is to be effected is stated in verses 14, 15 (R.V.): 'If any man obeyeth not our word by this epistle, note that man, that ye have no company with him, to the end that he may be ashamed. And yet count him not as an enemy, but admonish him as a brother.'

Similar to this is the command given to Timothy, 'Them that sin rebuke before all, that others may fear' (1 Tim. 5. 20). If unbelievers are present, they should be asked to leave.

To each member of any assembly the warning given in 1 Cor. 10. 12 ever applies, 'Wherefore let him that thinketh he standeth take heed lest he fall.' This being given in view of the backslidings of Israel, what need there is, especially when any disciplinary measures become necessary, to guard against the self-complacency that produces a careless condition of soul![1]

[1] See Note 9, p. 216.

CHAPTER X

FINANCE:
MAINTAINING THE WORK OF GOD

D. W. BREALEY

THE question of finance is, admittedly, a delicate one, and for this reason, few seem free to speak about it. Yet the Scriptures have much to say on the subject, and no trace of embarrassment can be detected in the writers who handle it.

In this chapter we suggest that we should first consider the teaching of Moses, then the teaching of Christ, and finally the teaching of the apostles. Taken together both unity and development will be noticeable.

The Teaching of Moses

In the Levitical economy there appears to be a distinction made between Tithes and Offerings: the Tithes were obligatory; the Offerings, in a sense, optional.

(A) TITHES. These covered the first-born of man and beast; the first-fruits of the earth; and the tenth.

(a) THE FIRST-BORN (Exodus 13. 1, 2).

God said of the first-born, 'It is Mine' (v. 2). The first-born of man had to be redeemed with a lamb; God accepted the slain lamb in its place (v. 15). Similarly the first-born of an ass might be redeemed with a lamb (v. 13), otherwise its neck must be broken, the Israelite might not retain it for himself, it was the Lord's. Every first-born of beast was to be sacrificed to the Lord (v. 15), 'the males shall be the Lord's' (v. 12).

So it clearly appears that when Israel offered to the Lord a lamb in the place of his first-born, or in the place of the firstling of his ass, or when he offered the first-born male of his cattle, he was not *giving* to the Lord, he was merely handing over to the Lord that which already belonged to Him.

(b) THE FIRST-FRUITS (Exodus 22. 29).

In like manner the first-fruits of the land belonged to the Lord, and without delay these had to be rendered to Him. God must have His portion before ever Israel had theirs.

(c) THE TENTH (Numbers 18. 20, 21).

For the maintenance of the priestly and Levitical service of the tabernacle of the congregation, God gave the tenth in Israel to the children of Levi. All that Israel had, they received from the Lord, but from that bounty He took a tenth for the maintenance of His work. Let us note the exact wording: ' . . . behold I have given the children of Levi all the tenth in Israel,' so that if words mean anything at all, that which Levi received was a gift from the Lord, not from Israel.

From these Scriptures we see that the first-born, the first-fruits, and the tenth, were the Lord's and that the rendering of these to the Lord *was not giving at all, it was tithing*, handing over to the Lord that which did not belong to them, but which always belonged to Him. Witholding any part of the tithe was, in God's estimate, robbery!

'Will a man rob God? Yet ye have robbed Me. But ye say, Wherein have we robbed Thee? In tithes and offerings. Ye are cursed with a curse: for ye have robbed Me, even this whole nation. Bring ye all the tithes (the whole tithe, R.V.) into the store-house, that there may be meat in Mine house, and prove Me now herewith, saith the Lord of hosts, if I will not open you the windows of heaven, and pour you out a blessing, that there shall not be room enough to receive it' (Mal. 3. 8-10).

Certainly, then, the tithe was obligatory.

(B) OFFERINGS. Over and above the tithe Israel had the blessed privilege of giving to the Lord. Their free-will offerings constituted their *giving*. They might give to the Lord after having disposed of the tithe, anything up to the limit of their willingness and capacity. 'If any man of you bring an offering unto the Lord . . . he shall offer it of his own voluntary will' (Lev. 1. 2, 3). According to his ability and willingness he might bring a bullock or a sheep or a goat, or turtle doves, among other things; great or small,

God would graciously receive from His people anything that their hearts prompted them to give Him.

We are prone to sing very glibly:

> Take my silver and my gold,
> Not a mite would I withhold,

but in the hearing of the present writer it was pertinently asked at a recent meeting in a farming district: 'Are you prepared to offer to the Lord a bullock?'!

THE TEACHING OF CHRIST

All that Moses taught was confirmed by the Lord Jesus Christ, as, indeed, it would be: for Moses was but the spokesman of God. 'Think not that I am come to destroy the law, or the prophets: I am not come to destroy, but to fulfil' (Matt. 5. 17).

In the particular matter of tithing, however, He seeks to bring back to a sense of proportion some who were very punctilious in this thing, but completely lacking in 'weightier matters.' 'Woe unto you, scribes and Pharisees, hypocrites! for ye pay tithe of mint and anise and cummin, and have omitted the weightier matters of the law, judgment, mercy, and faith: these ought ye to have done, and not to leave the other undone' (Matt. 23. 23). 'These' refers to the 'weightier matters,' but 'the other' to tithing which, says the Lord Jesus *must not be left undone*. Here, then, is Christ's authority for saying that tithing is obligatory. He does not specifically refer to the fact that the first-born and first-fruits are the Lord's, but rather points the way wherein is the true response to such a position. 'But seek ye *first* the kingdom of God, and His righteousness' (Matt. 6. 33).

He also has some pertinent things to say about giving, stressing not so much the fact and privilege of giving, as the conditions under which it can be acceptable to God.

(*a*) The life must be right if the gift is to be acceptable. 'Therefore if thou bring thy gift to the altar, and there rememberest that thy brother hath ought against thee; leave there thy gift before the altar and go thy way; first be reconciled to thy brother, and then come and offer thy gift' (Matt. 5. 23, 24).

(*b*) The motive must be right. 'Therefore when thou doest thine alms, do not sound a trumpet before thee, as the hypocrites do

. . . that they may have glory of men. . . . But when thou doest alms, let not thy left hand know what thy right hand doeth: that thine alms may be in secret: and thy Father which seeth in secret Himself shall reward thee openly' (Matt. 6. 2-4).

(c) There must be the due recognition and discharge of family obligations.

'Moses said, Honour thy father and thy mother . . . but ye say, If a man shall say to his father or his mother, That wherewith thou mightest have been profited by me is Corban, that is to say, Given to God; ye no longer suffer him to do aught for his father or his mother; making void the word of God by your tradition' (Mark 7. 10-13, R.V.).

(d) The gift must be impelled by love. An example of this is found in the offering of the penitent sinner in Simon's house. 'She loved much,' is our Lord's testimony (Luke 7. 47).

(e) The measure of the gift will be the degree of its acceptability. But the gift will be measured, not by its own intrinsic value, but by what is left when it is given.

'And Jesus sat over against the treasury, and beheld how the people cast money into the treasury: and many that were rich cast in much. And there came a certain poor widow, and she threw in two mites, which make a farthing. And He called unto Him His disciples, and saith unto them, Verily I say unto you, that this poor widow hath cast more in, than all they which have cast into the treasury: for all they did cast in of their abundance; but she of her want did cast in all that she had, even all her living' (Mark 12. 41-44). Jesus still sits 'over against the treasury'! Here in this poor widow's gift we have an example of the kind of giving God loves to accept; the giving to the point of extreme self-sacrifice. But the supreme example of all is found in the Lord Jesus Christ Himself. 'I am the Good Shepherd: the Good Shepherd *giveth His life* for the sheep' (John 10. 11).

As I pass on to the teaching of the apostles let me do so by quoting His words of exhortation and encouragement: 'Give, and it shall be given unto you; good measure, pressed down, and shaken together, and running over, shall men give into your bosom. For with the same measure that ye mete withal it shall be measured to you again' (Luke 6. 38).

THE TEACHING OF THE APOSTLES

The apostles continued the teaching of the grace of giving both by precept and by practice.

(A) BY PRECEPT. Every matter of vital importance for the child of God is dealt with exhaustively at least once in the Scriptures, often more than once. The subject of Christian giving is dealt with exhaustively by the Apostle Paul in 2 Corinthians 8 and 9. We commend those chapters to the careful and prayerful study of the reader, but for the present purposes we will learn from them certain principles which appear upon the surface.

The essential and primary thing in all Christian giving is the recognition that we are not our own (1 Corinthians 6. 19); hence the exhortation to the Romans: 'Present your bodies a living sacrifice' (ch. 12. 1), and the acceptance of this position by the Macedonian churches who 'first gave their own selves to the Lord' (2 Cor. 8. 5). If there is a clear understanding of that at the beginning, it will become equally clear that what we call our own is actually the Lord's and the most scrupulous care must be taken in the use of it. We will weigh up before Him the matter of our stewardship and settle in our minds what He would have us expend on ourselves and what should be done with the rest.

Having settled that question honestly before God, let us notice the principles in 2 Corinthians 8 and 9 which regulate Christian giving. I take the principles in the order in which they appear in these chapters, and the first of these is the principle of the *open hand* (ch. 8. 2), 'their liberality.'

The apostle comes back to this again before he closes the subject of giving, and as he begins, so he ends on the note of 'open-handedness' in Christian giving—'he which soweth bountifully shall reap also bountifully' (ch. 9. 6); 'being enriched in everything to all bountifulness' (v. 11), and 'your liberal distribution' (v. 13).

The supreme example of liberal giving, and the unanswerable argument for it, and incentive to it, is in the Lord Jesus Christ Himself: 'For ye know the grace of our Lord Jesus Christ, that, though He was rich, yet for your sakes He became poor, that ye through His poverty might be rich' (ch. 8. 9). 'Thanks be unto God for His unspeakable gift' (ch. 9. 15).

Let us also note carefully that liberality is not a grace limited to the rich who can afford to be liberal, but the very soil in which it flourishes is 'deep poverty.' 'Moreover, brethren, we do you to wit of the grace of God bestowed on the churches of Macedonia; how that in a great trial of affliction the abundance of their joy and their deep poverty abounded unto the riches of their liberality' (ch. 8. 1, 2). How constantly in Christian experience do we see this very thing obtaining.

The second is the principle of *the willing mind*. 'For to their power, I bear record, yea, and beyond their power they were willing . . .' (ch. 8. 3); 'a readiness to will' (v. 11); 'For if there be first a willing mind, it is accepted according to that a man hath and not according to that he hath not' (v. 12): 'Every man according as he purposeth in his heart, so let him give; not grudgingly or of necessity: for God loveth a cheerful giver' (ch. 9. 7).

This brings us to the third principle, namely, the principle of the *cheerful heart*. Those who give liberally and willingly will discover the joy of giving and the truth of the word, 'It is more blessed to give than to receive' (Acts 20. 35). Then as we give let us do it cheerfully; our hearts will be made glad and God will bless us.

In conjunction with this chapter consideration should be taken of 1 Cor. 16. 1-3 where three other principles are introduced, namely, Giving should be with *Regularity*: 'Upon the first day of the week let every one of you lay by him in store.' *Systematically*: '. . . lay by him in store.' *Proportionately*: 'As God hath prospered him.' My own conviction is, that, if under the law, the tenth was the minimum that Israel might render to the Lord in addition to the first-born and first-fruits, under grace it could not be less. And if, under the law, giving did not begin until this was disposed of, is it reasonable to suppose that we shall be accredited with giving until this same mimimum is handed over to God?

Then after that let us give proportionately as God has prospered us, yet not forgetting in this the discharge of all our earthly obligations so that yet another principle of great importance emerges, giving must be *honourable*. 'Avoiding this, that no man should blame us in this abudance which is administered by us: providing for honest things, not only in the sight of the Lord, but also in the sight of men' (2 Cor. 8. 20, 21). To give to the Lord's work at the expense of parents (Mark 7. 11-13), children and households (2 Cor. 12. 14; 1 Tim. 5. 8), tradesmen, etc. (Rom. 13. 8) would not be honest, neither would it be acceptable to God. The apostles taught not only by precept but by practice.

(B) BY PRACTICE. 'All that believed were together, and had all things common; and sold their possessions and goods, and parted them to all men, as every man had need' (Acts 2. 44, 45).

Acts 6. 1 speaks of a 'daily ministration' with needy widows particularly in view.

In Gal. 2. 9, 10, James, Cephas, and John gave the right hand of fellowship to Paul and Barnabas with the injunction that they 'should remember the poor, the same which I also was forward to do.'

In addition to the actual practice of the apostles themselves, the early Christians in apostolic days exercised this same grace, and collective gifts are mentioned in several places. In the church at Antioch, 'every man according to his ability, determined to send relief unto the brethren which dwelt in Judæa; which also they did, and sent it to the elders by the hands of Barnabas and Saul' (Acts 11. 29, 30). The church at Corinth sent a collective gift to the saints at Jerusalem (1 Cor. 16. 1-4) by the hands of Titus and another brother appointed by the churches (2 Cor. 8. 18, 19). On several occasions the church at Philippi sent collective gifts to the Apostle Paul (Phil. 4. 15, 16).

It is, moreover, worthy of note that apart from the Philippian gifts, the last of which was sent to Paul through the medium of Epaphroditus (ch. 4. 18) the other collective gifts were handled by two brethren, and in the case of the 'daily ministration' of Acts 6, 'seven men of good report, full of the Holy Spirit and of wisdom' (v. 3) were appointed over that business. This apostolic practice was both wise and good; it was wise that the church's money should be handled by at least two, appointed by their brethren; it would give confidence and close the mouths of any who might otherwise suggest that there was fraudulent dealing. Moreover, it was good that such a heavy burden and responsibility should be shared, and not be on the shoulders of one. It is very worthy of note that in that first appointment of deacons to handle the finance of the church, they were to be trustworthy men of unblemished character, 'of honest report'; spiritual men, 'full of the Holy Ghost'; and men of business acumen 'full . . . of wisdom' (Acts 6. 3).

Here, then, is an outline of Scripture teaching on the all-important subject of the grace of giving. It is the earnest desire of the writer that his own soul may be searched and brought into conformity to the Word of God, in this, as in all other matters; and it is his humble prayer that it may lead to the soul exercise of every reader.[1]

> Were the whole realm of nature mine,
> That were an offering far too small:
> Love so amazing, so divine,
> Demands my soul, my life, my all.

[1] See Note 10, p. 217.

CHAPTER XI

EVANGELISTS AND EVANGELISM

MONTAGUE GOODMAN

'Do the Work of an Evangelist'

BY far and away the most important function of the churches is to evangelize the world. As has been well said, 'Evangelize or perish' is the alternative with which they have ever been faced. Yet this most vital function of the churches is the most neglected, and in consequence the churches to-day show every indication of perishing. They are in a state of decay unprecedented in their long history solely because their members have ceased to propagate the Gospel as it was their province to do. In other periods, notably in the seventeenth and eighteenth centuries, Christian testimony in our land was at a low ebb indeed through a condition resulting from lack of zeal to propagate the Gospel coupled with crass popular ignorance on all religious questions. To-day the cause is the same, namely, church neglect to evangelize, coupled not with ignorance but rather with a high degree of national intelligence and education permeated throughout with a strong anti-Christian bias.

The Wesleys and Whitfield had but to preach the Gospel message broadcast through the land to countless thousands who were in utter ignorance of it to reap such a harvest as changed in a few short years the character of the nation and led to the Evangelical Revival of the century following. To-day we are faced with a far more educated population of men and women impressed from their youth with views concerning the unreliability of the Scriptures and the decadence of the Christian religion that make the work of the evangelist one of unprecedented difficulty. It is almost axiomatic to-day to say that the British public is not interested in Gospel meetings or missions and does not attend them. People are not usually actively hostile to the message but totally uninter-

ested. Organized Christianity is something as completely outside
the range of their concern as organized Jewry. And this condition
may be said to be general.

Yet it remains true that the main *raison d'être* of the churches'
presence on earth is to evangelize, to be witnesses unto Christ,
to preach the Gospel to every creature in all the world, and it is
equally true that the church is not doing so. What wonder that
sinners are so little concerned for themselves when they see so little
concern evinced for them by the church? Concern begets concern
and conviction spreads conviction. Under present conditions
it is not surprising if the world not only doesn't believe but doesn't
believe we Christians believe. Otherwise how could we show
such indifference to their unbelief and its terrible consequences?

What turned the world upside down in the first century was the
fact that the believers really believed and were eager to propagate their faith even if they suffered for it. In those early days
every believer was an evangelist. 'They that were scattered
abroad went everywhere preaching the Word' (Acts 8. 4). How
many professing Christians to-day ever open their mouths to tell
others the good news from heaven?

Is it not significant that in the enumeration of the special gifts
with which Christ endowed His Church through the Spirit, first
and foremost (after the foundation gifts of apostle and prophet)
should be named the evangelist? 'And He gave some, apostles;
and some, prophets; and some, evangelists' (Eph. 4. 11). The
pastors and teachers so prominent in organized Christianity to-day
are subordinate in order of precedence to the far less esteemed
evangelist. And truly his ministry is by far the most vital to the
world and, indeed, to the life and growth of the Church itself.
And the evangelist is and must be a peculiarly gifted man. It is
the province and imperative duty of all to evangelize in measure
but God has been pleased to gift and equip certain men in particular
for this vital ministry.

What, then, is the peculiar nature of the gift of an evangelist?
We see it exemplified in Scripture, often combined with other gifts,
in certain outstanding characters. Paul was an evangelist in addition
to being an apostle (Rom. 1. 15). Philip the deacon was an evangelist (Acts 21. 8). Timothy was both a pastor and an evangelist

(2 Tim. 4. 5). Wherein were these men evangelists in this distinctive sense? Truly they preached the Evangel (the Gospel) and in this sense they were, as all of us in our several spheres are called upon to be, evangelists. Yet there is a Spirit-imparted gift of an evangelist which not all who preach the Gospel possess. Our Christian assemblies are not lacking in preachers of the Gospel. Thousands of men are honourably engaged mainly in their leisure hours in teaching and preaching Christ. Yet it is probably true to say that the number of evangelists is lamentably few, and as a direct consequence our churches and fellowships languish. If we are to covet earnestly the best gifts then surely there is a call in these days for young men to covet, with a holy ambition, that rare yet greatly desirable gift of the evangelist among men. It was a notable British statesman and publicist who confessed that he would rather have been a humble Gospel preacher than to have had all the glory of his dazzling political achievements. And this is surely so. The effective evangelist, however lowly, is often doing greater patriotic service for his nation (to put it no higher) than half the Members of Parliament in Westminster.

What, then, are the outstanding, and in some part unique, marks and indications of the gift of an evangelist?

It is not easy, nor indeed appropriate to define or to comprise within the limits of precise terms any gift of the Spirit. Yet some attempt at an answer to the above question may be made however lacking in comprehensiveness if only that those we exhort to covet the gift may have some intelligent vision of what it is they are to desire earnestly.

Firstly, an evangelist must have *a consuming passion for the souls of men.* 'Give me souls or I die,' cried a famous Gospel preacher, and God granted him his request. The evangelist is no protagonist for a creed or cult. He is not a maker of proselytes to his particular form of religion. A preacher who will not evangelize except with a view to the creation or upbuilding of a church may be right in his ambition and admirable in his objective, but he has not the essential quality of an evangelist. The Apostle Paul had the evangelist's heart when he said of those who preached Christ of contention and envy and strife: 'What, then? notwithstand, every way, whether in pretence, or in truth, Christ is preached, and I therein do rejoice, yea, and will rejoice!' (Phil. 1. 18). His great yearning desire was that Christ should be preached. Woe unto him if he preached not the Gospel! He became all things to all men if by any means he might save some. The evangelist is not out to make co-religionists but Christians. He must long for souls. He must weep over them. He must spend himself to the utmost for them. I learned something of this on Salisbury Plain during the first World War. An American evangelist whom I met in Salisbury, prior to visiting the troops in camp, invited me into his room for prayer. As we knelt before God he began to pour out his heart but got no further than a sentence or two when he broke down in a torrent of tears. Then we went out to the men and he reaped them for Christ. He had the first and foremost indication of the gift of an evangelist. He had a passionate love for the souls of men.

Secondly, he must be *a man of one theme and that the Gospel.* There is much of the greatest importance that God would have His people learn concerning their Christian walk and worship and fellowship and to this end He gave some to be pastors and teachers. But the true evangelist is a man of one message. He must say with Paul: 'I determined not to know anything among you save Jesus Christ and Him crucified' (1 Cor. 2. 2, R.V.). This does not mean on the one hand that he should confine himself to a few Gospel texts and illustrations variously applied such as too often constitute the stock-in-trade of the travelling evangelist. Nor does it imply that he must content himself with expounding the way of salvation. It is one thing to preach *about* the Gospel and quite another to preach the Gospel. The evangelist is the bringer of good tidings. It is his province to proclaim it rather than to expound it. It is his gift to make the tidings appear to his hearers good tidings indeed 'worthy of all acceptation' rather than good doctrine worthy of their intellectual approval.

Thirdly, *he is essentially a winner of souls.* It is his gift *par excellence.* It is this that differentiates him from a preacher or teacher. Not that these latter may not have the joy of seeing men saved under their faithful ministry, but it is the essential quality of the evangelist that he is a soul winner. He not only preaches to men, he wins them. It is his to bring souls to the birth. This is his peculiar gift of God as marked and distinctive as the gift of tongues. He is a saviour of men. He convicts men by the power of the Spirit. He turns men from the error of their ways. He saves souls from death and covers a multitude of sins. It is a high calling of God in which he is careful to give God all the glory otherwise he will assuredly lose his gift. Like Elijah with the widow's son he can make the dead soul live and having played his part he departs as Elijah did after having delivered the newly-quickened son to his mother. Philip, the evangelist, pointed the eunuch to Christ then baptized him and then, the evangelist's work accomplished, 'the Spirit of the Lord caught away Philip and the eunuch saw him no more' (Acts 8. 39). Yet never was convert in more apparent need of guidance and instruction as to his future course of life alone in a heathen land.

Such, then, is the gift of the evangelist in some of the major aspects. But what of evangelism itself?

This, of course, is not the sole prerogative of the gifted evangelist. It is the work of the church and of every one of its members. It is, as has been already said, its greatest work and as such should have wholehearted attention such as a man gives to his business in life if he is to achieve success. That it does not commonly receive this attention must be generally admitted. No business venture could hope for any measure of achievement if entered upon in the manner in which the church approaches her task of evangelizing men. It is a fact which would be ludicrous were it not so tragic that the main effort of most churches and assemblies who set out to preach the Gospel (and how many churches fail to make even that effort) is to proclaim it weekly (and sometimes, alas, weakly!) in the last spot in the town in which they may reasonably expect to find the folk who need it! Indeed, the places of worship in a town are to-day, with rare exceptions, generally avoided by the outside public, who, in consequence, do not hear the great message of God's salvation from one year's end to the other.

A man who found the public refraining from entering his shop would be foolish to cast the blame upon the people who passed him by. He would achieve little by saying, 'Well, after all, my goods are available if they wish to buy; the loss is theirs if they neglect them.' This may be true, but *the failure will be his!* Would he not rather examine his shop and its position, his goods and their display, and his salesmen and their behaviour toward the public, and then adjust these matters with a view to commending his shop and his wares to the passers-by? Self interest alone would dictate this course. How much more would the conviction that his wares were not only desirable but vital to the public who were in danger of perishing for want of them if they did not buy!

Some of us would learn valuable lessons in evangelism by an occasional visit to any country town on market day in which a cheap-jack may be engaged in inducing the public to purchase the goods he has for sale. His glib, persuasive tongue does not fail to make his hearers feel their need of acquiring the article (often of trumpery worth) so that they can hardly refrain from purchasing it. Would that we purveyors of the Gospel were half as determined to achieve our aim! What a stir we should make in the market places of our land, much as Paul and Silas did at Philippi!

The fact is we need a drastic revision of our mode of approach and in our method of presentation of the Evangel if we are to evangelize men to-day. And that not so much in the direction of advance to new ways and means but of a return to the old. For in both method and message we have in these days travelled afar from the apostolic pattern. One trembles to think what the Apostle Paul would have to say were he introduced into the arena of some up-to-date Revivalist Mass Meetings. Or for that matter, were John Wesley, replete with wig and gown, to be there, what would he think? I am sure that both would be moved to indignation as they saw the auditorium wholly given up to laughter and hysteria!

There are two objections one would urge to much of the popular evangelism of to-day. First and most important, it is derogatory to the dignity of the Gospel. The Gospel is the noblest, grandest, most majestic and profoundest message that ever fell upon the ears of men and to present it in an atmosphere of lighthearted gaiety cannot but detract from these qualities in the minds of the hearers. It is a matter of vital and even desperate import to those to whom it is addressed and should be so presented. A proclamation from H.M. the King is always accompanied with all the solemn circumstance that befits its royal character and is the more readily heard by the Empire on that account. To-day more than ever is it necessary that men should know that the Mighty God has spoken and that His gracious Word must be given the more earnest heed as it comes with all the marks of its divine source. 'For if the word spoken by angels (at Sinai) was stedfast . . . how shall we escape if we neglect so great salvation . . . spoken by the Lord . . . and confirmed unto us by them that heard Him?' (Heb. 2. 2, 3).

The second objection is, that there is a more effective and at the same time, a more Scriptural mode of presentation. It is a striking reflection that neither our Lord Himself nor any of the apostles is represented as seeking to organize great crowds for the purpose of preaching to them. It is true that crowds came at times and the opportunity was used to the full, but crowds were not sought nor was any special significance placed upon them. Indeed, on more than one occasion our Lord discouraged them and sought to avoid contact with them. We read of great multitudes who followed Him only to be sent away disheartened and discouraged from further following after Him by the challenging character of the words He addressed to them. He showed no indication at any time of ingratiating Himself or courting popularity from however worthy a motive. It is not the least arresting statement concerning His ministry that we read, 'and Jesus went about *the villages* preaching' (Matt. 9. 35). The Lord Jesus in the rôle of a village preacher comes as a sobering reflection to many of us who are tempted to measure our success by our popularity.

The Apostle Paul preached to those who came to him in his own hired house, or in the market place, or wherever he found men to hear. His was never the rôle of the popular evangelist yet he proved mightily effective and the fruits of his labours stood the test of time.

There is something spectacular in great mass gatherings, and God has undoubtedly used such efforts greatly to His glory, but it is easy to over-estimate their value and effectiveness. The permanent worth of modern mass campaigns is a matter still in doubt, and such methods have yet to be vindicated by their effect upon the Church and, indeed, upon the country at large as distinct

11

from the immediate and often emotional influence upon the hearers as manifested by recorded 'decisions.' How many tens of thousands of such decisions must there not have been in England during the past twenty years as the outcome of outstanding Gospel campaigns. Yet the churches are still steadily on the wane and the country increasingly godless. When in South Africa before the war I found a sequence of popular evangelists had visited that country during the preceding years, each of whom had reaped widespread results (in one instance over 1300 in a fortnight) among a white community less in number than the population of one of our larger cities. Yet I found the churches still languishing and the people still godless and indifferent.

The truth is there would appear to be a kind of mass psychology attaching to the assemblage of great crowds in an atmosphere of religious enthusiasm that may even be subversive of the work of God in the souls of those present. The aim and culmination of the gathering is known by the whole assemblage to be the inducing of decisions, and when the appeal comes it has the backing of good will in the minds of all the audience, save for the comparatively small minority of the careless and indifferent present. The result is such an urge to respond as is hard for the more emotional of the audience (particularly the young) to resist. (It is not surprising—however deplorable—that some American evangelists do not hesitate to offer their services with 'results guaranteed'!) But the object of Scriptural evangelism is not the inducing of *decision*, which can be but a purely natural and mental response, and frequently imports little more than a desire, and perhaps a determination, to lead a better life. This may be evoked in all but the most depraved of men without any spiritual conviction or permanent outcome. The true object should be the producing of *conversion* which is wholly spiritual both in its inception and its result.

It is the Gospel message that is calculated to bring this about and strangely enough this message is often lacking in Gospel meetings. For appeals to men to decide for Christ, to give the heart to Jesus, to make a full surrender, to come out on the Lord's side, to give up their sins, etc., though unexceptionable and often very effective are none of them strictly speaking Gospel appeals in that they contain no evangel of glad tidings to the hearers, but an exhortation to them to *do* something, and that something which they will discover (if they have not already done so) as quite beyond their ability to accomplish. For the Gospel is good news to be received rather than good things to be done. 'I declare unto you the Gospel,' said Paul, 'which I preached unto you, which also *ye received* and wherein ye stand, by which also ye are saved' (1 Cor. 15. 1). And that Gospel he states to be that Christ died for our sins, was buried, and rose again. It is the Gospel of the finished work of Christ which alone can bring men to God, to peace, and to deliverance. It is this Gospel that the enemy does his best to obscure. He fears no other preaching however eloquent and sincere the preacher and however much it may evoke the response of the hearers. He knows that 'nothing but the blood of Jesus' can effectively set his captives free from the thraldom of his dominion over them.

What, then, are the methods needed in these days for the evangelizing of men?

Precisely the methods of the first century A.D., and no other. Outstanding among these may be named:

(a) *An overwhelming zeal on the part of the whole Church* for the spread of the Gospel and the salvation of their fellowmen.

Nothing will take the place of this, and until the Church of to-day awakens to a renewed concern for souls no revivalist methods will produce revival. It is the Church that is in dire need of revival. A revived Church alone will effect a revived nation. Such revival is a costly matter, and those who pray for revival little know what the answer to their prayer might mean for them. For a revived Church would mean a suffering Church. The Church to-day is tolerated unmolested by the world precisely because it is asleep. But a revived Church awakened to an aggressive concern for souls would mean:

(b) *A universal witness by all and every means*, in season out of season, by the rank and file of believers (in addition to the recognized preachers) to their fellowmen.

Suppose half a million Christians were to adopt the practice of accosting men and women everywhere in tram and bus and street, or from house to house, to ask them (of course with due courtesy) if they were at peace with God, would not that set the world (and the Press) talking! True, it would arouse indignant disapproval and would involve those who so acted in the greatest reproach. Like Paul they would soon become as the offscouring of the earth, but what of that, if it convinced the public, as it surely would, that there were men and women about them who believed sufficiently to suffer inconvenience and shame for their faith and its propagation in the world.

(c) *A bold and fearless preaching of Christ without apology or concession to modern opinion.*

The departure of the intelligentsia among men from faith in the revealed word of God has landed the world in a condition of unprecedented chaos, and it is high time that present day pseudo-scientific apologetics gave place to a return to the 'Thus saith the Lord' of the old prophetic preachers. 'Faith cometh by hearing and hearing by the Word of God.' What matters it that the modernist denies it to be such? No denial can alter the fact, and if men of conviction and determination would dare to proclaim the everlasting Gospel on the basis of its being not Pauline theology but the message of the living God, and if that testimony had the backing of a host of believers prepared to proclaim their faith in it at the cost of personal reproach, then I am convinced that what all the Gospel campaigns in the world will never achieve would be brought to pass and that in a surprisingly short space of time.

Before closing this chapter it might be profitable to consider the importance of what may be termed 'Specialized Evangelism.' We live in an age of specialization in almost all walks of life. Indeed, so complex is life in all its phases that in order to do effective service it has become almost essential that one's activities should be focussed on one special aspect of one's profession, be it medicine, surgery, law, scientific research or otherwise. It would seem wise therefore, that the would-be successful servant of Christ should devote his attention and activity in a like special manner if not exclusively, yet in large measure with a view to becoming expert 'a workman that needeth not to be ashamed, handling aright the word of truth' (2 Tim. 2. 15, R.V.). For it will readily be recognized that the mode of approach to different classes of the community whether of age, education, or social standing must of necessity vary, and that while the message is ever the same the mode of presentation must be adapted to the varying conditions. It was the recognition of this fact that gave to the Salvation Army its astonishing appeal to the lowest stratum of society, particularly in the early days. What the regular ministrations of the churches utterly failed to accomplish, the Army with its banners and bands, its cymbals and drums, its stirring songs and testimonies achieved among the most depraved and down and out of society in a manner that arrested the widespread attention of the world. The same may be said in varying degree of similar specialized efforts among other classes of the community. The preaching of the Gospel to children is an instance in point. When Mr. Payson Hammond came to this country as a children's evangelist less than a hundred years ago his efforts were looked upon with much disapproval and suspicion. But the outcome was the formation of the Children's Special Service Mission whose avowed purpose has been to specialize in this very sphere, and which it has done with astonishing success, so that its activities have become almost world-wide.

It is now the day of Youth Evangelism and Christian workers are rightly focussing attention as never before upon this branch of Gospel ministry. It is both needy and difficult. The need is great, even urgent, since the youth of our land are asserting increasingly an independence of thought and conduct that amounts, in innumerable instances, to open revolt against religion and authority. 'In my school,' said a public schoolboy to me, 'School Leaving Certificates are considered equivalent to church leaving certificates. We have had enough of both!' Yet these very young people are amenable to approach by those who have learned the technique and who practise it wisely, under the guidance and in the power of the Holy Spirit. But it is admittedly difficult and not the less so since there are certain initial obstacles to be overcome before any real hope of advance can be entertained. Three such obstacles may be named:

(a) *The Obstacle of Suspicion.* With a vast number of young people religion as such is suspect. The parson is suspect, the school chaplain is suspect, the Sunday School teacher and Bible Class leader are suspect. Their object is not understood except that they are out to make you religious, which is by no means a condition to be desired since it is thought to involve curtailment of liberty and a whole series of inhibitions. Moreover, religion carries little conviction of *truth* to the average young person to-day. It is something apart from the realities of life, as being in a separate category from ordinary existence, and therefore something to be avoided. Most boys, for instance, would far rather be thought wicked (within limits) by their fellows than peculiar, and religion tends to make you peculiar. This is an obstacle that must be overcome and it certainly can be. A public schoolboy after attending my class for a time remarked to me: 'What has attracted me here is that it is all *real.*' A tribute for which I felt deeply grateful for the first obstacle in that lad's case had been surmounted.

This problem of unreality is not to be met by aping the man of the world, by trying to be a good sport, by over-joviality, etc., all of which can be as unreal as over-piety or sanctimoniousness. It is overcome by just *being real.* Not over earnest, over serious, over religious, or 'over' anything, but just your real, healthy, sensible self. Anything else will be found out and suspected, but once a youth discovers you really mean and believe what you say he will listen to you with real attention and interest.

(b) *The Obstacle of Doubt.* It must be recognized that the young people of to-day have been brought up in an atmosphere of unbelief. The background of belief in the authority of the Scriptures and the general truth of Christianity has almost entirely gone. It is no longer sufficient to quote Scripture texts which will not carry any conviction, nor to make reference to Scripture facts or incidents of which most young folk are in complete ignorance. In other days evangelistic appeals could be made with the confidence that the young hearers had at least a mental understanding of the facts upon which the appeal was based. To-day the approach must be made with no such assumptions in support. Of course, the final solution of this problem is not found in the direction of Christian evidences or apologetics though these may be of value to impress the doubter that there are answers to be had. I think that in large measure the solution lies to-day, as in Pentecostal times, in the direction of personal testimony. The witness of those who have proved the truth of the Gospel in their own experience will often carry sufficient conviction to lead the doubter to taste and see for himself, much as the presence of other skaters will convince the hesitating onlooker that the ice will bear him too.

(c) *The Obstacle of Fear.* This is, perhaps, the most insurmountable of all the barriers that face young people to-day. For youth is imbued with the social spirit to an unexampled degree in these days of diminishing family life, and young people find their interests in groups and circles outside the home for want of the home interests of former times. Any true conversion to God accordingly involves a breach of social relationships which it is hard for most young people to contemplate. 'Must I give up my friends now I'm converted?' said a boy to me in some trepidation. I replied: 'Don't bother, they'll see to that!' And shortly after he came to tell me that they had! This problem is particularly acute among the poor whose interests are intimately bound up with the other lads of the street or village. One boy was bitterly persecuted on becoming a Christian on the ground that he had 'let down the gang.' The remedy to some extent has been found in the creation of a new circle of friends by means of Fellowships or Squashes, and, particularly in the case of boys from the street, in the formation of clubs where they can meet of an evening and get entertainment coupled with Christian fellowship and instruction.

Sufficient has been said to indicate the seriousness of the problems of the present day and of the specialized character which evangelism must take in any particular class of the community to be in any large sense effective. The Apostle Paul expressed the same principle when he said: 'I am made all things to all men, that I might by all means save some' (1 Cor. 9. 22). So the would-be successful evangelist must be prepared to adapt his methods to varying needs to become not only all things to all men but particular things to particular men that he may by particular means save some of them. But whatever the means, let us remember that the urgency remains that the churches' motto must be to-day more than ever it was, 'Evangelize or Perish!'

CHAPTER XII

THE
WITNESS OF A LOCAL CHURCH

E. W. ROGERS

'YE are My witnesses': so spake the Lord Jesus to the apostles who formed the nucleus of the first local church. In a special way, not common to believers now, they had seen Him prior to His death and subsequent to His resurrection. They could speak of the things they knew and testify of the things they had seen touching the King (John 15. 26, 27). While the Holy Spirit testified to the presence of the risen Christ in heaven, this group of apostles testified to having seen the risen Christ on earth. So they were found going everywhere preaching what they knew concerning Him.

But the church's witness is not only that which is heard from the lips; it is also that which is exhibited in the life. This was so, for example, with the church at Thessalonica. They proved the truth of their preaching by the manner of their living. The believers who comprised that church became imitators (1 Thess. 1. 6) of the apostles in that they also manifested in themselves the unusual combination of 'much affliction with joy,' which was found in Paul and Silvanus and Timotheus. Like Paul and Silas they were able to sing while they were suffering (Acts 16. 25). Their 'affliction' was the result of having received the Gospel message announced by the apostles, who to others seemed merely to be fanatical travelling Jews. Their 'joy' was the result of the Holy Spirit having taken up His residence within them when they believed that message. This union of two apparently contradictory principles was a most eloquent witness to the power of the message which they had believed.

It was an object-lesson both for the world and for believers. To the former the Thessalonian believers were a witness. To the latter they were an ensample (1 Thess. 1. 7). The impact of the

Gospel had made such an impression upon them that its mark—
tupos, dent—could be seen by all.

From them, moreover, the Gospel message echoed forth (v. 8)
rendering it needless for the apostles to say anything. The Thessalonian saints did not invent or propound any new doctrines.
What they had heard from the apostles was resounded by them.
It was an echo repeating the original apostolic message. The
apostles did not need themselves to repeat the Gospel message
elsewhere in the district for the report had been received (v. 9)
that the Thessalonians had 'turned to God from idols to serve a
living and true God' and were now waiting for His Son from
heaven (vv. 9, 10). Convincing witness to the fact and results
of conversion was being borne by the converts themselves, so that
the converts became preachers!

For the Thessalonians a silent tongue was impossible. There
had been created within them an earnest desire that others should
receive the same blessings as they had received. Necessity was
laid upon them to proclaim the Gospel.

It was not surprising that the believing Jews had suffered as the
result of receiving the Gospel: that was only to be expected for
their nation had murdered the very One whom they were now
trusting. What could they expect but persecution from their
fellow countrymen? What was it but treason to accept as Messiah
and to trust for salvation the One whom their nation had adjudged
an impostor, guilty and worthy of death? The Thessalonian
converts, however, were suffering in like manner from their own
countrymen (1 Thess. 2. 14). Their persecution made it plain
that in every nation all who trust the Lord Jesus Christ incur the
risk of suffering persecution from their own countrymen. Yet a
people that is prepared to suffer for 'another king, one Jesus,' is
always of great testimonial value.

Faith and love also marked them (1 Thess. 3. 6). Timothy
brought the good report to Paul and it rejoiced his heart. These
believers were characterized by a simple and unqualified belief in
the Scriptures and a simple and unfeigned love of their fellow
saints. What a testimony!

It would be a thousand pities if the gold of such a testimony
should become in any wise dim. The second epistle to this church,

however, shows that this sad possibility became a reality. One result of false teaching is to rob the saints of their Spirit-begotten joy; and occupation with the troubles of earth tends to divert the eye from the Lord who is coming from heaven. These things resemble the 'little foxes that spoil the vines' of testimony. Uncertainty on the part of believers as to divine truth, and self-pity among saints because of adverse conditions do not favourably impress the outside world: it is a bad display.

Although the Thessalonian letters were some of the earliest recorded writings of the Apostle Paul, Thessalonica was not the first city in Europe which he visited. He first went to Philippi where the Word of the Lord opened many a heart. Those who obeyed the Gospel there soon became its propagators.

They threw in their lot with the apostle who was set for the defence and confirmation of the Gospel (Phil. 1. 7). He defended it from opposers and confirmed it among believers. They all esteemed it a great favour, as Paul did, to be privileged to have their part also in spreading the good news which had reached and won their own hearts; and by so doing they became partakers of his grace.

In order to maintain church witness three things are necessary: (a) consistent behaviour; (b) unity of purpose; and (c) courage. For this reason Paul exhorted the Philippian saints to take care (a) that their citizen-behaviour should be worthy of the Gospel of Christ; (b) that they should stand fast in one spirit and with one soul should strive together for the faith of the Gospel; and (c) that in nothing they should shy (as a frightened horse) for fear of their adversaries (Phil. 1. 28).

The world is ever ready to bring against the believer a charge of inconsistency. What damage to the church's witness has been wrought by divisions! Satan knows that 'united' the saints stand; 'divided' their testimony falls. The rationalist despises inconsistency and refers with scorn to the numerous ecclesiastical divisions found in Christendom. Moreover, a fearful believer is a contradiction. If what he believes is true, why does he fear? God has not given him a spirit of cowardice. What havoc has been wrought by these three things: inconsistency, division, fear.

It may further be observed that the local church is made up of true believers who are considered as lights in darkness just as stars shine in the night (Phil. 2. 15). The darker the night the brighter they appear to shine. The light emitted by the believer is that which has first been put within, namely the illumination of the 'word of life' to which he is to bear testimony by 'holding it forth' (v. 16). Believers should not be 'wandering stars' (Jude 13) for such plainly are unreliable guides. The world in which they shine is 'crooked and perverse'; it is not straight (it is, indeed, crooked); nor does it desire to be made straight (it is, surely, perverse). In such a condition believers should shine as heavenly luminaries maintaining a fixed orbit and not departing from it. The believer is neither a comet nor a meteor. It is known where he should be and what course he should take.

In association with this idea is that of an earthen vessel wherein is placed 'the light of the knowledge of the glory of God in the face of Jesus Christ' (2 Cor. 4. 6, 7). When the vessel becomes broken the light shines out even more clearly. Gideon's army of three hundred selected warriors with a similar number of trumpets and torches did exploits and routed the enemy. Trumpets and torches must ever go together as must preaching and living, and oneness must be unbroken if a local church is to triumph similarly.

Connected, also, with the idea of luminaries is that of the local church being a lampstand (Rev. 1. 12). A lampstand is plainly for the purpose of giving light in the darkness, though its radiation is far more restricted than that of a star. A lamp can shine only if it is adequately supplied with oil; in like manner the church can only effectually bear witness to a dark world proportionate to the extent of its receiving 'power from on high' (Luke 24. 49); that is, as the Spirit of God is afforded opportunity unrestrictedly to operate in and through those who form the local church. The source of all true shining is 'first love' to Christ (Rev. 2. 4). Abandonment of this love ruins the testimony.

If saints forget that they were once darkness, though now they are light in the Lord (Eph. 5. 8) their shining will surely be defective. They will need the exhortation given to the Corinthians not to receive the grace of God in vain (2 Cor. 6. 1). God has imparted grace to the believer in order that he may, in the present 'acceptable time' and 'day of salvation,' spread abroad the same

Gospel in order that others, too, may receive that same grace.

Yet another figure emphasizes this truth. The local church of the living God is the pillar and ground of the truth (1 Tim. 3. 15). Everyone in the district where such a church is located should be aware of its existence because, being a pillar, it is conspicuous. It is like a city set on a hill which cannot be hid. It is made up of people who know the truth, for they each and all have come to Him Who is the Truth (John 14. 6). The world around them is hastening on to the day when they will 'believe the lie' (2 Thess. 2. 11). If, through the operation of the Spirit of God, an unbeliever should become uncertain of his present convictions the local church ought to be able to give to him out of its store of truth that which his soul needs. The sinner should know where to turn for the truth; the church is its pillar; the church should be able to dispense it. Not that the local church is an authority or that the local church can demand the submission of men. It is not a source but a channel. Those in the local church have learned what sin is; what its penalty is; how sin can be forgiven; and why; and on what terms. They know the truth, and having the Spirit of truth, can speak the truth in love. The church is a company of people who themselves have submitted to the truth of the Scriptures.

Truth searches the conscience and places a soul in the light of the presence of God. Because of this it is feared by some. 'Of the rest durst no man join himself' to the early local church at Jerusalem (Acts 5. 13). In that church resided the Spirit of God Who exposed all falsehood and hypocrisy. The record of Ananias and Sapphira is a case in point. Sincerity and truth must mark God's house; the place for those who will have none of these things is outside. A local church walking thus in the fear of the Lord to-day would find itself relieved from the menace of false brethren creeping in unawares. Carelessness or unfaithfulness on the part of those within opens the door to grievous wolves (Acts 20. 29), and wolves are no attraction for lost sheep.

Moreover, if the local church functions as it should do, it will not only go out to the world with the Gospel but it will welcome sinners as spectators of its central ordinance of fellowship, where the saints proclaim or preach or announce the Lord's death till

He come. The poetess's words approached the truth when she wrote:

No Gospel like this feast,
Spread for Thy Church by Thee:
Nor prophet nor evangelist
Speaks the glad news more free.

There is no Gospel like that ordinance which tells so eloquently of the love of the Father and of the Son as demonstrated by the death of the Lord Jesus, who subsequently rose from the dead, ascended up on high and is soon to return. The unbelieving onlookers would behold a company of loyalists to a rejected King engaged in the solemn act of remembering Him in His absence. They would learn that His body, denoted by the bread, was bruised at the hands of sinners, and that His blood, denoted by the cup, was shed for the forgiveness of sins. It is true that there is much they would not understand but they would behold a silent witness to the righteousness and grace of God, a righteousness which demanded the exaction of sin's penalty: grace which made it righteously possible for the guilty to avoid that penalty.

Indeed, when a local church is functioning as it should, the oral ministry will be in such power that the unlearned or unbelieving onlooker will declare that God is among them of a truth and, falling down, will worship Him (1 Cor. 14. 25). The absence of heathen rites will be a testimony to the subjection of the company to their One Lord to which also the silence of their women, with their long hair and covered heads, will be an added eloquent witness. Their manifest love to one another will declare plainly that they are His disciples, for it is by that means that the world is able to recognize the disciples of the Lord Jesus (John 13. 35).

In days, later than those of the New Testament, there was much departure from the pattern given in the Scriptures. The world and the church became mixed; wheat and tares grew together. Obsolete Judaism became mingled with corrupt paganism and was Christianized. Christian ordinances were distorted out of all recognition. An accumulation of unauthorized rites and ceremonies was made to obscure Scriptural simplicity. Those who loved the Lord and who sought to obey His commandments were compelled to separate themselves from such things. Although they were accused of causing schism the guilt was not theirs but that of those who went beyond the things written (1 Cor. 4. 6, r.v.). Wherever a local church is found meeting together in simple accordance with New Testament principles it is in itself a protest against the departure of Christendom from the truth and pattern of the Scriptures.

The local church should also bear witness to the unfailing care of the Great Shepherd Who provides all that is requisite for the well-being of His sheep. The Risen Lord, with a view to the well-being and development of all the members of His body, ensures, by giving gifts to the church, a continuity of ministry. His own chosen ministers are trained by His Spirit for the work of ministering; and this will continue without interruption as long as there is any need for such ministry (Eph. 4. 12). Thus the church bears testimony to the fact that the Lord Jesus is, indeed, El Shaddai, the all-sufficient God.

The pooling of the material resources of the saints did not continue for long in the early Church. The cause and rightness of this need not here be discussed. Suffice it to say its abandonment was no error. Paul did not enjoin community of wealth but had words of counsel of a different kind for those that are rich. He everywhere encouraged, and indeed enjoined, the saints to care for the poor among them and gave careful directions concerning widows in their midst (1 Tim. 5. vv. 3 ff) and also as to needy believers in distant parts (Rom. 15. 26). He himself was glad to be the travelling trustee of the gifts of the saints. A local church should follow the example of the Lord Jesus who in grace for their sakes, though He was rich, became poor in order that they might, by that great stoop of His, become rich. With such an example left to them the saints should be moved to impoverish themselves for the relief of others. Those who oppose the Gospel can say nothing against such conduct for it is truth translated into deeds.

Similarly, if local churches act aright they will regard it as their duty and privilege to honour and to care for those who minister to them; and they will not ask the unbeliever to contribute toward the maintenance of their teachers.

Inasmuch as men commonly think in terms of material gain, the mercenary trend of many religious organizations creates the impression that all who name the name of Christ must be actuated by the same base motive, notwithstanding that the Scriptures refer clearly and significantly to filthy lucre or base gain gotten by such means. If, then, men see, as they should, a local church providing sufficient funds for the relief of its poor and for the expenses of the ministry without making any appeal to the public, directly or indirectly, what can they say? The value of such practice far exceeds anything which may attach to mere precept.

CHAPTER XIII

THE CHURCH AND YOUTH

A. RENDLE SHORT

IT is not proposed to include under this heading Sunday School work, or evangelistic efforts specially directed to the winning of young people. Both these subjects are far too important to be dealt with by a brief reference in the midst of other matters. We shall confine ourselves here to the place of young people within the church fellowship.

At what age should children be brought by their parents to the regular Sunday services, and in particular, to the Breaking of Bread meeting? Now, quite a number of infants are brought by their parents to our morning service for worship, and they are not always silent. By way of answer to our question, let it be emphasized that the happy church is one where the family spirit is most manifest. Nothing pleases young mothers like friendly notice being taken of their babies. We do not believe in christening or infant baptism, but let there be a dedication service when children are a few weeks old, either on a Sunday or on a week-day, preferably on a Sunday.

Again, let it be observed that if children are not brought to the Breaking of Bread at an early age, it will probably be very difficult to persuade them to start attending later. Also, if they stay at home, some adult will have to stay away from the meeting to look after them. Babies will often sleep through the meeting in a pram outside, or in a vestry. Children from twelve to twenty-four months old are always a little difficult to control anywhere, and if they are very fractious and disturb a meeting too much they may be better away; or it might be possible to bring them and put some one person in charge of three or four of them in a schoolroom. As soon as this stage is passed, let them be brought. If a number of children are present in a meeting, an occasional word suitable for them will quite likely be of the Spirit's leading. The discipline of sitting still is no bad thing for children.

At what age should children or adolescents be admitted to baptism, or to the Lord's Table, or to regular membership with the local church? In some quarters it is argued that baptism in New Testament times followed almost at once on a profession of faith, as in the case of the Ethiopian eunuch, or the jailor at Philippi and his household, and that children who make a profession of conversion which seems genuine need not be kept waiting. Those who believe that baptism is essential to salvation *could* not well keep anyone waiting. Certainly baptism is spoken of in the New Testament once or twice as though it had a bearing on salvation (e.g., Mark 16. 16: 'He that believeth and is baptized shall be saved'); but the case of the penitent thief, and the testimony of a number of passages announcing the way of salvation in which baptism is not mentioned, leads us to conclude that baptism is not indispensable to a title to heaven. We heartily believe in child conversion. It is, perhaps, normal in a godly family that children may be born again at such an early age that they cannot clearly remember the occasion. Those who question candidates for church fellowship often find this to be the case. But though we believe in child conversion we are not by any means sure that we can distinguish inherited faith from personal faith, in children. In apostolic times there were gifts of the Holy Spirit which attested the fact of conversion so plainly that as Peter said, 'Can any man forbid water, that these should not be baptized?' (Acts 10. 47). In our day, a period of observation is necessary, to see whether the life brings forth the fruit of the Spirit. There is an exercise of soul when a lad or girl chooses to apply for baptism and church membership, that is more likely to be a lasting blessing, when they have become old enough to make their choice for themselves after careful consideration. In most cases this may be during their later years at school, but some children mature early, and are very responsible at twelve or thirteen. If young people brought up in Christian homes or in the Sunday School do not come forward by the time they are twenty, we are fearful for them.

What special care should the church take of its younger members, beyond that which members of any age have a right to expect, and what service may it rightly expect from its youngest members? There are exhortations several times repeated in the epistles that

12

those who are more experienced and older, and take oversight in the church, should be highly esteemed and obeyed, and this is obviously the will of the Lord. Attendance at meetings, particularly at the Breaking of Bread but also at a certain number of other meetings, is plainly commanded in the Scripture: 'This do in remembrance of Me' (Luke 22. 19); 'not forsaking the assembling of ourselves together, as the manner of some is' (Heb. 10. 25); and so on. Service, and financial contributions, ought to be rendered by young as well as old. But unless these duties are performed of a willing mind, they are of little value. The church has to convince all its members that these courtesies are not being claimed by men as due to themselves, but to the Lord. And it has to win allegiance by showing a sympathetic under-standing of the point of view of the younger members, and by putting forth an effort to meet their special needs. Best of all, some suitable work must be found for them to do.

To bring all this to practical issues, one must recognize that there is a difference between churches. In one, recently formed it may be, there is not much variation in age; all are between sixteen and thirty-five, shall we say. In another, perhaps in a rural area, the average age is high and there are only three or four members under twenty-five. In a long-established city meeting, there will probably be quite a number of old, and quite a number of young, in the fellowship.

Is it right and wise to have a young people's meeting once a week? This cannot be decided outright by saying that there is no precedent for it in the New Testament. The New Testament lays down some very definite principles with regard to Christian worship, but it is singularly silent with regard to what we may call a classification of meetings or methods. Where do we find a precedent for a Sunday morning Breaking of Bread, a Sunday afternoon school for children, a Sunday evening Gospel meeting, and a week-day meeting for prayer? Do we find a Christian marriage service described? Were hymns sung? Must we conclude that all these are wrong? Of course not. Under certain circum-stances, at particular stages of church history, they are right. Under other circumstances, at another period, they were not practised; perhaps rightly. To repeat our question, then, should there be a young people's meeting, and if so, should the octogenarians in the fellowship be invited to attend?

In the type of assembly where all are in the first half of life, in my judgment, there is no need for a special young people's meeting. Where the young members are very few, it could scarcely be a success. The question really arises, when the membership is large, and all ages are well represented. Thirty or forty years ago, I stoutly advocated the young people's meeting. My opinion is just the same to-day, and for two main reasons. It is only natural for young people to find their friendships amongst those of about the same age. They are more influenced by the opinions and example of those not very much older than themselves. If they do not find their close friends, and their life partners, within the church of God they will look for them elsewhere, which is a first-class disaster in some cases. The present generation of lads and girls growing up amongst us has a very hard fight to maintain faith, and to preserve Christian habits of life. More likely than not they were taught at school more about evolution than about God, and the Bible was discredited. Christian ways of living were laughed to scorn. Wherever they study, or earn their living, they will almost certainly find genuinely converted young people in a tiny minority. (There are happy exceptions, especially in the Universities.) If they do not intend to marry except in the Lord, their choice is far more restricted than that of a worldly person. Surely those who have to face these difficulties deserve our deepest sympathy and everything possible should be done to help them spiritually. If they think that a young people's meeting will best meet their needs, why put difficulties in their way, even if we think them wrong?

The other reason is that it is more important to teach people to think than to give them information, if they think rightly. The best way to help them to think, is, usually, to encourage them to speak in public however small the audience, to write, or to take part in discussions. When young people are addressed by much older speakers they are apt to allow that to take the place of thinking for themselves, and what is said is only half believed, and soon forgotten. They are more likely to think for themselves if they are meeting regularly with those of the same age.

It is easy to criticize, and to foresee disasters. A young people's meeting may be suspected of creating a division between the young and old. Much more probably, it does not create the division; it was present, though out of sight, already. If the rift widens it usually means either that undue repression has been exercised by elder brethren, or that the young people have chosen bad leaders. If a church allows the use of its premises to the junior members, it certainly should be a condition that the leaders are acceptable. It is a happy thing if one or two men can be found, aged between thirty and forty, who have the affection and respect of their juniors and the full confidence of their elders.

It may be feared that the ordinary week-night evening services may not attract those who have a meeting specially for themselves. The remedy is so to improve the quality of these regular assembly services, that everybody will wish to come.

A young people's meeting should not be invaded by elderly folk unless they are asked to come, or have reason to be quite sure that they are wanted.

Time and place must vary a good deal. Often, a week-night meeting is suitable. Or, an after-service gathering on Sunday evening may be better. A room in a private house gives a happy atmosphere if it is intended to get outsiders in. Subjects considered should cover a wide field. Christian biography is stimulating. Missionary work should be regularly considered.

It is only to fairly large meetings, with a good many members of all ages, that the foregoing remarks apply. When there are only two or three under twenty-five years of age, some other way must be found to help them. To give them *too* much praise and prominence in hopes of keeping them in a good humour, may have the result of turning their heads. It will be well if united meetings for young people of a whole group of assemblies can be arranged. The complaint, 'I, even I, only am left' is specially discouraging to the young. The Holiday Conferences, such as have been held now over a period of thirty-five years, and which it is to be hoped will become more numerous and more accessible, are particularly valuable for lonely souls.

A church has by no means fulfilled its duty to its junior members if it tells them in effect, to take possession of the premises once a week and do the best they can. There should be hospitality, instruction, and opportunities for service. Some of us can remember, when we were away from home for the first time in uncongenial lodgings, how we blessed those kind folk who asked us to tea and supper on a Sunday, especially if there were others of our age to be met there. We would have attended almost any church to earn such a reward. Here is a service which can best be rendered by young married people in the assembly. If they cannot afford it, it would be well worth while to finance them out of assembly funds.

It might be thought that Christian instruction of a character that would be helpful to young and old alike would be comparatively easy to provide, but many meetings do not find it easy. We have a convention, or tradition, that Christian instruction is out of place on Sunday mornings, except for ten minutes at the end, and out of place on Sunday evenings, when the Gospel should be preached, often to people who are not there. If a good company can be collected on a week-night evening, the difficulty is met, but for one reason or another, there will always be those who do not or cannot come out on that particular evening. We are stating a difficulty without solving it. More useful, perhaps, is the suggestion that instead of leaving speakers to choose their own subjects, the younger generation, and others, should be invited to send in lists of subjects they think would be profitable, and then try to find someone competent to take that particular line. You feel obliged to attend, if the subject for the occasion was suggested by yourself. There should be a clear explanation, from time to time, of why we worship as we do, and why we believe certain methods of church government and service to be the will of God. We do not hear enough about practical Christian living. I do not mean vague exhortations to consecration, but such subjects as the Christian view of marriage, the use of money, why we keep Sunday, or why we are not Christian Scientists or Roman Catholics.

There are many forms of service besides preaching or taking a Sunday School class, important as these are. Beginners need to be helped and taught how to speak in public, how to prepare, and how to teach a class. But there are other ways of helping. The minister of the best attended church in one of our large cities recently called at a house and asked the woman to attend his meeting next Sunday evening. She could not come, because she had a baby to mind. He immediately undertook to send along one of the church baby-minders to set her free, and she came, though she said she was an agnostic. Probably she was glad of an evening off. Cannot some of our young women volunteer to be baby-minders? Then, there are probably folk within reach who are elderly, or crippled, or cannot walk far, but would come if a bright, cheerful lad or girl called for them with a car, or even with the church bathchair. Then, the local hospital, or public assistance institution is well worth a regular visit, and the inmates much prefer that some, at any rate, of the visitors should be young and cheerful. I have known religious services in the wards stopped because the visitors were all so old. But hospital visitation, though capable of doing great good, is a special art, and a mistake may close the doors for ever. There should be some tactful and experienced Christian worker in charge, and his directions should be carefully obeyed. He will probably say: 'Don't push in where you are not wanted. Don't say anything to frighten patients. Don't stay long in any one ward.'

'The things which thou hast heard from me . . . the same commit thou to faithful men, who shall be able to teach others also' (2 Tim. 2. 2). That means, to men younger in the faith. It may be possible to hold a short course for Bible Study for younger brethren in the assembly, or in several assemblies, who show promise, and something like a Preachers' Preparation Class. A practised speaker may take a lad with him when visiting elsewhere to preach, and give him the opportunity to face the audience and read the Scripture, give out the hymns, or lead in prayer. If younger brethren show a little enterprise, and launch out on schemes of their own, they should only be discouraged for very serious reasons.

We may conclude the whole matter, by reiterating that in the happy and spiritual church the older will be as fathers and mothers of the best type to the younger, and the younger will remember Peter's admonition, 'Likewise ye younger, be subject unto the elder. Yea, all of you gird yourselves with humility, to serve one another' (1 Peter 5. 5, R.V.).

CHAPTER XIV

THE CHURCH AND MISSIONS

A. PULLENG

THE church, indeed, has a mission. Its primary, but not sole duty, is to evangelize. To discover how that duty is to be fulfilled it is necessary to consider first of all the purpose of God.

The clear testimony of Scripture is that the incarnation and death of Christ had in view the whole world. At the Saviour's birth, Simeon, with wonderful intuition, declares Him to be, 'A light to lighten the Gentiles' (Luke 2. 32), whilst John Baptist in his earliest message states that, '*all* flesh shall see the salvation of God' (Luke 3. 6).

The men of Samaria, having heard Him for themselves, wonderingly exclaim, 'We know that this is indeed the Christ, *the Saviour of the world*' (John 4. 42). The Lord Himself, having in mind the death He should die, answers: 'And I, if I be lifted up from the earth, will draw *all* unto Me' (John 12. 32). Ere the Ascension He declared, 'it behoved Christ to suffer, and to rise from the dead the third day: and that repentance and remission of sins should be preached in His Name among *all* nations' (Luke 24. 46, 47).

Paul announces that 'Christ Jesus . . . gave Himself a ransom for *all*' (1 Tim. 2. 6). It is Paul also, erstwhile Pharisee, who brings home to our hearts a glorious catholicity as he speaks of the grace and apostleship received unto obedience of faith among *all* nations (cf. Rom. 1. 5). When at Antioch in Pisidia, Paul and Barnabas decided to turn to the Gentiles, they claimed that the Lord had commanded them saying: 'I have set thee to be a light of the Gentiles, that thou shouldest be for salvation unto the ends of the earth' (Acts 13. 47). Thus the purpose of God is that the knowledge of the Christ who came into the world to save sinners should be made known to all the world. But how?

The plan is enshrined in the Lord's commission to His disciples, given after His redeeming work had been accomplished, when

He said: 'Go ye therefore, and make disciples of all the nations, baptizing them into the name of the Father and of the Son and of the Holy Ghost: teaching them to observe all things whatsoever I commanded you: and lo, I am with you alway, even unto the end of the age' (Matt. 28. 19-20, R.V.). In Mark's Gospel the commission is expressed more briefly: 'Go ye into all the world, and preach the Gospel to every creature' (Mark 16. 15). The commission is indeed a comprehensive one, but first there is to be noted the crucial part in the plan each believer is expected to fill. It has been said: 'Christ alone can save the world, but Christ cannot save the world alone.'

For the fulfilment of the plan apparently the co-operation of all believers as witnesses is essential. If they fail God seems to have made no other provision. Consequently, it is an integral part of the plan that 'all are to go and they are to go to all.'

This commission, set forth at the close of the Gospels, is supplemented by wonderful words spoken by the Lord immediately prior to His Ascension, and recorded in Acts 1. 4-8. The disciples were to wait for the promised bestowment of the Holy Spirit, and then, when the Holy Spirit had been received, they were to be 'witnesses unto Me both in Jerusalem, and in all Judæa, and in Samaria, and unto the uttermost part of the earth,' thus it was vital to the achievement of the plan that all disciples were to witness, that is, to tell what they knew of the Lord, to tell of His saving merit and power. The scope of that witness was to be worldwide.

The commission is an unabrogated command, and the intent of God is that each succeeding generation should hear the Gospel from the lips of believers of its own generation. How grievously the Church in all ages has failed, and still lags behind.

To fulfil God's plan it is significant to note that there is no suggestion in the New Testament of the need for an elaborate organization. The testimony and witness of believers is described in the 'simplest' terms, and probably it was simple in fact. For example it is said of the apostles in Acts 5. 42 (R.V.) that, 'every day in the temple, and at home, they ceased not to teach and to preach Jesus as the Christ.' In Acts 8 we read of the disciples being scattered from Jerusalem by a fierce persecution. This does not, however, silence their testimony, for they went everywhere preaching (lit., speaking) the Word. This testimony was rendered by the ordinary rank and file believer, for the apostles remained in Jerusalem. In the same chapter it is recorded of Philip that, 'he preached Christ unto the inhabitants of the city of Samaria'; and also that 'he preached Jesus' to a solitary individual.

The witness of Paul and his companions is described with a greater variety of expression. To the cities of Lystra and Derbe, they 'preached the Gospel'; in the region around Antioch of Pisidia, 'they published the Word of the Lord'; in Perga they 'preached the Word'; at Thessalonica Paul testifies that, 'this Jesus whom I preach unto you is Christ'; at Athens he preached 'Jesus and the resurrection'; at Ephesus he disputed in the synagogue 'concerning the Kingdom of God.' Thus in Paul's ministry of the Gospel there is no evidence even of organized services in the inception of the work in any place, but of taking full advantage of occasions and places where people were wont to gather in order to witness to them that Jesus was the Christ.

Instruction, also, was an essential part of the commission. Converts were to be taught to 'observe all things whatsoever I have commanded you' (Matt. 28. 20). Consequently we read that Barnabas and Paul gathered with the assembly at Antioch for a whole year and taught much people. At Corinth, Paul remained eighteen months, 'teaching the Word of God.' It was evidently a settled practice to revisit churches, to confirm the souls of the disciples and to exhort them to continue in the faith (Acts 14. 22); to confirm the churches (Acts 15. 41); and to establish the churches in the faith (Acts 16. 5).

For the successful prosecution of the plan a living power was essential. Only as it is acknowledged that such a power animated those early disciples, can the spread and triumphs of the Gospel be understood. It was a mere handful of followers to whom the commission was given—without influence, for the most part unlettered, and indeed without any of those advantages which the majority of people would deem essential for such an enterprise. They were to meet fierce opposition from the Jews, and the studied indifference of heathen philosophy and learning. Yet the Gospel won its way throughout the then-known world within a short space of time. False faiths were deprived of devotees in such numbers as to cause considerable alarm to those who thus found their means of livelihood threatened.

Indeed, it can be justly claimed that the Gospel, as its truths were preached and practised by those early believers, effected a complete transformation in the Roman Empire. Moral standards were lifted, slavery diminished, and many evil customs and practices were largely abandoned, whilst both war and the degradation of women were greatly modified. Truly the Gospel brought forth fruit in all the world. And the weapons of the disciples were not carnal; they were not forged in the world's arsenals, but they were 'mighty through God to the pulling down of strongholds' (2 Cor. 10. 4). All this could only have been accomplished through the operation of the Holy Ghost. He was sufficient for every emergency and crisis, pervading the whole story of the Acts of the Apostles. When Peter and the other apostles were arraigned before the High Priest and challenged to declare by what power the healing of the lame man as recorded in Acts 3 had been wrought, Peter bears witness, as one filled with the Holy Ghost, and, as a result, those that heard marvelled, and took knowledge of them that they had been with Jesus.

Scripture is never given to exaggeration, neither is emphasis laid upon numbers: yet it is evident that very many turned unto the Lord. As Peter preaches in the power of the Holy Spirit on the day of Pentecost men were pricked in their hearts and cried out: 'Men and brethren, what shall we do?' (Acts 2. 37). About three thousand souls received the Word and were baptized. In a second address, consequent upon the healing of the lame man, Peter answers the unspoken question of the people who thronged him, and their numbers rose to five thousand.

Further, we see the Spirit at work not only in the conversion of large numbers and of notable individuals such as Sergius Paulus, but also in many other ways. As the disciples were filled with the Holy Spirit they were welded together in a true unity of one heart and of one soul; incipient hypocrisy as displayed by Ananias and Sapphira which, unchecked, would have ruined the testimony of the church, was exposed and judged; Stephen being full of the Holy Ghost was enabled to die so triumphantly that the goads began to prick the heart of Paul the persecutor; guidance was afforded by the Holy Spirit in a marked way to Philip and Paul. It is the Holy Spirit who says: 'Separate Me Barnabas and Saul for the work whereunto I have called them' (Acts 13. 2), and the important decision reached at the conference at Jerusalem is represented as being due to the Holy Spirit (Acts 15. 28). Further, spiritual gifts such as evangelists, pastors and teachers, necessary for the work of the Gospel, the perfecting of the saints, and the edification of the Body of Christ, were provided by the immediate operation of the Spirit 'dividing to every man severally as He will' (1 Cor. 12. 11).

It is important to observe the principles enumerated in the New Testament for the consummation of God's purpose to call out a people for His Name. In the Acts of the Apostles and in the Epistles only a very limited number of incidents are recorded of all that transpired in those momentous years. It may, therefore, be deduced that those which are recorded are intended to be of abiding application. The manner of the *call to missionary service* is of fundamental importance. From what is recorded of the call of Paul and Barnabas in Acts 13. 1-4, and of Timothy in Acts 16. 1-3 much that is significant may be learned. The church at Antioch was in a most prosperous spiritual condition, being served by a number of gifted men, filled with the Holy Spirit. There was a spiritual response to that ministry, for the church is seen gathered together in an attitude of prayer and fasting. In all likelihood such was not an isolated occasion. It was in such an atmosphere that the Holy Spirit was able to designate to the church those whom He was calling to a new sphere of service. The fact of the call would seem to have been revealed to the church before Paul and Barnabas expressed their own convictions. In this incident the emphasis is laid upon the call being from God made known by the Holy Spirit. The call came to those who were already serving in the assembly, being conspicuous for their devotion, zeal, and love to the Lord, demonstrating that in the varied experiences of life and service for the Lord, they were being fitted and equipped by the Holy Spirit for enlarged activities.

Further, the call was recognized by the assembly. In connection with the release of Paul and Barnabas for their service two interesting expressions are employed, they 'laid their hands on them'

(Acts 13. 3), and 'they were recommended to the grace of God' (Acts 14. 26). The laying on of hands was clearly not by way of ordination for service, for Paul and Barnabas had already been engaged in special ministry at Antioch for over a year (Acts 11. 26). Nor did it secure the impartation of the Holy Spirit or of some special gift. They had already given abundant evidence of the enduement of the Holy Spirit, and of the possession of gift for service. It was, however, a solemn recognition of the fact of a divine call, and also an expression of identification with the missionaries in the service in which they were about to engage. Such identification is of value, so far as effective support of the missionary is concerned, only if there is in the assembly a general conviction that God has called. It is not merely that the individual or even the elders also should be persuaded of the call, but that the conviction should be shared generally by the assembly. When such is the case a sense of partnership between the assembly and the outgoing missionary will develop. There will be a recognition that the work in which the Lord's servant will be engaged is one in which the assembly collectively will share, and it will be regarded as an overflow or extension of assembly activities.

When Paul and Barnabas returned from their first missionary journey, recognizing the intimate association subsisting between themselves and the assembly, they took the initiative in convening a gathering to rehearse all that God had done with them. It is then that we learn that, at their first valedictory meeting the assembly had committed them to the grace of God. It must have been an inspiring gathering, with a full attendance of the assembly all instinctively feeling that an event of unusual significance was impending. Even so, neither the assembly nor the missionaries could have had any idea of the variety of experiences which would be theirs, some pleasant but many irksome and dangerous; of bitter opposition to be endured, of trophies of grace to be won, and of hardships to be borne. The assembly could not do more than hand them over solemnly to the all-sufficient grace of God.

In the case of Timothy it would seem that the will of God was made known through Paul, but this does not mean that either Timothy, or the assemblies at Lystra and Iconium did not recognize that the call was of God. The significant feature of Timothy's call and commendation was that he was evidently well known and well reported of by a number of assemblies. It is still vital that the potential missionary should have a good report in respect of home, assembly, and business life. A grave responsibility rests upon elders of assemblies, particularly to-day, to discern whom, amongst the many who are coming forward and expressing a desire for missionary service, God is calling. It, indeed, behoves all those exercised as to missionary service to seek and to wait for full assembly recognition and fellowship ere taking a decisive step.

Another matter which is of importance is that of the missionary's *guidance and control*. Whilst the most intimate fellowship existed between Paul and the assembly at Antioch it is manifest that he was not under the control of, nor did he look for guidance in his service to the assembly at Antioch, or Jerusalem, or to any council of elders such as met together on the occasion of the conference recorded in Acts 15. He looked to God for direction and guidance in his service. In Acts 16. 6-10 we see Paul, Silas and Luke most uncertain as to their future course. In that dubiety they push in several directions only to discover that the way seems barred, until clear light is finally vouchsafed, and the testimony is that 'after he had seen the vision, immediately we endeavoured to go into Macedonia, assuredly gathering *that the Lord had called* us for to preach the Gospel unto them.' It may be thought that in those days no other course was practicable. There was no postal service or any rapid means of communication with the elders at Antioch. This, no doubt, is true, but not more so than was the case in the early days of missionary service in most lands. Many a missionary has felt that Mission Boards in the home-lands, despite the best of intentions, have often been completely out of touch with the real position obtaining on the mission field, and quite unable to appreciate fully the nature of the problems and the choices confronting the missionary. There is little doubt that this control from the home base had much to do with David Livingstone and Hudson Taylor severing their connection with the missionary societies with which they were originally associated; whilst between Carey, Marshman, and Ward, at Serampore, and the Baptist Missionary Society at home there was grievous friction over the same question for some years. To-day, with the advent of the aeroplane, knowledge of problems and needs may be swiftly obtained, and decisions are more likely to be in accord with the real position than was formerly the case. With such facilities for obtaining accurate information speedily, there may appear to be great advantages in more control from the home base, but the removal of obvious disadvantages does not render nugatory the principle of New Testament practice that the missionary shall look directly to God for his guidance.

With guidance and control there is intimately linked the matter of *the support of the missionary*. There are a number of references to this important subject scattered throughout the New Testament. The cardinal principle unfolded is that whilst the missionary's call is from God, and he looks also to God for guidance and control so likewise he is to look to God alone for the supply of his material needs. Not even in this matter is any individual or group of believers to be allowed to come between him and his Lord. The New Testament affords no precedent or authority for the guaranteed support of the missionary by any church or body of Christians. There is no explicit reference even to any monetary support of Paul and Barnabas on the part of the assembly at Antioch.

Paul sets forth the principles in I Cor. 9. 14 that 'they which preach the Gospel should live of the Gospel' and that the servant of God should not be expected to go a warfare at his own charges. On the contrary, having sown to a church in spiritual things, he might expect to reap of things for the body (I Cor. 9. 11). Nevertheless, Paul does not press any such claim. He declares to the Corinthians that he has not availed himself of any of these things. He would rather 'suffer all things, lest we should hinder the Gospel of Christ' (I Cor. 9. 12). Possibly his fear of compromising the testimony was due to the practice of a class of religious teachers, mere mystery-mongers many of them, who travelled from town to town lecturing and collecting money. If there was the slightest danger of Paul being classed amongst such, and regarded as one who preached the glad tidings for base gain, he would prefer to labour with his own hands for his material support. This he often did (I Thess. 2. 9).

Where, however, a church was ready spontaneously to minister to his temporal support, Paul was quite happy to receive such help.

The church at Philippi seems to have been a pattern, and possibly quite exceptional amongst apostolic churches in this matter. It was not, however, the only church which sent to Paul for he says to the Corinthians: 'I robbed other churches, taking wages of them, to do you service' (2 Cor. 11. 8). Paul does, however, refer to a number of occasions when the saints at Philippi ministered to him of their substance. Whilst he was labouring in Thessalonica they sent at least twice (Phil. 4. 15, 16); the gift was repeated when he was labouring with so much discouragement at Corinth; whilst Epaphroditus was their messenger on that hazardous journey to seek out Paul then a prisoner in Rome. Paul writes gratefully of their 'fellowship in the Gospel from the first day until now' (Phil. 1. 5), a fellowship maintained over a long period of time despite difficulties of communication. He describes the gift which Epaphroditus brought as 'an odour of a sweet smell, a sacrifice acceptable, well pleasing to God' (Phil. 4. 18), as though, before he would even use it he would offer it to God. It is worthy of note that this ministry of giving is not represented as one-sided in its blessing, as though the recipient only is blessed and helped, for Paul speaks of it as fruit abounding to the account of the Philippian believers. When Paul unfolds the principles of Christian giving in 2 Cor. 8-9 he speaks of those who sow bountifully, reaping also bountifully, and that through this grace believers experience an abounding sense of the grace of God, rejoice in an increase in the fruits of righteousness and thereby glorify God.

The question may be raised as to whether these principles are intended to be of permanent application, and whether it is practicable even to follow them in the vastly different conditions obtaining to-day. The teaching unfolded in the Acts and in the Epistles concerning apostolic methods of Gospel work, forms part of the 'faith once for all delivered unto the saints' (Jude 3, R.V.). It may, therefore, be claimed that there is no authority to go beyond the things thus written. If there be an attempt to do so the problem to be faced immediately is, whose conclusions or ideas shall be followed?

As to the practicability of these principles it has been proved abundantly that they are workable in any country. Mr. W. E. Vine remarks: 'The simple, unencumbered methods employed by the apostles under the Lord's injunctions and the guidance and control of the Spirit of God, have never proved unsuitable in any nation or age.' It is interesting to observe that in consequence of nationalistic trends in all lands, Governments are now claiming a greater measure of control over foreign missionaries, whilst native Christians are seeking a greater share in the activities of the Christian Church. Many missionary societies have, therefore, deemed it advisable to change their policy drastically, and to adopt practices much more closely allied to those set out in the New Testament. Hitherto, missions with their foreign workers have been divorced from the native church; so much so that in a report of a council meeting of a well-known interdenominational mission it is stated that the question was raised 'whether we should consider ourselves as actually part of the Church'! After discussion it was agreed that 'where the Church desires it missionaries may accept church membership and serve as members of the Church Council, diaconate or other similar body.' Another question propounded was: 'If there is a Church, ought we not as fellow-labourers to be working through it?' And the confession is made: 'We have been slow to grasp the truth, with all its implications, and its application has lagged also, because we have not seen it with sufficient clearness.' This change of attitude, induced by modern conditions means that the work of this mission, as of other societies, is not now so much mission-conscious as church-conscious. Or, in other words, they are finding it more practicable to draw close to New Testament principles of missionary service than to pursue the practices hitherto followed.

In conclusion it must be stressed, as a matter of solemn import, that the successful application of New Testament principles of missionary service is dependent primarily upon a high level of spirituality being maintained in the assemblies of the homelands. Only as assemblies manifest the characteristics of the church at Antioch will the Spirit be able, unfailingly, to indicate those whom God has called to missionary service so that none go forth unbidden, and only thus will those who do leave for heathen lands be truly men and women of God. Only as assemblies exhibit the same exercise as that at Philippi, will the support of missionaries by intercession and giving be such as will maintain them as men and women of prayer, and furnish the means, not only for the maintenance of life, but also for the prosecution of an aggressive work for God.

The spiritual condition of the home assemblies will certainly be reflected in the state of the work in other lands. Paul indicates this in 2 Cor. 10. 15, 16, when he says: 'As your faith grows so we shall be enlarged unto further abundance so as to preach the Gospel in the regions beyond you'; as though until there was a growing interest and concern he felt restricted and confined in his labours and unable to reach out into new fields.

O Master of the waking world,
Who hast the nations in Thy heart,
The heart that bled and broke to send
God's love to earth's remotest part—
Show us anew in Calvary
The wondrous power that makes men free.

On every side the walls are down,
The gates swing wide in every land,
The restless tribes and races feel
The pressure of Thy pierced hand.
Thy way is in the sea and air,
Thy world is open everywhere.

O Church of God! Awake! Awake!
The waking world is calling thee.
Lift up thine eyes! Hear thou once more
The challenge of humanity!
O Christ, we come! Our all we bring,
To serve our world and Thee our King.

Frank North

CHAPTER XV

CHURCH HISTORY AND ITS LESSONS

F. F. BRUCE

'THE real history of Christianity is the history of a great spiritual tradition. The only true apostolical succession is the lives of the saints. Clement of Alexandria compared the Church to a great river, receiving affluents from all sides. The great river sometimes flows impetuously through a narrow channel; sometimes it spreads like a flood; sometimes it divides into several streams; sometimes, for a time, it seems to have been driven underground. But the Holy Spirit has never left Himself without witness; and if we will put aside a great deal of what passes for Church History, and is really a rather unedifying branch of secular history, and follow the course of the religion of the Spirit and the Church of the Spirit, we shall judge very differently of the relative importance of events from those who merely follow the fortunes of institutionalism.'

With these words of Dr. W. R. Inge[1] we may set ourselves to consider some of the lessons to be learned from a bird's eye view of the history of the Christian Church.

Naturally, within the limits of one chapter, nothing like a detailed survey of Church history can be attempted; the phases here selected, and the morals drawn from them, probably depend on no better principle than the present writer's interest and caprice, as, for example, in the frequent references to Scottish Church history. For a thorough-going treatment of the whole subject readers are most emphatically recommended to have recourse to *The Pilgrim Church*, by the late E. H. Broadbent,[2] a book whose character is more exactly indicated by its sub-title: 'Being some account of the continuance through succeeding centuries of churches practising the principles taught and exemplified in the New Testament.'

[1] *Things New and Old* (1933), pages 57 f.
[2] London: Pickering & Inglis. First published 1931. It is most gratifying to know that a new edition has appeared (1946).

These words, 'practising the principles taught and exemplified in the New Testament,' are noteworthy; they enshrine a vital principle frequently recurring in Church history, to which the name Reformation is given. This use of the term 'Reformation' may be illustrated from the following enviable testimonial which John Row, writing about 1640, gave to the Scottish Reformers of the previous century: 'They took not their pattern from any kirk in the world; no, not from Geneva itself; but laying God's Word before them made reformation thereto.'

Reformation according to the Word of God is a principle which constantly needs to be put into operation. We must not imagine that those who stand for the maintenance of the Reformed Faith are simply asserting sixteenth century principles. They stand for the maintenance in every century of the principles which the Reformers of the sixteenth century sought to practise at the risk of their lives—the abiding principles of the divine Word.[1] These Reformers themselves were far from claiming finality in their application of these principles; when John Knox and his friends published the *Scots Confession* of 1560, they begged that any deviation therein from Scriptural principles might be pointed out to them, so that their Reformation according to the Word of God might be yet more complete.

When the term 'Reformation' is thus understood in its full sense, its perpetual necessity will be better recognized. For if Church history teaches one thing more than another, it is that there is a constant tendency to deterioration in ecclesiastical as much as in all human affairs. The price of liberty, here as elsewhere, is eternal vigilance; and such vigilance can best be maintained by unceasing reference to the Magna Charta of our faith, the Holy Scriptures. Thus Reformation according to the Word of God is no harking back to the dead past, whether of the first or sixteenth century; the Word of God is living and powerful to-day as ever, and speaks to our condition in the twentieth century as much as in the centuries gone by. We can still prove the truth of John Robinson's

[1] The related term 'Protestant' is also commonly misunderstood; it does not primarily denote one who protests *against* something, but (in the etymological sense of Latin *protestatur*) one who *bears witness for* the truth of Scripture. If this were borne in mind, it would do away with the well-meant objections to being so described, sometimes made by Christians who earnestly desire to bear witness to the truth of Scripture.

words spoken over three hundred years ago to the Pilgrim Fathers at Delft Haven: 'I am verily persuaded the Lord hath more truth yet to break forth out of His Holy Word.' The lessons to be learned from that Word are not yet exhausted. And one way of viewing Church history is to see it as the record of constant departure from, and as constant returning to, the principles of Holy Scripture considered as the only rule of faith and obedience.

We propose, then, to consider historically how 'Reformation according to the Word of God' affects (a) the Form and Ministry of the Church; (b) the Relation between Church and State; and (c) the Church's Mission in the World.

THE FORM AND MINISTRY OF THE CHURCH

When the Reformers of the sixteenth century found it necessary to re-state the meaning of the term 'Church,' they did so by reference to the Scriptures. For, as Bishop Pearson rightly saw at a later date,[1] 'the only way to attain unto the knowledge of the true notion of the Church, is to search into the New Testament, and from the places there which mention it, to conclude what is the nature of it.' So they found that the Church Universal,[2] in its widest scope, consists of the whole company of God's elect, of all realms and all ages; so far as the local and visible manifestation of the Church Universal was concerned, they recognized it by three outstanding notes—the preaching of the pure Word of God, the right administration of the sacraments according to Christ's ordinance, and the maintenance of godly order by the proper exercise of Church government. These notes certainly distinguished the local churches of New Testament times.

But we cannot read the later books of the New Testament without becoming aware of ominous tendencies within the Apostolic Churches. Paul's warning to the Ephesian elders as early as A.D. 57, that 'grievous wolves' would ravage their flock and that from their own ranks false teachers would rise and lead many astray (Acts 20. 29 f.), prepares us for the developments reflected at a later date in the Johannine writings. Most menacing

---

[1] *An Exposition of the Creed* (1659), Article IX.

[2] The epithet 'universal' or 'catholic' seems first to have been applied to the Church by Ignatius (c. 115), to whom we owe the epigram: 'Where Jesus Christ is, there is the Catholic Church' (*Letter to Smyrnæans,* 8. 2).

towards the end of the apostolic age was the form of teaching called Docetism which, asserting the inherent evil of the material order, denied the reality of Christ's Incarnation. The apostles themselves had their opponents; in Asia Phygellus and Hermogenes led a revolt against Paul (2 Tim. 1. 15), and Diotrephes, three decades later, refused to receive the delegates sent by John (3 John 9).

How were these tendencies to be dealt with? Paul referred the Ephesian elders to the divine Word (Acts 20. 32); and in 2 Tim. 2. 2 he envisaged a true and spiritual apostolic succession, i.e., a succession of faithful men perpetuating the apostolic teaching. This succession idea, however, soon became stereotyped into something more formal, as is evident as early as about A.D. 115, in the letters which Ignatius, bishop of Antioch, wrote to various churches on his way to Rome to be thrown to the lions. Ignatius, in his anxiety to maintain orthodoxy within the churches and debar heresy, laid great stress on the function of the monarchical bishop, an office which first appears at the beginning of the second century. He insisted that the bishop, or someone delegated by the bishop (presumably someone who saw eye to eye with him in these matters), was the only church official who might conduct a valid baptism or Eucharist.[1] The bishop or his representatives were thus in a position to refuse the holy ordinances to heretics. The apostolic succession as commonly interpreted in episcopal churches thus had its origin in an effort to keep heresy out of the Church.[2] A bishop who could trace his succession through the previous bishops of his see back to the apostles was in a position to claim apostolic validity for his acts. (This differs in one respect from the later idea of apostolic succession, which lays emphasis on the continuity of episcopal *ordination*; then the emphasis was on the *succession* of bishops in a particular local see, by whomsoever they had been ordained.)

As time went on, the tendency was to shift the emphasis from

[1] 'Let that be held a valid Eucharist which is under the bishop or one to whom he shall have committed it. . . . It is not lawful apart from the bishop either to baptize or to hold a love-feast' (*Letter to Smyrnœans*, 8. 1, 2). 'Six of the seven letters are filled with exaggerated exaltation of the authority and importance of the bishop's office. . . . To Ignatius the monarchical episcopate is an *idée fixe*' (B. H. Streeter, *The Primitive Church*, 1929; pp. 164, 173). For all that, Ignatius has no thought of any episcopal succession, an idea which first appears later in the second century.

[2] It was the same concern for the exclusion of heresy that led to the requirement of fairly elaborate credal tests in place of the primitive confession of allegiance to Jesus as Lord.

the actual maintenance of the apostles' teaching and fellowship to the external fact of historic continuity. Where the Reformation was most thoroughgoing, therefore, the original emphasis was restored at the expense of the latter. 'It is by making Scripture the rule of faith that the Reformed Church stands in the true Apostolic Succession.'[1]

The rise of the monarchical episcopate was historically a development within the elderhood of the local church.[2] The presiding elder, or an elder who was outstanding among his fellow-elders in experience, personality, or in some other way, might easily pass from being *primus inter pares* to be *primus* pure and simple. We can infer from the New Testament, for example, that James, the brother of our Lord, must, in practice, have played a dominant part among his fellow-elders at Jerusalem; although, to be sure, he and his colleagues and successors in the first Jerusalem Church, down to the refounding of the city by Hadrian in 135, were in their lifetime not called bishops but simply elders. (This was but natural, as 'elder' has a Jewish background, while 'bishop' has a Gentile background.) It is, indeed, warmly contended by some scholars that monarchical bishops did not arise in this way, but that they were formally the successors of the apostles, appointed by them to continue the apostolic ministry in a local form.[3] This cannot be upheld, however, if only because the New Testament usage of Greek *episkopos* points uniformly in the other direction. In New Testament Greek the *episkopos* (bishop or overseer), and *presbyteros* (elder) are one and the same. (This is reflected in the fact that even to-day a bishop in the Roman Church does not possess *different* Orders from a presbyter or priest, but possesses the *fulness* of the presbyterate to rule a diocese as its chief pastor.) The more thoroughgoing Reformers, therefore, replaced the monarchical episcopate by the Scriptural government of each church by a presbytery or body of elders (1 Tim. 4. 14), none of whom enjoys a superior status to the others.

The restriction of the valid Eucharist to the bishop and his representatives had more serious implications than Ignatius could

[1] D. T. Jenkins, *The Nature of Catholicity* (1942), page 37.
[2] See, for example, J. B. Lightfoot, *The Christian Ministry* (1868), pp. 23 ff.
[3] This is the thesis, for example, of the symposium *The Apostolic Ministry*, edited by the Bishop of Oxford (1946).

have envisaged. 'The rise of officialdom and formalism,' says Professor Angus, 'must be regarded as a contributory cause to the evolution of sacramentarianism.'[1] In the New Testament there is not the slightest hint that the administration of the sacraments is to be restricted to any particular class of Christians. The ministry of the Word is to be exercised by those divinely called to that service, and so with the other ministries; but nothing is said about who should undertake the ministry of the sacraments. This is the more remarkable, as even in very many of the Reformed Churches, where wide liberty is enjoyed in the preaching of the Word, the celebration of the sacraments is conditional on the presence of those who are specially set apart for this purpose. The New Testament implication is that the true ministers, say in the celebration of the Lord's Supper, are the members of the Church themselves. A sense of spiritual fitness would teach that those who lead the congregation in this solemn act of worship should be such as are spiritually fit to do so; but this is a very different matter from restricting valid celebration to a special class of men. This departure early in the second century unfortunately coincided with a tendency for ecclesiastical practice in many Gentile churches to be influenced by the contemporary mystery cults. In these cults the due performance and interpretation of the Mysteries (or sacred dramas) were the province of hierophants, men specially set apart for this purpose. It was at least to some extent under such influences that the Christian minister, as Angus says,[2] 'assumed the office of priest as the dispenser of grace-conferring rituals and as the custodian of the kingdom of heaven entrusted with the dread "power of the keys."' The well-meant injunction of Ignatius thus chimed in only too well with 'the magic fashion of the days when,' to quote the same writer,[3] 'on the cessation of the primitive spiritual manifestations, the outward rite was correspondingly highly esteemed, and when the idea from the Mysteries had taken permanent root in Christianity that no member of the brotherhood could be saved or benefit by the grace or blessings of the religion except through participation in its rituals of initiation and rebirth.' To be sure, the extent of the influence of the Mystery Religions on the

[1] S. Angus, *Religious Quests of the Græco-Roman World* (1929), p. 151.
[2] *Op. cit.*, p. 152. [3] *Op. cit.*, p. 217.

Church has often been greatly exaggerated, but some influence from those quarters there certainly was.[1]

This tendency naturally obscured the New Testament doctrine of the priesthood of all believers; and the reaffirmation of this truth was one of the most urgent tasks of the Reformers. It is noteworthy that the New Testament writers studiously avoid the use of the Greek word *hiereus* (priest) as a title of a Christian minister.[2] The only Christian applications of this word in the New Testament are (a) to the unique High Priesthood of Christ, and (b) to the common priesthood of all believers. All believers are priests, though by no means all are public ministers of the Word. And this is why in the New Testament the priestly acts are not restricted to any one class within the Christian community. Those Christian bodies which give most practical effect to the priesthood of all believers are in this respect the most truly reformed.

This principle marks a deep cleavage in Christendom, a cleavage which does not always follow denominational boundaries. There are those 'unreformed' communities whose ministers are primarily sacrificing priests, and there are those 'reformed' communities whose ministers are primarily preachers of the Word. This distinction is often reflected even in the architecture of their places of worship, according as the altar or the pulpit occupies the central place.

The truly reformed churches therefore can harbour no proper distinction between clergy and laity. A high esteem of the holy ministry of the Word is right and proper; the Scripture enjoins that elders 'who labour in the Word and in teaching' are to be accounted worthy of special honour (1 Tim. 5. 17).[3] And alongside these are those elders who, while they may not have the gift of public utterance, place the Church under a heavy debt of gratitude by their wise rule and guidance. Church history demonstrates abundantly how disastrous an error it is to think that a church can

[1] See, for example, E. Hatch, *The Influence of Greek Ideas and Usages upon the Christian Church* (Hibbert Lectures, 1888), pp. 283-309.

[2] It is unfortunate that the English word 'priest,' which in the English New Testament represents only Greek *hiereus*, a sacrificing priest (Latin *sacerdos*), is used in the Book of Common Prayer and the Ordinal in the sense of Greek *presbyteros*, from which, indeed, it is derived. This verbal ambiguity has probably facilitated the growth of sacerdotalism in the Church of England.

[3] The word 'honour' (Greek *timé*) in this verse may include the idea of 'honorarium.' (Cf. W. E. Vine, *Expository Dictionary of New Testament Words*, Vol. II, p. 230.)

ever dispense with sound government for the due preservation of order and discipline, according to the Scriptural pattern.

CHURCH AND STATE

No lesson can be read more plainly in the records of the Church's history than that the Church must constantly be on her guard against encroachment on her liberties by the State.

The Church and the State are both instituted by God for the accomplishment of His will on the earth. Both are subject to the dominion of Christ, who is not only 'Head over all things to the Church which is His Body' (Eph. 1. 22 f.) but also 'Prince of the kings of the earth' (Rev. 1. 5, quoting Psa. 89. 27). Of the institution of the Church an account is given elsewhere in this volume. Her sphere is clearly prescribed by God. Her weapons are spiritual; her calling is eternal. The civil ruler, on the other hand, exercises a temporal authority; the weapons committed to his hand are material. His divinely appointed duty is the maintenance of justice and order in a fallen community (Rom. 13. 1-7, 1 Pet. 2. 13-17). It is arguable that in an unfallen community the State would be superfluous, but that is beside the practical point. The civil ruler's jurisdiction does *not* include the regulation of divine worship, although (to quote from the Schedule annexed to an Act of the British Parliament in 1921)[1] it is 'the duty of the nation acting in its corporate capacity to render homage to God, to acknowledge the Lord Jesus Christ to be King over the nations, to obey His laws, to reverence His ordinances, to honour His Church, and to promote in all appropriate ways the Kingdom of God.' The Church exists on earth to bear witness to Christ, her sole Head and King, to proclaim the Word of God, and to confront mankind with the claims of His kingdom and righteousness.

So long as Church and State fulfil their respective functions and do not transgress upon each other's jurisdiction, all is well. But this does not always happen. When the State departs from the justice which it ought to maintain it may well resent the Church's insistent proclamation of the righteousness of God, and attempt to curb the Church's freedom. Or the Church may yield to the temptation to play the political game, and run the risk of discrediting herself and her proper mission in the world.

[1] Church of Scotland Act, 1921.

Church history shows the undesirable consequences that arise when one of these two tries to dominate the other. The Church's attempt to dominate the State is seen at many times in the record of the Roman Church, supremely in the endeavour to practise the high doctrine of Hildebrand.[1]   (It must be conceded that in the history of the Roman Church it is often difficult to disentangle the Christian community from the largely political Papal system which sits on her shoulders like an Old Man of the Sea.)   The opposite error, an excessive deference by the Church to the State, has had unhappy results, for example, in the history of German Christianity from the time of Luther onwards.   The doctrine (commonly called Erastianism) that a Christian ruler, because of his secular authority, has automatically a ruling voice in the councils of the Church (a doctrine as old as Constantine), is totally wrong. It finds expression in some Lutheran countries where the king as such is Chief Bishop, and it finds expression nearer home as well. A Church which, in practice at any rate, entrusts the appointment of her chief pastors to whoever happens to be Prime Minister for the time being, can hardly substantiate the claim, made emphatically for her by some of her members, to be the most Scriptural Church in the world.

Until Constantine acceded to the supreme power in the Roman Empire, in 312, the Church was faced with a generally hostile State. For longer or shorter periods between the time of Nero (A.D. 54-68) and Galerius (305-311) there might be a lull, but persecution was always liable to break out, and the passage of years did not diminish its fury. The last imperial persecution was the fiercest. The root of the trouble was the Christians' refusal to accord to the Emperor (regarded as the sacred incarnation of the Empire) such homage as in their eyes amounted to divine honours. Offering a pinch of incense in his honour, swearing by his *genius*, giving him the title 'Lord,' which he claimed in a divine sense— such things they refused to do. Some of us to-day might consider them unnecessarily obstinate in refusing to perform such trivial outward acts. It might similarly be argued that Shadrach, Meshach,

---

[1] He ruled as Pope Gregory VII, from 1073 to 1085; it was he who humiliated the Emperor Henry IV at Canossa in 1077. 'With imperious courage Hildebrand conceived of the world as a single Christian polity governed by an omnipotent and infallible Pope' (H. A. L. Fisher, *History of Europe* [1936], p. 199).

and Abednego ran quite unnecessary risks in refusing to bow before Nebuchadnezzar's image. They might have reasoned thus: 'An idol is nothing in the world; this act is therefore a matter of indifference to us; let us conform outwardly to save trouble.' But they did not; for they saw exactly what was at stake—their witness to the undivided sovereignty of the true God. The early Christians followed their example. The grand phrase, 'The Crown Rights of the Redeemer,' had not been coined in so many words at that time, but they vindicated those Crown Rights full well. Nor is such a predicament as theirs even yet a thing of the past. It is not so long since a very similar crisis confronted the churches in the Japanese Empire, not to mention other parts of the world; and what has happened once can happen again.[1] In this realm, as much as in the political, the surest way to ensure the coming of such undesirable consummations is to say complacently: 'It can't happen here!'

But the tension between Church and State changed its character in the fourth century, and the temptation assumed a more subtle form. Less than fifteen years after the last imperial persecution ended, the Roman Emperor Constantine was found presiding at the Council of Nicæa (325). By what right? Because of his spiritual stature in the Church? No, but because, although then still unbaptized, he was the ruler of the Empire, who had departed from his predecessors' repressive policy and decided to extend his patronage to the Church. The Crown Rights of the Redeemer, maintained for three centuries against the threat of direct persecution, were now confronted by a more insidious but none the less dangerous menace.

We cannot here review the century-long tension between Church and State in the Middle Ages. We can learn some lessons, however, from British history at a later period.

When the Church of England threw off the Papal allegiance in the sixteenth century, it found itself more strictly governed than before, under the rulers of the Tudor dynasty, especially Henry VIII (1509-1547) and his masterful daughter Elizabeth (1558-1603). The royal supremacy in ecclesiastical as well as in political causes was stoutly asserted and exercised. Those Reformers who envisaged

---

[1] Striking parallels between the situation of Christians under the Roman and Japanese Empires, in both of which Emperor-worship was enjoined by the State, are drawn by Dr. John Foster in his book *Then and Now* (1942), pp. 84-103.

a more thoroughgoing and Scriptural Reformation were like to be given short shrift. Such men were Robert Browne, author of a *Treatise of Reformation without Tarrying for Anie* (1582), whose strength and spirit were at last broken by repeated imprisonments, so that he finally conformed to the Elizabethan Settlement; and Henry Barrowe, John Greenwood, and John Penry, all three of whom were hanged in 1593 for stubborn refusal to conform.[1]

In Scotland, on the other hand, the Reformation of 1560 was carried through *against* the will of the government. From the outset there was in Scotland a strong insistence on the liberty of the Church from State interference. When James VI of Scotland (1567-1625) desired to enjoy such authority in the Scottish Church as Elizabeth did in the Church of England, he met with strong resistance. This found forceful expression in the words of Andrew Melville, who told the king during an interview with him in 1596: 'And thairfor, sir, as divers tymes befor, sa now again, I mon tell yow, thair is twa Kings and twa kingdomes in Scotland. Thair is Chryst Jesus the King, and his kingdome the Kirk, whase subject King James the Saxt is, and of whase kingdome nocht a king, nor a lord, nor a heid, bot a member!'

The spiritual independence of the Church could not be more explicitly stated, with the corollary that a Christian ruler, so far as his secular status is concerned, is in the Church 'not a king, nor a lord, nor a head, but a member.'

However, James was ultimately able to assert his power and compel some measure of submission to his policy. The episcopal system, as he saw it operating in England, was to his mind better calculated to support the royal authority in the Church—a viewpoint which he summed up in the aphorism: 'No bishop, no king!' When he went to England in 1603 as James I, he found the Anglican leaders more respectful than the leaders of the Kirk. For example, the language of the Epistle Dedicatory 'To the Most High and Mighty Prince James,' prefaced to the Authorized Version of the

---

[1] R. W. Dale, *History of English Congregationalism* (1906), pp. 120 ff. Barrowe has left the following definition of a local Church which should not be forgotten: 'A true-planted and rightly-established Church of Christ is a company of faithful people, separated from unbelievers, gathered in the name of Christ, whom they truly worship and readily obey. They are a brotherhood, a communion of saints, each one of them standing in and for their Christian liberty to practise whatsoever God has commanded and revealed unto them in His Holy Word.'

Bible, forms an eloquent contrast to that of Andrew Melville, who plucked him familiarly by the sleeve and called him 'God's sillie vassall.' Yet in England, too, there were those who shared Melville's opinion, though they may not have expressed it with Melville's great freedom of speech. Such a man was Thomas Helwys, one of the first English Baptists, who, in 1612, presented James with very similar arguments to Melville's in a book entitled *The Mystery of Iniquity*.

But both in Scotland and England blood and tears had to flow before some degree of spiritual liberty was won. The conflict which had to be waged is associated in Scottish history with the memory of the Covenanters, and in English history with such names as those of the Pilgrim Fathers of 1620, the Ejected Ministers of 1662, and the illustrious Tinker of Bedford. These stiff-necked men, as they appeared to many of their contemporaries, might have compounded with the government had they been willing to acknowledge in some small practical way its right to lay down conditions for the Church's life and work. But this was the very issue at stake, and on this they would not compromise.

Even after the Revolution of 1688-1689, the various secessions in the Scottish Church, culminating in the Great Disruption of 1843,[1] were not due (as some ignorantly suppose) to any fissiparous tendency innate in Presbyterianism, but to a resolute contention at all costs for the spiritual independence of the Church. As for the Disruption, while lay patronage of parochial incumbencies was its immediate occasion, its real cause was the persistent overriding by the State legislature of the Church's own decisions. The rightful cause triumphed at last; whatever our views may be on the general principle of ecclesiastical establishment,[2] it is worth noting that the Church of Scotland is probably unique in being at once legally established and yet spiritually free, statutorily subject to no ruler but Christ, in that it 'receives from Him, its divine King and Head, and from Him alone, the right and power

[1] Secession takes place when part of the Church severs its relation with the parent body; disruption is the severing of the link between the Church and the State. If the whole Church of Scotland had followed Chalmers in 1843 to form the Free Church .this would still have been a Disruption—an even greater Disruption than actually did take place.

[2] The leaders of the Disruption firmly believed in the principle of Establishment: 'We quit a vitiated Establishment,' said Chalmers, 'but would rejoice in returning to a pure one.'

subject to no civil authority to legislate and adjudicate finally, in all matters of doctrine, worship, government, and discipline in the Church.'[1]

For various reasons, English Church history has had to run a different course. Among the less desirable features of the Oxford Movement in England, which was roughly contemporary with the Disruption conflict in Scotland, should be noticed one praiseworthy point at any rate which was common to both, an earnest contention for the Church's freedom from State control. The Erastianism which seems so constantly to accompany Anglican Evangelicalism, and which is none too pleasant to contemplate, may be due in part to misgivings lest the removal of State control should lead to the dominance of the High Church party. Those of us who are free from such embarrassments should thank God, and neither envy nor criticize our Evangelical brethren in the Church of England.

But history shows clearly that it is not to the interest of any Church to be too closely linked to the ruling power. It is obviously undesirable in India, for example, that Christianity should be too closely identified in the popular mind with the late British Raj. It has been suggested that the favour shown to Christian missions in China by Chiang Kai-Shek's government might not be ultimately for the advantage of the Chinese churches if that government were replaced by another. The history of the Russian Church illustrates the point very well. While the Marxian thesis is opposed on principle to all religion, and indeed considers that the purer the religion the more deadly an enemy it is, yet the downfall of the Russian Church after the Revolution of 1917 would have been less easily compassed if that church had not been so hopelessly implicated in the worst features of the Tsarist régime.[2]

It is a melancholy fact, but one which is worth pondering, that all too often those Christian bodies which have wielded political power or been able to influence the civil rulers have used their influence intolerantly. It is said that C. H. Spurgeon once declared that the Baptists could claim to be the only denomination that had never indulged in religious persecution—adding, when the applause

[1] Schedule annexed to the Church of Scotland Act, 1921.
[2] Things have changed since then, and it is to be hoped that the Russian Church in our day will not repeat the mistake of an earlier age.

died down, 'because they have never had the chance!' An earlier Baptist wrote to George Washington: 'Religious ministers, when supported by force, are the most dangerous men on earth.' And Jonathan Swift said: 'I never saw, heard, nor read that the clergy were beloved in any country where Christianity was the religion of the country. Nothing can render them popular but some degree of persecution.' The lesson of these quotations needs no pressing.

One further lesson, on the other side, to be learned from the history of relations between Church and State, is that spiritual liberty is more likely to be preserved where the Scriptural principle of the administrative independence of each local church is maintained.[1] This is, of course, not at all inconsistent with the utmost Christian fellowship and co-operation between churches. But if the State be adversely disposed it can more easily paralyse a centrally organized corporation than a multitude of unfederated congregations, each independently governed and administered by its own elders and deacons. And it would be well if this consideration were borne in mind when governments try to press some measure of federation upon independent churches, as has happened in recent years in several countries of Europe, as well as in other continents.

The Church's Mission in the World

The Church's main function in the world is to bear witness to her Lord and Master, by carrying out faithfully the commission with which He charged her after His resurrection: 'Go ye therefore, and make disciples of all the nations, baptizing them into the name of the Father and of the Son and of the Holy Ghost: teaching them to observe all things whatsoever I have commanded you' (Matt. 28. 19 f., R.V.). An impossible task, surely, for such an absurdly small and uninfluential body as the infant Church was to all outward seeming. But the New Testament shows how actively and successfully the infant Church set about this business, undeterred by any discouragement. As time went on the Church found all the might of the Roman Empire stirred up against her, and attempts

[1] That this is a Scriptural principle has been shown by E. Hatch in *The Organization of the Early Christian Churches* (Bampton Lectures, 1880), and by F. J. A. Hort in *The Christian Ecclesia* (1897), among others.

were made in one persecution after another to suppress the Christian name altogether. But such was the Church's survival-power that the last imperial persecution, the severest of all, had barely come to an end when the Empire bowed in acknowledgment of the Church's victory. This, as we have suggested, did not prove an unmixed blessing for the Church, but the wonder of the fact remains.

The Christians of the first three centuries had little, if anything, to aid them in their advance which we have not. We have the Gospel, as they had; we have the Holy Spirit, as they had; and we have a spiritually hungry and disillusioned world around us, as they had. True, in their day the greater part of the civilized world was politically united as it is not to-day, but we have in turn those conveniences of modern civilization which were denied to them.

We are tempted to feel to-day that the tide has set strongly in opposition to Christianity. Not so strongly as in the first three centuries A.D.! A review of Church history is a splendid tonic for despondent hearts. Such a review is afforded by Professor K. S. Latourette in his monumental History of the Expansion of Christianity.[1] Dr. Latourette portrays the expansion of our faith as a series of alternating advances and recessions.

The first advance lasted from the beginning of the apostles' preaching till nearly A.D. 500. By the end of this period the majority of the subjects of the Roman Empire professed Christianity and the faith had spread outside the Empire—to Ireland on the west, and to Ethiopia, South Arabia, Persia, and India on the south and east. Christianity had begun to influence Imperial Law. It may be questioned in what sense, if any, it is ever right to speak of a Christian nation; but if the spirit of Christianity is written into a nation's laws and constitution, a case may be made for describing such a nation as Christian. At any rate, Christianity has in this way extended its influence down to the present day in all those lands whose laws have been influenced, directly or indirectly, by Roman Law.

During the first recession (c. 500-950) the Christian communities were actually scattered over a wider area than ever; but the solid block of Christendom round the Mediterranean shores was broken

[1] 7 vols., Eyre & Spottiswoode, 1939-1946. Dr. Latourette has presented his main thesis in conveniently small compass in The Unquenchable Light 1945). See also Dr. John Foster, World Church (1945), for a study along similar lines.

up. The invaders of the Empire were largely pagan. The Goths had been evangelized before they captured Rome in 410, but such races as the Huns, who ravaged the Empire on the North, and the Vandals, who overran North Africa, were pagan. The recession in North Africa was hastened by the incursion of Islam in the seventh century. The fate of the African churches which had produced such giants as Tertullian and Augustine was a colossal tragedy. But it is not without its lessons. The Christian communities of Egypt and Ethiopia survived, although in an enfeebled condition, because they were indigenous and had the Scriptures in the vernacular, whereas in the Roman province of Africa (corresponding to modern Morocco, Algeria, and Tunis) Christianity seems to have been the religion of the dominant Roman caste, rather than of the native races, and the Bible was read only in Latin. The moral? Indigenous churches and a vernacular Bible are indispensable for lasting Christian work.

On the north-western borders of the Empire, too, many churches were submerged by the pagan tides, first by the Angles and their kindred, and later by the Scandinavians. Yet this period of recession was not lacking in signs of progress. The barbarians were gradually assimilated, if not converted, to Christianity; the Picts and Anglo-Saxons in Britain received the Gospel from Ireland and Rome; the evangelization of the southern Slavs began, and the Nestorian Church carried the Gospel to Central Asia.[1]

These signs of progress were fulfilled in the second great advance (950-1350). Reforming influences began to operate in the Western European Church with the foundation of the monasteries of Cluny and elsewhere, and other Puritan movements, some of which broke away from the Roman communion. In Northern Europe the Scandinavians were evangelized, not only in their homelands but also in their settlements in Iceland and Greenland. The eastern Slavs (Bohemians, Poles, Wends, and western Russians) and also the Magyars in Hungary received the Gospel. In the thirteenth and fourteenth centuries the Nestorians were active in China, which was also visited by Franciscan missionaries. The Christian Way was followed from Greenland to China.

[1] On the evangelistic activity of the Nestorian Churches of Syria and the East, well into the Middle Ages, see *Nestorian Missionary Enterprise: The Story of a Church on Fire*, by Dr. John Stewart (1928).

14

This age was followed by a second recession (c. 1350-1500), in which Christianity disappeared from Greenland, while at the other extremity of its extension Nestorian Christianity began to shrink. The Byzantine Empire was crushed by the Muslim Turks, who captured its capital, Constantinople, in 1453. The Roman Church was weakened by inward strife, and corruption was rife within it. The Renaissance brought to many a sceptical attitude towards the traditional beliefs. Yet this age of recession is illuminated by bright spots, such as the names of Wyclif and Hus. And the discovery of the Americas towards the end of this period was the harbinger of a greater expansion than ever. At the end of the fifteenth century, however, Christianity was almost confined to Europe, and even there its condition was none too promising.

But the following 250 years (1500-1750) were marked by the greatest advance yet. In Europe, the Reformation is the great movement which gives character to this advance. The colonization of the Americas carried Christianity beyond the Atlantic; the Gospel spread into East Russia and Siberia, and was carried to the western, southern, and eastern shores of Africa, to South India and Ceylon, South-East Asia, Indonesia, and Japan.

The third recession (1750-1815) was the shortest in duration and the least in extent. In some of the mission fields there was shrinkage, as in South America and Japan; and in Europe there were strong influences inimical to Christianity, such as the rationalist spirit which played so important a part in the French Revolution. But even so, it was this period which saw the rise of the great evangelical and missionary movements associated with the names of the Moravians, Wesley, Carey, and others, which were to blossom so amazingly in the next period of expansion, the fourth advance, during 'The Great Century' from 1815 to 1914, when the influence of Christianity made itself felt throughout the world to a much greater degree than ever before.

The period since 1914, marked by such disastrous war and unrest on a world-wide scale, may possibly be looked upon as the beginning of a fourth recession, though whether a world-view would justify this is doubtful. At all events, a survey of Church history gives us ground for confidence in the future of the Gospel. Dr. Latourette has demonstrated 'that each peak in its effect has been higher than the preceding peak, and that each recession has, on the whole, been marked by smaller losses than its predecessor.'[1] And within each period of recession can be traced the seeds of the following advance. And the present 'ebb, if ebb there be, is not so pronounced as any of its three major predecessors. . . . In the past each ebb has been followed by a fresh advance and each advance has set a new high mark for the influence of Jesus in the total life of mankind.'[2]

This should encourage us to forge ahead with the missionary enterprise committed to us by our Lord, not to sit back in complacent assurance that this pattern of ever greater advances and ever smaller recessions will go on reproducing itself indefinitely with no effort on our part. It does give us confidence that the Lord continually works with those who obey His commission, and grants them accompanying signs. A study of Church history from this angle confirms the truth of His assurance that the gates of Hades shall not prevail against His Church (Matt. 16. 18), and the abiding validity of His promise: 'All authority has been given unto me in heaven and on earth . . . and lo, I am with you all the days, even unto the consummation of the age' (Matt. 28. 18, 20).

---

[1] *Anno Domini: Jesus, History and God* (1940), p. 219.
[2] *The Unquenchable Light*, pp. 124 f.

CHAPTER XVI

THE UNITY OF THE CHURCH

HAROLD ST. JOHN

THE structural pillars on which our subject rests are four in number and may be summed up under the following heads:

What was the mind of the Good Shepherd as to the oneness of His flock?

What was the teaching of St. Paul in regard to it?

What has history to say as to the Church's response to the doctrine preached by the Redeemer and the apostle?

What is the present position and where is the path of faith to-day?

THE MIND OF CHRIST

The authority of our Lord is the standard by which we test all matters which concern God or man; the final word must be spoken at His judgment bar. Our true starting point, then, will be found at His feet listening to His Word.

Turning to the later records of His ministry, as preserved to us by the evangelist John, we find that the Ransomer bore a heavy burden on His heart in relation to the unity of His flock.

The earlier Gospels have little, if anything to say on the subject, but the fourth Gospel contains three notable passages in which the thoughts of Christ are revealed.

(a) In chapter 10. 14-17 we read that 'the Beautiful Pastor' knows His sheep, lays down His life for them, and that the reason for this action is that 'there shall be *one* flock and *one* shepherd.'

Bishop Westcott has reminded us of the serious damage done to the cause of truth by the false rendering, given in our common version. A fold is a man-made device by which sheep are herded and held together by walls of wood or stone. The members of a flock are not bound by force, but are held by personal attachment to the shepherd. The closer each sheep keeps to its master, the nearer it will find itself to its companions.

(b) The voice of a false shepherd is heard in chapter 11. 51-52, but none the less it is truth that is spoken. The high-priest 'for that year' prophesied that it was expedient that Jesus should die 'for that nation.' John explains that His death would result in the wider work of gathering together into one the scattered children of God.

(c) In the priestly prayer, recorded in John 17, our Lord uses the numeral 'one' four times and always in relation to the unity of His people:

That they all may be *one*, even as we   -   (v. 11)
That they all may be *one* . . . in us   -   (v. 21)
That they all may be *one* even as we are -   (v. 22)
That they may be perfected into *one*   -   (v. 23)

These four clauses, in their contexts, may be summed up as follows: First, the Holy Father, in His keeping power, will unite the men whom He has given to His Son, in the closest bonds of communion. Second, after His departure, the preaching of His apostles would attract a countless host of adherents to His cause. Third, the Son had shared with the first generation of His followers, and with their successors, the glory which the Father had given Him. In that gift, there resided a binding quality, in the power of which, the members of the pilgrim Church would be welded into one and be indwelt by the Son, as He Himself had been by the Father. The final fruit of this indwelling would be that all His people, perfected into one, would so impress the world, that it would be brought to believe in the mission of Christ and to discover that God loves Christians as He loves Christ.

All down the ages, true children of God have been forced, either by the claims of conscience or by the teaching of Scripture (as they see it), into positions of isolation from the mass of their fellow-believers. Surely these farewell words of Christ should humble all of us who are in that state. It is our clear duty to stand apart from what we judge to be evil, but we are equally bound to recognize and to support all that is good. We tend to turn the microscope on the failings of our fellow-Christians and thus enlarge them: we are prone to overlook our own graver faults of pride, self-satisfaction and a censorious spirit. Let us remember our Lord's parable of the mote and the beam. When chips are flying in the carpenter's shop, the man from whose eye a house-beam is protruding, is scarcely the right person to deal with the speck of dust which has settled in his fellow-workman's eye.

The motto of the Pharisee is 'stand by thyself, come not near to me, I am holier than thou'; this is an abomination in the eyes of the Lord. The real barrier to spiritual unity amongst believers is not a matter of the intellect, it is an affair of the heart. Do I share the passion of Christ, 'that they all may be one'? Do I venture to the utmost legitimate limit to foster living, loving fellowship with all who bear His Name?

The Mind of Paul

The master-theologian of the early Church handles the subject of unity in his letters to the Christians at Corinth.

He begins by exposing the shameful results of division among the saints in that city. He tabulates these as follows: party spirit, sectarianism, railing and carrying personal quarrels into pagan law-courts. Gluttony, drunkenness, and immorality follow in sad succession.

The schisms began by a practical displacement of Christ: the Corinthians were ranging themselves under party banners, bearing the names of conspicuous servants of Christ, just as to-day men say, I am of Luther, I of Calvin, and I of Darby (see 1 Cor. 4. 6).

The apostle then corrects these abuses by showing how practical unity may be attained, both in the local assembly and in the Church Universal.

First, intellectual unity: 'I beseech you . . . that there be no divisions among you; but that ye be perfected together in the same mind and in the same judgment' (ch. 1. 10, R.V.).

Second, spiritual unity: Paul had sent Timothy to Corinth to remind the believers of his ways which were 'in Christ even *as I teach everywhere in every church*' (ch. 4. 17, R.V.). The pattern of the pathway of Jesus had been displayed in the character and conduct of the apostle (see 4. 16; 11. 1; Phil. 3. 17; 1 Thess. 1. 6; 2 Thess. 3. 9).

Third, domestic unity: the writer ordains *in all the churches* that the Christian household, father, mother, and children, must be marked by practical piety and peace (ch. 7. 17 and 15).

Finally, ecclesiastical unity: dealing with the church in session he ordains *in all the churches of the saints* that there must be an identity of custom and of outward order. The section covering chs. 11. 2 to 14. 40 deals with such subjects as the Lord's Supper, His control over those who minister the Word and the part to be played by women in the church. These commandments of the Lord (ch. 14. 37) will test whether a man is spiritual or not.

The Roman Catholic church, with its incomparable worldly wisdom, has seen the importance of this last principle. If a visitor enters any church in the Roman obedience, in any part of the world from China to Peru, he will find absolute sameness of form and ritual. I do not suggest that Rome is trammelled by an excessive reverence for the commandments of the Lord as laid down by Paul: in fact she flatly disobeys one of them by conducting her services in a language which not only is unknown but is dead. (Contrast 1 Cor. 14. 4, 9, 19).

LIGHT FROM THE LAMPS OF HISTORY

From earliest times the church has divided and subdivided, but we may distinguish three main 'ages of division' in or about the fifth, eleventh, and sixteenth centuries.

At first there were four outstanding churches, all in one common communion but each pre-eminent in its own area as a centre of light, authority and influence. These were Antioch in Syria, Alexandria in Egypt, Rome in the Western and Constantinople in the Eastern Mediterranean. The church in Jerusalem enjoyed a peculiar prestige at the beginning, but it ceased to be missionary-minded, and after the siege and sack of the city in A.D. 70 its candlestick was removed. For its lack of spiritual progress see Acts 21. 20-25.

In view of later developments it is worth noting that when the Council of Nicæa declared Alexandria, Antioch, and Rome to be patriarchal sees, the latter was the least important of the three. In fact, the early Roman Church was merely a colony of Greek Christians and Græcized Jews; the very name 'pope' is not Latin, but is the Greek title given to every minister in the Orthodox Church. In short, that church was 'the aged tree beneath whose shade the rest of Christendom has sprung up,' the perpetual witness that the East is the mother and West the daughter.

The Syrian churches were largely Nestorian, that is, their doctors stressed the humanity of our Lord in such a way as to weaken faith in His true divinity.

By the fifth century the Eastern churches had branched out into five sections (Persian, Armenian, Jacobite, Coptic, and Abyssinian Coptic) each standing apart from the other and largely out of touch with Western Christendom. The East looked to Constantinople as its metropolis, and the West (Gaul, Britain, and Spain) to Rome.

Until the year 1054 there existed an outward unity between these two great centres, but even this was marred by ceaseless political and religious disputes. Then the great schism occurred, and this has never been healed, all attempts at reconciliation having broken down on Rome's fixed demand for 'unconditional surrender.'

In the sixteenth century, Western Christendom also split into two parts: on the one side stood Rome and on the other, the Reformed Churches. These latter grouped themselves into various national folds (French, German, Anglican, and Scottish) or into federations of churches, called after the names of their leaders. One of the noblest of these was William Farel, and of him John Calvin said: 'There will never be a Farelite'; this was his lasting glory!

These divisions weakened the Protestant cause, and correspondingly strengthened its enemies, but it is pleasant to record, that, on the whole, these bodies exhibited much unity of spirit and displayed a noble charity to one another. On several occasions, common confessions of faith and articles of belief were drawn up by committees of theologians selected from various Reformed churches.

Time would fail to speak of countless other schisms; the issues at stake were sometimes frivolous and sometimes fundamental: Arius and Athanasius, Calvin and Arminius, waged war against one another, but the theological problems lay upon the surface, while the deeper causes were spiritual pride, lust of wealth and power, intolerance, and ancestral prejudices. In milder forms these are still the root reasons why we Christians refuse to recognize one another. German measles is milder than smallpox, but both alike weaken the patient's powers!

THE CHURCH IN THE TWENTIETH CENTURY AND (?) AFTER

We have reviewed the words of Christ and the teachings of Paul in relation to church unity. We have seen from the annals of history how poorly His professed followers have answered to His mind. It remains for us to humble ourselves under the mighty hand of God, to trace His way in revival and healing in the past, and to apply these ways to the present situation; then alone we may learn what we have a right to expect in the future.

(a) Under the first point, I will quote two Scriptures which, when first spoken, inaugurated mighty movements of power amongst God's people.

'*If My people*, upon whom My Name is called, shall humble themselves, and pray, and seek My face, and turn from their wicked ways; then will I hear from heaven, and will forgive their sin, and will heal their land' (2 Chron. 7. 14).

'And now for a little space grace hath been shewed from the Lord our God, to leave us a remnant to escape, and to give us a nail in His holy place, that our God may lighten our eyes, and give us a little reviving in our bondage' (Ezra 9. 8).

The pessimist will scoff and say that it is too late for any recovery; the optimist will launch schemes of 'Corporate Reunion,' but God will hide His face from both of them: the poor in spirit will stand in the council of the Lord and mark His word (see Jer. 23. 18-24).

(b) It is important to see how Scripture uses the word revival; if we look for more than that to which we are entitled we shall be put to shame.

When Habakkuk prayed, 'O Lord, revive Thy work in the midst of the years, in the midst of the years make known' (Hab. 3. 2.), he expected that God would break the Babylonian yoke, and bring the exiles of Judah back into their land, there to enjoy the right of divine worship, to rebuild a humble shrine (Ezra 6. 3, 4), and to offer sacrifice after the manner of their fathers. He did *not* expect that the schism between Judah and Israel would at once be healed, nor that a temple 'exceedingly magnifical' would be erected. These things would only be brought to pass at the coming of the Messiah.

The later epistles of the New Testament do *not* encourage the hope that a united, spiritually powerful church will welcome the Lord when He comes; on the contrary, we find that divisions will abound, the love of many will wax cold, and that an apostate church in close alliance with 'the kings of the earth' will make war against the Lamb (Rev. 17. 14). Let us briefly recall some notable revivals of the past, and see how partial, limited, and flecked with failure they were; at the same time, we find that each recurring tide carried the high watermark a little higher up the beach.

The deliverances of the Book of Judges usually affected one district in Palestine, broke a single tyranny for a term of years, and the instruments used were marred by grave personal weaknesses; the last was the most fragile of all, yet the power of God shone even in Samson.

The five revivals recorded in the second book of Chronicles (under Asa, Jehoshaphat, Joash, Hezekiah, and Josiah) were definite exhibitions of restoring grace, but the light soon faded and gross darkness settled down afresh.

Even after the supreme glory of the coming of the Holy Spirit at Pentecost, there followed a sad history of strife, division, and heresy.[1] For details see Acts 6. 1; 1 Cor. 4 and 15, and especially Rev. 2 and 3.

No historian would make light of the work of Francis of Assisi in the thirteenth century. Very moving are the words of a biographer: 'While it was yet dark, a figure appeared on a little hill above the city, dark amid the fading darkness . . . he stood with hands uplifted to God, about him was the burst of birds, and behind him was the break of day.' A pure stream of fresh faith in God, and a new hatred of sin had flowed into Western Christendom, but the fountain soon dried up because there was no attempt to give the Scriptures to the people and hence no clear witness to the Gospel.

The Reformation of the fifteenth century dealt with both of these supremely important matters, but the share taken by the secular princes, the hideous wars of religion, and strife between the leaders weakened the movement. The work of God through the Wesleys and George Whitfield probably saved this country from horrors

[1] See Note 11, p. 218.

such as those of the French Revolution, and is beyond our praise in its clear testimony to holy living, but again there was a settling down and the temperature fell.

About one hundred and twenty years ago, the so-called brethren movement began; the Gospel was preached with great fulness and power and, for the first time, the oneness of all saints was practically set forth in action. If we are honest, I fear that we must confess 'we have as it were brought forth wind; we have not wrought any deliverance in the land.' A sectarian spirit has crept in by the back-door and the stream has dwindled.

These witnesses from Church history suggest that we may not expect a world-wide return to Pentecostal power, nor a general 'union of churches.' We can count upon God to gather His people together in our generation and to enable them to exhibit the Spirit of Christ in their mutual relations. First, let us turn to our own country; the religious condition of any average city in Britain will tell us what we need to know.

We find the streets sprinkled with churches bearing the names of great Christian leaders (Wesley or Calvin), of forms of church government (Presbyterian or Episcopalian), of some special doctrine (Baptist), of a geographical region (Anglican or Roman), with many smaller societies. In almost every case these bodies came into existence by reason of some protest uttered by the Spirit of God; some truth of Scripture had been diluted, distorted, or denied; at the price of persecution and pain the godly in their day restored that truth to its proper niche within the temple of Christian doctrine. This subject can be pursued further by reading the various denominational histories compiled by the critics or the adherents of such churches.

It is important to see that the primitive church maintained intact all the doctrines and loyalties for which these bodies stand, *but declined to use any of their party labels.*

It is being brought home to the conscience of many Christians that the present situation is intolerable, a grief to our Lord and a grave weakness to His Church. It must suffice to illustrate this latter point by looking at the mission field.

We send forth the strongest of our sons and the fairest of our daughters to lay siege to the fortresses of darkness in the pagan world, but, as they start from their base we cut the nerve of their endeavour.

The Moslem mullah mocks the missionary, and contrasts the feeble and divided forces of the Church with his own serried and unbroken ranks.

The African and the Hindu are perplexed as they listen to the agents of rival societies, in some cases far more anxious to propagate special schemes of church government or details about the sacraments, than to preach and to produce repentance towards God and faith in our Lord Jesus Christ. Can we wonder if the convert feels that these good men are more concerned with their mission than with their Master?

All normal Christians agree that our Lord's farewell words: 'Go ye into all the world and preach the Gospel to every creature,' still stand, and that we are called to imitate the apostle whose ruling passion it was to spread the fame and to proclaim the message of his Master to the utmost bound of the everlasting hills.

If our lack of unity is the chief hindrance to full obedience to our commission, it is clear that our first business is to confess our failure, to seek the present mind of Christ and to deal faithfully with ourselves and others in this regard. If we are prepared to do this, we may be sure that He will work and, at least, will lower many of these barriers.

There are already signs that the Spirit of God is dealing with the collective conscience of the Church: I may mention a few of the brighter spots on the horizon.

For over seventy years, at Keswick in Cumberland, a flag with the motto, 'All one in Christ Jesus' has floated above the Convention Tent. The cynic may say, 'Yes, but if it is right to preach this unity for one week in each year, why not manifest it always?' The reply is obvious: 'You are quite right, but Rome was not built in a day; the same grace which can reveal an annual glimpse of our basic oneness could undertake the even harder task of turning you into a spiritually helpful person.'

In 1920 the Lambeth Conference, representing the leaders of the Church of England, issued a formal statement to the effect 'that we recognize all who believe in our Lord Jesus Christ, and who have been baptized into the Name of the Holy Trinity, as members with us in the Universal Church, which is His Body . . . we acknowledge all who preach the Word in the power of the Holy Spirit, and who share in our common sacraments, as true ministers of the Gospel.'

The recently published pamphlet *Towards the Conversion of England*, issued as a memorial to Dr. Temple, late Archbishop of Canterbury, contains the following definition: 'To evangelize is to present Christ, in the power of the Spirit, so that men shall come to put their trust in God through Him, to accept Him as their Saviour, and serve Him as their King, in the fellowship of His Church.' Is not this the faith once for all delivered to the saints?

Much more might be said, but these fugitive lights in the sky must suffice. I am in deep sympathy with the inward work of God which they represent, but I am convinced that something more radical is needed: let me sum up what I judge to be the message for the moment, a word for the Lord's watchmen in this hour.

First, let us recognize that a real and irrefragable unity does exist; the sevenfold unity of Eph. 4. 3-6 and the one loaf upon the pure table are the inward and outward evidence that we are really one. We cannot reach uniformity, but we must give diligence to maintain the unity of the Spirit in the uniting bond of peace.

Second, we can educate ourselves to accept and to absorb our Saviour's warnings against evil speaking, censorious or patronizing judgments passed upon our fellow-Christians.

Third, as far as is possible, we can decline to use the sectional names which only serve to emphasize our differences; it may be necessary, in order to be understood, that we must use them sometimes, but as seldom as possible. I have friends who take pride in calling themselves Strict and Particular Baptists, and I once met a Muggletonian, but surely the worthy Name by which we are called sounds better![1]

Fourth, let us foster the kindliest relations possible with our fellow-Christians in our own localities and make it our habit to pray for them by name in our private and public prayers.

[1] It is worth noting that every title given to God's people in the New Testament, such as Christians, saints, brethren, believers or disciples, tends to *unite* them and could not be claimed by any party or sect. On the other hand, all the names, coined by men, such as Anglican, Romanist or Open Brother, serve to divide them and could not be applied to all Christians.

In our contacts with Christians further afield, let us beware of trade unionism, namely, of belonging to some federation of assemblies. It is convenient to know where to find believers who are seeking to build churches on New Testament lines, but the following story may have a certain point. Someone told the late G. V. Wigram (a well-loved saint of the last century) that 'so-and-so has compiled a list of assemblies.' The old man shook his head and said: 'That is the death-knell of the testimony.'

Fifth, let us see to it that the Christians with whom we walk, welcome to their fellowship all who offer evidence that Christ has received them. Would any one of us care or dare to say to some visiting believer: 'I freely admit that Christ has received you, but I decline to do so'?

The holiness of God's house is best secured by the characters of His people: the carnal and the worldly professor will never be at home in an atmosphere of spiritual power. In the early church the presence of Christ was such a blazing reality that 'of the rest durst no man join himself to them, but the people magnified them.' The reception question settled itself.

Brethren, I close with this word of warning: I have offered no panacea for the ills of the present hour, no easy way of healing the sorrows of the Church. I have suggested an attitude of humility which would soften the harshness of our judgments. We are living in a day of rebuke and of blasphemy; the worship of money and music, of pleasure and of power, of science and of sin have intoxicated the Western nations and in the biting phrase of Gen. 19. 11: 'Men weary themselves to find the door.' Pride and the neglect of God have plunged our own nation into two world-wars in a single generation. Our fathers used to sing the *Te Deum*, their children prefer to raise the *Me Deum;* yesterday we sang 'Lord of all being, throned afar,' but now we substitute 'Glory to man in the highest, for man is the master of things.'

The Christian Church stands by, impotent, unconcerned, and ignored. If we are content with our church life, may God have pity upon us, and blast it into fragments, thus awakening us to life's realities. If we are marked by a holy discontent, let us 'afflict ourselves before our God, to seek of Him a right way for us, and for our little ones, and for all our substance' (Ezra 8. 21).

Contents of Appendix

APPENDIX

MATTHEW 18. 20

I AM not persuaded by the arguments adduced to show the *eis* in such cases as this (Matt. 18. 20) is no more than the equivalent of *en*. 'In the Name' (Matt. 21. 9; John 5. 43; Acts 3. 6; 4. 10; 10. 48, for example) means 'by the authority of.' It has other uses, of course, such as in those passages in which it describes the relation between the believer and the Lord, of which Romans 6. 11, 23; 8. 1 are examples, but with these we are not now concerned. *Eis* seems everywhere to retain its suggestion of motion towards. Thus in Acts 19. 4-5; 1 Cor. 10. 2 for example, 'into association with' is expressed by *eis*, as it is in Matt. 28. 19 in keeping with the idea of motion inherent in the verbs it follows, 'baptize,' and in our present text, 'gathered together into (association with) My Name.' In Scripture, and, indeed, in common use, name stands for character, as in Psalm 9. 10, 'they that know Thy Name will put their trust in Thee: for Thou hast not forsaken them that seek Thee.' It seems as though the Lord were here suggesting that just as His people know Him first as the forgiver of their sins, so their first privilege and responsibility in the churches would be to cherish a forgiving spirit: they might well be assured that for its exercise occasion would not be lacking.

It is true that the Lord did not use the word forgive, but Peter apparently grasped the underlying thought and immediately suggested a limit to forgiveness, a limit which the Lord promptly repudiated. The parable that followed shows that those whom God forgives receive with the forgiveness the Spirit of the Forgiver, this being one of the ways in which 'the Spirit Himself beareth witness with our spirit, that we are the children of God' (Rom. 8. 16). Where the will to forgive is absent we may examine ourselves whether we are children of God at all, for these—Forgiveness and the Spirit of the Forgiver have been joined by God and cannot be received by man apart one from the other: therefore we read that 'if any man have not the Spirit of Christ, he is none of His' (Rom. 8. 9). Those who have had any experience of church life will justify the wisdom of the Lord in associating this first word concerning the gatherings of His people with their first and most pressing need, the love that 'seeketh not its own, is not provoked, taketh not account of evil' (1 Cor. 13. 5, R.V.).

The Lord's use of the phrase 'in the midst' may well have startled the disciples for it is of frequent occurrence in the Old Testament, where it is said many times of God in His relations with Israel. (Exodus 33. 3; Psalm 46. 5; Zeph. 3. 5, 17 are examples). Its use by the Lord can only be construed as a claim to be able to do what only God can be conceived as doing. More, indeed, for whereas

God was in the midst of the people in the land, the Lord declared His presence in the midst of two or three wherever they might be gathered.

Again conditions are implied. The Lord is indeed the Mighty One Who will deliver His gathered saints and Who will rejoice over them with singing (Zeph. 3. 15-17), but He is also the righteous One (v. 5) Who dwells with him that is of a contrite and humble spirit, 'He hath respect unto the lowly' but 'the haughty He knoweth from afar.' He is 'of purer eyes than to behold evil and cannot look on perverseness' (Isa. 57. 15; Psa. 138. 6; Hab. 1. 13).

How easy it is to claim to have the Lord in the midst and yet to fail to hear Him say, as He said to Israel: 'I will not go up in the midst of thee; for thou art a stiffnecked people: lest I consume thee in the way' (Exod. 33. 3). Therefore 'let us have grace (gratitude), whereby we may offer service well-pleasing to God with reverence and awe: for our God is a consuming fire' (Heb. 12. 28, 29). When we are tempted to dwell on our privileges overmuch it is salutary to remember the warning, 'be not highminded, but fear' (Rom. 11. 20). While we are in fellowship with Christ we cannot compare ourselves with others to their disadvantage, for then we shall be learning 'in lowliness of mind each to esteem the other better than himself' (Phil. 2. 3). The significance of this ought not to be overlooked lest we suppose that a church is a place where a man can get his own way! On the contrary it is where each has the privilege of yielding to others, in love preferring one another: where no one desires his own way but where all are ambitious to be (to desire the honour of being) well-pleasing unto the Lord (2 Cor. 5. 9).

Pursuing these thoughts we perceive that Matt. 18. 20 is among the most heart-searching, awe-inspiring texts in the Scriptures. How often it has been made a shibboleth whereby to identify a party! Should we not rather tremble at such a word? If the Lord is indeed 'in the midst' of us He is there to cleanse His people, calling upon us to put away from ourselves everything that grieves Him: our pride, self-seeking, covetousness, our factions and our strifes and all those 'works of the flesh' that mar alike our fellowship with Him and our testimony to the world. If we feel the weight of His Word, if we have any sense of its solemn reality, we shall come together with humbled hearts that we may escape His judgment by anticipating it.

The presence of the Lord in the midst is the essential of the Church. His purpose is that each church should be a corporate witness to the life that pleases God and that in it should be fulfilled His Word, 'by this shall all men know that ye are My disciples, if ye have love one to another' (John 13. 35). A church is thus to be a mirror to reflect the glory of the Lord: alas, that it should so often be made a wall to obscure it!

The disciples to whom the Lord spoke formed the nucleus of the church at Jerusalem—they are named again in Acts 1. 13 as met together with many more unnamed. The promised Spirit came upon them, making them the first worshippers, then witnesses to the resurrection of the Lord. The response to their testimony, and to the convicting power of the Holy Spirit was such that about three thousand souls were baptized and added to the original company. Steadfast continuance characterized them in the apostles' teaching, in their fellowship associating themselves with the apostles, sharing their burdens as well as their blessings: in the breaking of the bread as the Lord commanded and which is to be observed 'till He come.' They were, moreover, a people who realized their dependence on God, for prayer is the evidence that the soul has come to know its own emptiness and that its resources are in God alone.

The world outside was impressed, for here was not merely a people with a new creed: they had a new power that awed the beholder, and a new love among themselves. At first their mutual care showed itself in a community of goods, though it is carefully noted that family life was not interrupted, for they broke bread at home, words which, as what follows makes clear, refer not to the Supper appointed by the Lord (as in v. 42) but to the food which they took with gladness of heart. Later on ministrations to the necessities of the poorer members of the community were organized, as is recorded in chapter 6, but though its expression changed the mutual care remained. C. F. HOGG

Note 2

MATTHEW 18. 20

THE preposition *eis* is much more elastic in its significance than *en*, and it sometimes becomes a matter of interpretation, to decide in any given passage whether it simply stands for *en.*, or whether it has a different meaning. There are instances like Luke 9. 61 where *eis Ton oikon mou* can have no other meaning than 'in my house.' In a considerable number of instances it can have no other meaning than 'into,' e.g., Matt. 18. 8. There are other varieties of meaning, which I need not enumerate, but the very fact of these varieties show that we can scarcely take *eis* in Matt. 18. 20 as simply equivalent to *en*, and this is particularly so where the substantive governed by it is figurative instead of local.

Robertson turns down the meaning 'into' (p. 593), but I cannot follow him there. He rightly says: 'It is absurd to take *eis* as "into" in Matt. 12. 41, *eis kērugma Iōna,*' but he is not justified in putting Matt. 18. 20 into the same category. W. E. VINE

Note 3

COLLECTIVE USE OF *EKKLĒSIA*

ACTS 9. 31, R.V. is read by some as an exception to the rule that Scripture does not use the word 'church' in the collective sense to describe the churches in any country or province. But is it really so?

The verse should be viewed in connection with Acts 8. 1, 2 and with 1 Thessalonians 2. 14 and Galatians 1. 22.

The church was scattered by persecution from Jerusalem but there is no record of the formation immediately of other churches as such in the places to which the scattered saints fled. Is it not probable that they are still described as the church which had been located in Jerusalem? The cessation of persecution did not mean that they would be formed at once into so many churches. There was scarcely time for that, with all that it would involve. The church, scattered from its place and still comprising persecuted believers 'had peace, being edified; and walking in the fear of the Lord and in the comfort of the Holy Ghost, was multiplied.' That description would be applicable as indicative of general conditions of a change from persecution, but it does not justify the idea of the formation of a number of churches. The Lord still looks on them as His scattered church though robbed of many of the privileges they had corporately enjoyed in Jerusalem.

With the passing of the years the settlement of these believers in their new localities and the additions of disciples won through their testimony in the Gospel, churches would be formed with a distinct Samaritan and Judæan individuality so that in 1 Thess. 2. 14 and Gal. 1. 22 we read of 'the churches of God which are in Judæa,' a description paralleled elsewhere in other groups of churches, e.g., Macedonia, Galatia (2 Cor. 8. 1; 1 Cor. 16. 1).

Note 4

BAPTIZED FOR THE DEAD
1 Cor. 15. 29

THE principal obstacle to the acceptance of the solution of this hard saying by the change of punctuation put forward is that it does not fairly face the phrase *huper tōn nekrōn*. Sir Robert Anderson in *The Bible or the Church?*, adopts this interpretation and gives the text this turn: 'It is for corpses if the dead rise not: why are they, then, baptized for them?'

F. F. Bruce (*Expository Times*, Sept., 1943) remarks: 'Anderson's *for corpses* does not take account of the definite article before *nekrōn*. "The article with *nekrōn*," says Parry (Cambridge Greek Testament *ad loc.*), "and the simple reference in *autōn* . . . alike prevent us taking the words to be merely=death, in relation to death." And he adds, "In fact all such evasions are wholly due to the unwillingness to admit the practice of baptism by proxy and still more such a reference to it by Paul without condemnation."'

The natural sense of the apostle's words certainly suggests a practice of being baptized on behalf of those who have died. The difficulty of accepting this interpretation is clearly perceived, as is the fact that the same reluctance is responsible for the attempts to evade the plain meaning of the words.

Another explanation which has a presentable case is that which looks upon the Christian community as an army in which the places of those removed by death are immediately filled by new recruits. (See G. G. Findlay, *The Expositor's Greek Testament*, *ad loc.*, but even this does not satisfy the sense of the crucial phrase.)

Note 5

RECOGNITION OF ELDERS

IT appears agreeable to the Scriptural teaching and practice on this subject that younger men in the local assembly who manifest the qualifications of overseers should be encouraged by the existing body of overseers to join them in their gatherings for prayer and conference relating to matters connected with the assembly's welfare. The names of those thus recognized should be publicly announced at the next church meeting or on some other convenient occasion, so that the assembly may recognize and acknowledge those who 'labour among them and are over them in the Lord' (1 Thess. 5. 12).

Note 6

DEACONS

It is usual to regard the appointment, in Acts 6, of the seven brethren to 'serve tables' in the assembly's daily ministration to needy widows as the first indication of the functions of those afterwards known as deacons. The actual term, however, is not employed in Acts 6.

The reference in Phil. 1. 1 to deacons and in Rom. 16. 1 to a deaconess are the only allusions in the earlier epistles of Paul. They do no more than indicate:

(a) That thus early deacons were as clearly recognizable a group in the assembly as were the elders.

(b) That the service of sisters was recognized as well as that rendered by brethren. It cannot, however, be established from Rom. 16. 1 that Phoebe held any official position in the assembly at Cenchreae.

In 1 Tim. 3. 8-13 the required qualifications are in line with those demanded of the seven in Acts 6; suitable, that is, to those whose work is to be the equitable and understanding disbursement of the assembly's bounty to the needy.

The word 'deacon' is, of course, a transliteration of *diakonos*, a servant. This word is related to *doulos*, a bondservant, *diakonos* being the servant in relation to his work and *doulos* the servant in relation to his master. All service which members of an assembly render to each other is deaconing, but it seems clear that a recognized work of deaconing came into operation very early in the Church's history. It would also seem that after 'proving' their readiness and fitness for such service deacons were appointed as a result of the choice of the assembly.

The office has much less prominence than that of the elder and may have been devised as in Acts 6 to assist the overseers.

Perhaps it may be safely said that deaconing included services rendered to the saints other than that of government, and probably consisted mainly of the ministration of temporalities.

Note 7

THE SERVICE OF CHRISTIAN WOMEN

The writings of Paul furnish the principal guidance and there are wide divergencies of interpretation of his directions, some dismissing them as temporary orders given to curb irreverence and disorderliness among the women of the Corinthian church, while others extend the prohibition of 1 Cor. 14. 34 to cover practically every possible public activity in which women might otherwise take part.

Two things seem clear: (a) that in the assembly met together as such, women are not permitted to take individual and audible part either in address to God or to the saints (1 Cor. 14. 34); (b) teaching or any activity by which a woman takes the lead over the men-folk is likewise debarred (1 Tim. 2. 12); to which may be added that in prayer meetings the men-folk take the lead and not the women (1 Tim. 2. 8).

On the other hand there were occasions (presumably other than church gatherings) when women *did* take public and audible part (1 Cor. 11. 5). On these occasions, however, the woman is enjoined to wear a head-covering in token of her recognition of the divine economy of Headship (1 Cor. 11. 3). Praying and prophesying are the exercises specified, presumably public prayer and address. Philip the evangelist had four daughters gifted as prophetesses (Acts 21. 9). Paul acknowledges the services of 'those women which laboured with me in the Gospel' (Phil. 4. 3). Deaconesses are indicated in 1 Tim. 3. 11; Phoebe of Cenchreae was one of these, whose service apparently took the form of succour or protection to the saints (Rom. 16. 1). So that a very wide range of spiritual activities is open to Christian women. We would judge that to-day Gospel work among women and children invites the service of consecrated sisters. Circumstances may and do obtain in foreign lands in which none but a woman is able or available to use the presented opportunity for service in the Gospel, and it need hardly be added that a vast deal of necessary though unpublic work can be best done by women. We should keep before us the prohibitions clearly prescribed in the Scriptures as regards activity in the assembly, and on the other hand watch against extending these prohibitions beyond the sphere in which they have force.

To the cavil that 1 Cor. 14. 34 was a local and temporary veto laid on Corinthian women only, to subdue their irreverent spirit of chattering, it is enough to draw attention to the solemn claim made in the immediate context that the things Paul is writing are not the jaundiced prejudices of an embittered bachelor but the commandment of the Lord. Moreover, the things he enjoins on the Corinthians are in line with his directions to other Christian churches (1 Cor. 14. 37; 7. 17; 11. 16; 14. 36).

Note 8
THE LAYING ON OF HANDS

THE act of laying on of hands, whether in the Old or New Testaments, was symbolic and not magical; it was never more than a sign. It did not of itself belong to the essence of the matter, but it publicly attested something (the thing being determined by the context). It is an act signifying identification, representation, as, for example, when the high priest laid his hands upon the head of the live goat, on the Day of Atonement, and confessed over him all the iniquities of the children of Israel (Lev. 16. 21; see also 1. 4, etc.). The sins were not, of course, literally conveyed or transferred to the animal, that would have been impossible; but they were confessed and thus outwardly transferred to the goat by an act of identification, and the animal bore them away into a solitary land.

In the New Testament the rite sets forth the same thing essentially. The Lord Jesus laid hands on people, but not by any means upon all those whom He healed, showing again, that this was not the essential element in the healing. His laying on of hands signifying His gracious association in spirit with those needing His aid (see Matt. 8. 17); but there is no suggestion in the Gospels that the physical act, of itself, conveyed any blessing.

The occurrences in the Acts give similar teaching. The apostles thus declared their association with the seven who had been chosen to serve tables (ch. 6. 6). The converts in Samaria were allowed to await the symbolic act before receiving the Spirit, so that they should learn their link with the believers in Jerusalem as they grasped the oneness of the work done in both cities; thus ancient barriers were broken down, in the development of the new fellowship (ch. 8. 17). Ananias conveyed to Saul of Tarsus a token of his new association with the disciples (ch. 9. 17). The early missionaries went forth conscious of the identification with them in their ministry of the church in Antioch (ch. 13. 3). The twelve men whom Paul encountered in Ephesus were not at that time Christians, at least in the full and normal New Testament sense; the fact that they knew only the baptism of John indicates that they were unaware of the power and meaning of the Resurrection of Christ and the coming of the Spirit at Pentecost. But they eagerly received this fresh teaching, and it is clearly implied (ch. 19. 4) that there and then they believed on the Lord Jesus. Thus they were baptized and the symbolic act of laying on of hands brought them full recognition as fellow-believers (ch. 19. 1-6). In the case of Timothy, both the body of elders, and Paul himself, signified in this manner their full satisfaction with his call to public ministry, and they identified themselves with him as he went forth (1 Tim. 4. 14; 2 Tim. 1. 6). In his ministry at Ephesus he was exhorted to 'lay hands hastily on no man,' that is, in appointing to eldership, lest his precipitate action should turn out to be association with other men's sins (1 Tim. 5. 22-25). In all these passages a common meaning can be discerned: the disciples, or missionaries, were made aware of the fellowship of others; there was a recognition of the oneness of all true service for Christ. And it is well to remember the comment of Dr. James Orr that 'no ground is afforded by this symbolic action for any sacrament of "Orders".'

The inclusion of the act among 'the first principles of Christ' (Heb. 6. 1-3) has caused some to imagine it to be in the category of a fundamental of the faith, but this is to misunderstand the plain import of the passage, besides giving to an outward rite a place never so given in the New Testament. The context speaks of the immaturity of the Hebrews to whom the letter was sent, and they are exhorted to press on to full growth. The foundational matters specified are all things which Judaism had in common with Christianity, and they fall into three couplets: repentance and faith; the teaching of washings (R.V., margin), and of laying on of hands; resurrection and eternal judgment. The reference in the two middle items is not to Christian ordinances but to Jewish ceremonial washings and the ritual act of laying on of hands as under the Old Covenant. (Note the plural word, *baptismoi*, whereas the singular word, *baptisma*, is always used of Christian Baptism.) Then the reference is, not to either of these ceremonies in itself, but to the teaching of them, i.e., what they stood for and represented. The significance of ceremonial ablutions was, of course, purification, while that of the laying on of hands (by either priest or offerer) was, as we have seen, representation, implying the deeper thought of substitution. We find, therefore, not an exhortation assuming the perpetuation of these outward ceremonies, but a recognition of their spiritual teaching, purification, substitution.

Taking the three couplets in this light, the 'first principles of Christ'—things essentially connected with the Messiah in the minds both of Jews and Christians —are an experience of repentance and faith; the basis for the experience in purification and substitution; and the final issues of resurrection of the dead and eternal judgment. The disciples were to go forward unto a greater apprehension and experience of their distinctively Christian inheritance, bound up with the personal knowledge of Christ.

There is no command in Scripture for the observance of the laying on of hands (contrast the case in regard to Baptism and the Lord's Supper). Its misuse in Christendom has frequently led to an assumption of priestly power. Sanday wrote: 'It is, no doubt, a widespread idea that this denotes *transmission*—the transmission of a property possessed by one person to another. But it cannot really mean this. It is a common accompaniment of 'blessing'—i.e., of the invoking of blessing. It is God who blesses or bestows the gift; and it is in no way implied that the gift is previously possessed by him who invokes it.' (*The Conception of Priesthood*, p. 167).

The essential thing is that there should be a true spiritual fellowship among God's people. This may be present with or without the laying on of hands. Remembering that the physical act of itself conveys nothing, where this fellowship is present, the non-essential character of the rite may determine that churches can dispense with it without loss. Hort has wisely remarked that it was 'highly probable that (as a matter of fact) laying on of hands was largely practised in the Ecclesiæ of the Apostolic Age as a rite introductory to ecclesiastical office. But as the New Testament tells us no more than what has already been mentioned, it can hardly be likely that any essential principle was held to be involved in it.' (*The Christian Ecclesia*, p. 216).   G. C. D. Howley

Note 9

DIVORCED PERSONS AND CHURCH FELLOWSHIP
Matt. 5. 32; 19. 9

It is clear that the divine intent was that marriage should be indissoluble save by death, but when sin came in, and considering that the original ideal had failed of its accomplishment, permission was given under the Law for divorce, owing to the hardness of men's hearts, and for the avoidance of the corruption that is in the world through lust. The concession was not perfect, ideally, but practically necessary in view of moral conditions.

The Lord, in answering the enquiry of the Pharisees whether divorce was permissible for every cause, cleared this solemn step from the trivialities that had become associated with it, and specified the one sin by which the institution of marriage was itself broken, as the only ground of divorce.

There may be grave reasons why a Christian should take advantage of this concession in order to remarry, and in such a case fellowship at the Lord's Table should not be denied, where he or she, as the innocent party, has had recourse to this legal action in order to become free. Seeing that no moral obliquity attaches to a person under such circumstances, any public services rendered previously would not necessarily terminate on that ground alone.

On the other hand, there may be to a soul in real fellowship with God a higher question as to whether it may not be more according to Scripture and to godliness to refuse to take advantage of this concession, and to endure patiently and humbly such an unspeakable trial for the Lord's sake, especially in a day like this when the tendency is all the other way. Higher interests than their own, will, no doubt, prevail with those who occupy any prominence in an assembly and are looked upon as representative in any measure of its life and testimony. On the analogy of Lev. 21. 7-14, and 1 Tim. 3. 2, a high standard is required of those who walk before the saints as ensamples to the flock, and they will be ready, as far as in them lies, to forego their right in order to preserve their spiritual place and influence. It is a serious thing anywhere, and especially in heathen lands, to close the door for ever against the return of a repentant erring spouse. God Himself has left the door open in the case of Israel (Jer. 3. 1).

The plea that the obtaining of a divorce by the innocent party will enable the guilty one to form a regular union instead of an irregular one, has no force. Human law may legalize the fresh union, but it cannot sanctify it. 'Whoremongers and adulterers God will judge.'

W. E. Vine and W. R. Lewis

Note 10

THE ADMINISTRATION OF CHURCH FUNDS
(Acts 6. 1-6; Acts 11. 27-30; 1 Cor. 16. 3, 4; 2 Cor. 8. 16-24; Phil. 4. 18)

THE passages quoted above give guidance for the administration of church funds. While they refer principally to the relief of widows, needy saints, and the support of the Lord's servants, the principles underlying them cover all the financial undertakings of the local assembly.

(a) The administration of church monies should be in the hands of more than one brother (Acts 6. 3; Acts 11. 30; 2 Cor. 8. 18).

The exception in Phil 4. 18 makes us believe that there was not, however, a hard and fast rule. Nevertheless the wisdom of appointing two or more brethren for this service is clear; it gives confidence to the assembly by avoiding temptation to dishonesty (2 Cor. 8. 21) and avoiding blame by those that are without (v. 20).

(b) This is not everybody's work but requires special qualification; 'honest report,' unblemished character; 'full of wisdom,' business acumen; 'full of the Holy Ghost,' divinely controlled and directed (Acts 6. 3).

The late Dr. A. T. Pierson characteristically describes these qualifications as Integrity, Sagacity, and Spirituality. He says: 'Secular men have absolutely no place in the administration of the affairs of the church of Christ, all of which are "sacred" to the Holy Spirit.'

To sum up: As a matter of proper safeguard, and to avoid all 'appearance of evil' the administration of church funds should be the responsibility of at least two brethren.

Those who are chosen for such service should be chosen because of their suitability—suitability of character, 'honest' men; suitability as to their natural endowments, men of 'wisdom.' Above all they should be spiritual men whose every action is under the control of the Holy Spirit.

Note 11

HERESIES AND SECTS

THE root idea of the word heresy (Greek *hairesis*) is that of choice or the act of choosing, and in Scripture it is used in three ways:

(a) In the Old Testament the word is translated 'freewill offerings' (Lev. 22. 18, 21), i.e., what you choose to give.

(b) In the New Testament, especially in the Book of Acts, it describes any school of thought or set of persons holding particular opinions, whether true or false, such as Nazarenes, Pharisees, or Sadducees.

(c) In the Epistles, it is the name applied to one of the works of the flesh (Gal. 5. 20) or of gross false doctrines (2 Peter 2. 1). In the first passage cited above it is bracketed with schisms and means factions or party-spirit in a local church (vv. 18 and 20).

If applied to any (professed) body of believers we should explain whether we use it in its neutral sense (b), or in its wholly evil meaning. In the latter case the word might be applied to such a movement as 'Christian Science,' provided the speaker were in a very humble frame of mind.

Heresies are necessary in the same sense that the Fall was necessary, if there was to be a history of redemption; that the poor must always be with us, if we are to be 'forward to consider them': that darkness is necessary as a background for the light. Under the Law of Leviticus God put a plague of leprosy in a house (ch. 14. 34); this was a tragic necessity due to the neglect and uncleanness of the occupants. In the first Corinthian Epistle, Paul exposes the disorders and immoralities found in that House of God, in the second he cleanses the Assembly —the priest of God must be a master of diagnosis and of healing.

H. St. John

Note 12

THE COUNCIL OF JERUSALEM

THE Council of Jerusalem, of which we read in Acts 15, is sometimes adduced as an argument against the position maintained in this volume regarding the administrative independence of each local church. It may, therefore, be helpful to say one or two things about it.

In the first place, the Council of Jerusalem was not (as has been imagined by some) a body of apostles and elders meeting in permanent session in the metropolis of Christianity. It was a special gathering convened for a special purpose.

In the second place, the Council of Jerusalem does not represent any superior authority enjoyed or exercised by the Church of Jerusalem over the other churches of apostolic days.

The Council of Jerusalem was a conference held between delegates from the Church of Antioch (including Paul and Barnabas) with the apostles and elders at Jerusalem, to reach agreement with regard to the terms on which Gentile believers might be welcomed to full Christian fellowship. The stricter Jewish Christians of Jerusalem and Judæa had insisted that these Gentiles should be circumcized. Failure to reach agreement on this point might have resulted in a schism between the Church of Jerusalem and her daughter-churches in Judæa on the one hand, and the Church of Antioch and her daughter-churches in Asia Minor on the other hand. The conference agreed, however, that no ritual or ceremonial conditions were to be required of Gentile converts; the principle 'of grace alone, by faith alone' which had been sufficient for their salvation was to be sufficient for their recognition as full sharers in the Christian fellowship. A recommendation of a practical nature was added which would make it easier for Jewish and Gentile believers to enjoy full Christian and social intercourse.

Had the Jerusalem members of the conference thought differently, it would have put grave difficulties in the way of fellowship between the churches, but Paul would obviously have refused to accept their views as binding on the churches which he founded. As it was, however, all could rejoice that the conference, under the guidance of the Spirit of God, had reached such a happy decision.

One further point is to be noted. As a result of the conference, the apostles and elders of Jerusalem sent a letter to the Church of Antioch and her daughter-churches. Apostles as such wielded an authority that was not locally restricted, but here the apostles and elders write as leading members of the Church of Jerusalem. The terms in which they write the letter are therefore interesting. 'The New Testament,' says Dr. Hort (*The Christian Ecclesia*, p. 82), 'is not poor of words expressive of command . . . ; yet none of them is used. It was in truth a delicate and difficult position, even after the happy decision of the assembly. The independence of the Ecclesia had to be respected, and yet not in such a way as to encourage disregard either of the great mother Ecclesia, or of the Lord's own

Apostles, or of the unity of the whole Christian body.' What they say, therefore, is: 'it seemed good to the Holy Spirit, and to us.' If the mind of the Spirit be humbly sought, ascertained and followed, fellowship between churches will be promoted, as it will not if a church is subjected to the authority either of another church or of a group of churches. And the mind of the Spirit to-day is expressed in the Word, interpreted by that same Spirit. For the Spirit in the Word, as John Knox said to Queen Mary, 'is never contrarious to Himself.'   F. F. Bruce

BIBLIOGRAPHY

(Many of the books listed are out of print, and only procurable second-hand)

The Bible or the Church? - - -	Sir Robert Anderson
The Christian Ecclesia - - -	F. J. A. Hort
The Church and the Ministry in the Early Centuries - - - - -	T. M. Lindsay
The Organization of the Early Christian Churches - - - - -	Edwin Hatch
The Pilgrim Church - - - -	E. Hamer Broadbent
The Nature of Catholicity - - -	Daniel T. Jenkins
Essays in Orthodox Dissent - - -	Bernard Lord Manning
Bishops, Priests, and Deacons - -	William Hoste
The Christian Ministry - - -	J. B. Lightfoot
The Church's Ministry - - -	T. W. Manson
The Local Assembly - - - -	G. H. Lang
The Church and the Churches - -	W. E. Vine
Fellowship - - - - -	C. F. Hogg
The Charter of the Church - - -	John R. Caldwell
God's Principles of Gathering - -	George Goodman
Light for Dark Days - - - -	Edited by W. Hoste and W. E. Vine
George Muller of Bristol - - -	A. T. Pierson
The Divine Plan of Missions - -	W. E. Vine
The Free Church Tradition in the Life of England - - - - -	Ernest A. Payne
The Church Universal and Local - -	A. M. Stibbs
The New Testament Order for Church and Missionary - - - -	Alex. Rattray Hay
The Unquenchable Light - - -	K. S. Latourette
What Saith the Scripture? - - -	C. F. Hogg
Outlines of Christian Doctrine - -	H. C. G. Moule
An Expository Dictionary of New Testament Words - - - -	W. E. Vine
Then and Now - - - -	Dr. John Foster

221

INDEX OF SUBJECTS

INDEX OF PERSONS

16

INDEX OF SCRIPTURES

227

APPENDIX: THE EDITOR OF THIS SYMPOSIUM

Mr. J.B. Watson (1884-1955)

My father's oral gifts as a minister of God's Word were immense, and between the two World Wars he spoke to many thousands of people of all ages, helping them to a deep devotion to Jesus Christ whom John calls the Word.

Some years after my father's death I began to feel that his spoken ministry was forgotten and that the few books which he had written, sometimes in co-operation with others did not adequately record his very special gifts in oral ministry. I have therefore put together the following series of articles (previously published in *The Witness*) so that his spoken ministry over forty years may be remembered more effectively, and something of his love for Jesus Christ, which was always the purpose of his talks, may be recalled.

I warmly welcome a reprint of these articles by John Ritchie Ltd as an Appendix to his symposium, The Church, in which he drew together the teaching on this subject by many of his friends with whom he had often ministered.

Sept 1999

John R. Watson
23 Leaks Close
Southwell
Notts

J.B. Watson
Preacher

My father from the earliest days of his ministry preached five or six times a week. On Sundays he would often minister at the Lord's Supper, and later in the day preach at an evangelistic service somewhere in the London area. During the week he would minister on several occasions at meetings in local churches and at special conventions for Bible teaching. Added to his daily work as a Customs Officer in the London Docks it made up a formidable programme, but he maintained it for about 40 years until his health began to fail in 1949.

In spite of his heavy programme, however, my father never went to preach unprepared and the notes he left behind speak volumes about the work which went into his sermon preparation. His life was too full of more important things for him to have catalogued his sermon notes, but each set of notes is a masterpiece of note-making. The main points of each address and its main objectives are as clear today to the reader as they must have been in his own mind, but the flesh on the bones (a phrase he often used) was built around the skeleton once he was on his feet.

All his notes are well sprinkled with illustrative material, mostly personal experiences, historical anecdotes and, above all, poetry. His poetical 'windows' brought much light into his sermons and were an outstanding feature of his preaching. They were culled from many sources but were usually so apt that they acted upon his hearers like nails fixed in sure places. An incidental pleasure of browsing through his notes is to read his poetical illustrations again and to recall the peculiar power which poetry exerted in his preaching. As an example, here is his comment on the priority of fellowship with the Lord over all other Christian occupations. His own words are pinned home to the conscience by a few lines of poetry.

'If I could have my life over again, I do not say I would preach less, but I would pray more. And probably I might find in fellowship with Him that I would accomplish His will better by fewer and more manifestly guided activities.

And this inward fellowship with God rises to its height in those blessed experiences (all too rare with most of us) in which

> *We ask no prayer,*
> *For all is given.*
> *Thyself all fair;*
> *And that is heaven.*

This is the height of adoration when
Silent at His feet we lie,
Lost in love's immensity.'

Another feature of my father's notes is that important paragraphs like the one just quoted, and very frequently final paragraphs, are written out in full, for he regarded every sermon at some point as a challenge to the hearer to action. His own phrase was 'tying the knot in it' which was his way of saying that he wanted the full force of God's Word to be brought home to those who heard him preach. Listen to his closing word to a congregation of young people to whom he had ministered on the lost opportunities in the life of Jonathan:

'I look into your faces, young, eager, full of hope. Some will fail of their early promise: see that it isn't you. Some will turn their back upon the very Christ whom now you praise; see that it isn't you. Some will fling away the chance to mean something for God in order to cling to some social toy, some worldly purpose, some unhallowed companionship, some point of pride, some unwillingness for the reproach of Christ; will it be you? Do you want to have a place by Him when he appraises the loyal service of His servants? Then be ready to go all the length to pray whatever price is needful.'

I hope to bring you some of the treasures that have lain buried in J.B. Watson's notes for a long time. We shall look at him in his many roles as a preacher – as evangelist, expositor and teacher, and also in some of the special opportunities that his ministry increasingly brought him. I hope to give some glimpses of those extraordinary powers which by the Spirit of God brought the truth of God to bear upon hundreds of his hearers during his itinerant ministry of forty years.

I close this first article with a prayer which he offered at the beginning of a meeting for the ministry of the Word. The occasion warranted a written prayer and we can regard it as his own considered desire for his own ministry too. It lays bare his view of the needs of the human spirit and the way that these can alone be met by our Lord Jesus Christ through the Word of God. In his own style of updated Elizabethan English he reveals those desires which were the motive forces behind all his own spoken ministry.

'Father and God, we come to Thee. We are Thy children and we have learned that Thou knowest how to give good gifts to them that ask Thee. We are bold therefore to ask Thee for bread, even the Living Bread, whereof if a man eat it he shall live for ever. We are an hungered and we look to Thee for sustaining, refreshing, strengthening food. Grant us this boon, we humbly pray.

We have been in contact with the world and are aware of the drain on our inner man that this contact entails. We have met here, not so much to meet each other as to meet Thee and receive from Thee that replenishment which will re-equip us for the needs of the way. Be gracious, O Lord: open Thine hand to us and bless us.

This also we ask: our pilgrimage has this effect upon us. We tend to see the temporal as the only real things, and to lose touch with the spiritual and invisible world. Unseen verities become distant, dim, unreal, unsubstantial, and we ourselves as those that are without spiritual vision. We pray Thee to reverse all this. Give us fresh hold of ultimate realities. Chase from us the pressure of the seen, the temporal, the visible. Make us to stand among the verities of the Kingdom which cannot be shaken; cause us to possess our possessions.

May Thy Name be for ever blest for Him who is the central Reality, our Lord Jesus Christ, the same yesterday and today and for ever. Magnify Him in our midst this day and grant us such an experience of Him as shall renew our faith, rekindle our hope and redouble our love.

Take Thy servants into Thy keeping, O Lord. Fill them – their minds with Thy truth, their mouths with Thy word, their hearts with the power of Thy love. Make them Thy free channels through which Thy word shall flow to us. And when this precious hour has fled may we find the confidence of our souls in Thee and may the certainty of Thy purpose make us buoyant and joyful in Thee. Hear us, O Father and answer speedily, for the sake of Him – our Lord Jesus Christ. Amen.'

Evangelist

In these living recollections of my father as a preacher I must begin with his evangelism since I heard him preach the gospel again and again when, as a boy, I accompanied him on his Sunday evening preaching engagements in the London area. I did not only listen but often on the journey home we would discuss what had been said; and my father, in typical manner, would recall passages of his sermon or even particular phrases that could have been expressed better. Little did I realize at the time that I was discussing the work of a master!

Even in his later life when he was sought by so many people for his Bible-teaching ministry, my father was still an evangelist at heart and he loved to preach Christ as man's Saviour. The wonder of his own conversion never left him and he would refer to it as the impulse that made him the preacher he was. Here is a full account of it in his own words evidently prepared in his later life. His own experience was as fresh as if it were yesterday.

A Personal Testimony

I am an ordinary, average man, neither brilliant nor much-learned. I hark back, now that I grow old, to the greatest day of my life. I had for over two burdened years been thinking of the personal problems of life and being upon which I have touched tonight. They brought me where they are bound to bring every honest seeker early or late – face to face with the stupendously challenging claims of Jesus Christ. Shake off my concern I could not: the eager round of distractions of the day brought back the problem of God and my soul more vividly when I lay down at night to rest. And so it went on: reading, thinking, trying to pray now and then; another time immersing myself in a round of distractions. But God had his grip on me. I was being followed by what Frances Thompson daringly called 'The Hound of Heaven'.

> *'Nigh and nigh draws the chase*
> *With unperturbéd pace*
> *Deliberate speed, majestic instancy:*
> *And past those noiséd Feet*
> *A voice comes yet more fleet*
> *Lo, nought contents thee, who contentest not Me.'*

Till I had to turn and face God. I could take you to the spot. I can tell you the hour of the clock, the day of the week, the month of the year, the year itself. God's messenger to me was an old grey-bearded blacksmith and his message was an invitation to accept Christ at His own valuation of Himself, as able to give me all I sought of peace, knowledge and certainty of God's forgiving acceptance. He used a word from the Book to clinch the matter – the word in the Gospel of John which says 'These are written that ye might believe that Jesus is the Christ the Son of God, and that believing ye might have life through His name'.

There and then I accepted Him at His word. Many things I did not understand, many questions remained, but the vital thing was clear – Jesus Christ offered me life on acceptance of His Saviourhood and Divinity. And I made the venture – an act of faith.

Over 40 years have sped since then. It still remains the most treasured memory of all. I count everything as having begun there. All that has been good and worthwhile sprang thence. Everything worth doing I have ever accomplished had its rise there. All my peace of heart rose from that fountain.

Almost at once he began to preach the gospel himself and within a few years his life in London began and we find him busily engaged in this sacred task in his spare time. In those early days he conducted many missions for children and as a result his search for simplicity which began then never left him. As he preached the gospel his expository gifts were often temporarily hidden as he took a Bible incident or topic which provided a suitable means of illustrating the grace of God in salvation. But always he strove for a simplicity and directness that would challenge his hearer to reach a decision. Here are the notes of an explanation he once gave of what it means to believe in Christ – a phrase which he described as 'often meaningless to unconverted persons'.

(1) It is to credit the historic record of His life.

(2) It is to believe He was what He claimed to be.

(3) It is to believe that He did what He said He came into the world   to do.

(4) It is to believe that He means what He says.

At this point my father brought in some basic gospel texts, adding that having come so far 'Belief means personal trust. It means the committal of my soul to Him for all it needs'.

In all his evangelistic sermons my father preached for a decision and this is reflected in the care with which he prepared his final paragraphs. His convictions were based on his understanding of the responsibilities of the evangelist but he also longed for the fruit of individual lives yielded to Christ and great would be his joy if he returned home knowing that someone had received Christ as Saviour as a result of his preaching. Listen to his appeal to his hearers at the close of a gospel talk from the unlikely text 'Beginning at Jerusalem'. In it he refers to a young man whom he led to the Lord some time previously.

'I stood with a young man one night years ago and talked to him long and earnestly about this matter. He had listened silently for a long time. At last I said "You know you ought to begin. I am going to say a last word to you in my Master's name. In the name of Christ, I ask you – will you make a beginning?" A long, long silence, in which he looked on the ground and scratched among the pavement dust with his cane. And then he looked up at me and said "Yes". That was all. After a few more words he went his way and I went mine wondering how much was in that "Yes". But he has never looked back. He had begun! He was through! And tonight I ask it of you, my undecided friend. In my Master's name I speak "Will you make a beginning now?" Who says "Yes"?

As I look through the notes of my father's evangelistic talks I am struck by the fact that there are several sets of notes of the same sermon. Although he used the same themes on several occasions, he never relied on the unction of yesterday but refashioned his instrument with the care an archer might give to every arrow in his quiver. The parallel notes shew signs of additional thought or modification to suit different occasions and it is easy to see that he regarded each service he led as a new opportunity requiring new grace from the Lord.

The outline address with which I close is a wonderful example of this careful preparation, for I have found several sets of notes and I know that they were used on occasions many years apart when the conviction came upon my father that this was God's word for the occasion. Even in the outline (and I cannot give more) one can see his use of imagination, sense of human need and grasp of the essentials of the gospel of Christ. Of all the examples I might have chosen I feel that this one best illustrates his evangelistic preaching at its highest and most appealing; and in making my choice I have the assurance that the Lord used this sermon to bring some to a knowledge of Christ as Saviour.

It is called 'A Sunday Evening Walk' and is a meditation on the resurrection incident of the two disciples on the road to Emmaus (Luke 24.13-35). The atmosphere of that evening is made real and relevant to the hearer.

(1) *The Unfinished Journey.* 'Two of them went'.
Life likened to an uncompleted journey.

(2) *The Unsolved Problem.* 'They communed together and reasoned'.
All life's travellers have unsolved problems about the soul in its relation to God.

(3) *The Unrecognized Presence.* 'Jesus Himself drew near...but their eyes were holden that they should not know Him'.
Christ is present and can meet our need although we may not recognize Him.

(4) *The Unopened Book.* 'O fools, and slow of heart to believe all that the prophets have spoken'.
The answers to life's deepest problems are all answered in the Scriptures if only we will look there.

(5) *The Unveiled Mystery.* 'Ought not Christ to have suffered these things'.
The meaning of Christ's cross and resurrection.

(6) *The Unrepeated Opportunity.* 'He made as though He would have gone further'.
Christ gives the opportunity to recognize Him which may not be repeated.

(7) *The Unspeakable Gladness.* 'Did not our heart burn within us?'
The deep joy of knowing the living Christ and the forgiveness He gives.

Expositor

Almost as soon as my father began to preach the gospel of Christ he became a student of Holy Scripture and set out on the pathway that eventually brought him to that time in middle and later life when he spoke with humble yet convincing authority from the Book of all books. Early in life he saw that Holy Scripture was itself the divine authoritative revelation to mankind, and that his task was simply to lay bare its message and to apply it to the human heart. He has left a note of that early conviction which set him on this course and which involved him in seeking, first of all, to understand for himself the divine Word:

'The Bible is the subject of such contentions in Christendom that we are forced to take up a definite attitude towards the Book, and that very early in our Christian pilgrimage. And I can conceive nothing that will go so far to solve the problem finally for one who loves the Lord Jesus Christ and desires to follow Him and obey Him, as to see clearly what was His attitude to the Scriptures.

A long, long time ago now, I had to settle this matter for myself. It is a good thing to pass through these times when we shape our course. They are often times of painful uncertainty, sometimes of doubt and deep exercise. But if we face them and endure them and are brought victoriously through them we have gained incalculably by the experience. And we in our turn will be enabled to help others who have to pass the same way.

Dr. Moule, that great saint who was Bishop of Durham when I was in my first few years of Christian experience, went through this same valley of decision. And his experience became a decisive help to me in my problem-solving crisis. One day I came across these words of his on the matter in hand: "When my Lord Christ first became a living, and an unutterable reality to me, I remember that one of my first sensations of profound relief was this: *He absolutely trusted the Bible*; and though there are things in it inexplicable that have puzzled me much, I am going, not in a blind sense, but reverently, to trust the Book because of Him".'

From this beginning, it was inevitable that his ministry should not only be founded upon the text of Scripture but that it should have as its goal the glory of Christ which he saw to be the final objective of the whole of divine revelation.

Whether therefore my father was carefully examining the text of Scripture, or weighing up one of its great themes, or tracing the course of one of the prominent characters in Bible history, his ultimate aim was to uphold and honour the Christ whom he worshipped.

'He fills it all. It exists for Him. All roads in it lead to Him. Until you know Him you cannot really know the Book. Know the purpose for which the Book is in your hands is that you may get to know Him ever more deeply. Great as the Book is, He is infinitely greater.'

As I have searched through my father's notes left behind like the trusty weapons of a fallen warrior, one sermon came to light which crystallised his whole attitude to the task which God gave him. There were three sets of notes; one in the careful handwriting of his youth with large headings in a bolder hand; one typed out and dated 13th October, 1923 when he was 39; and another in the typing of his later years with a telling quotation from B.B. Warfield but otherwise scarcely changed in outline form from the other two. These notes spell out his ministry. What was his task? To bear witness to the greatness and glory of Christ and to do it by means of expounding the God-breathed Scriptures.

THE INCARNATE WORD AND THE WRITTEN WORD

(1) *Both bear the title 'The Word'.*
     Christ...John 1.14 – many deeds, discourses etc. ONE WORD.
     Bible...Heb 4.12 – many authors, books, prophecies. ONE WORD.

(2) *Both were given through the action of the Holy Spirit.*
     Incarnate Word...Luke 1.35. Written Word...2 Peter 1.21.

(3) *Both are of Jewish birth yet Universal in their appeal.*
     Incarnate Word...2 Tim 2.8 Jewish; John 12.32 Universal.
     Written Word...Rom 3.2 Jewish; Romans 16.26 Universal.

(4) *Both are Human and also Divine.*
     Incarnate Word...1 Tim 3.16 Divine; 1 Tim 2.5 Human.
     Written Word...2 Tim 3.16 Divine; Jude 3, Gal 6.11 Human.

(5) *Neither will ever be superseded.*
     Incarnate Word...Heb 13.8. FOR EVER.
     Written Word...1 Pet 1.24,25. FOR EVER.

(6) *Neither can be understood nor appreciated by man apart from Divine illumination.*
     Incarnate Word...Matt 11.25-27.
     Written Word...1 Cor 2.9,10,14.

(7) *There are difficulties in connection with both which human reason cannot solve.*

Incarnate Word...1 Tim 3.16.

Written Word...2 Peter 3.16.

(8)   *Conclusion. Each attributes infallibility to the other.*
Christ's testimony to the Scriptures...John 10.35.
The Scriptures' testimony to Christ...Col 2.9.

Of course, as a faithful teacher of the Word of God my father ministered on many passages of Scripture or on topics not directly concerned with the Person or work of our Lord but even then he would take opportunity – sometimes in surprising ways – of exalting Christ. With a few deft words attention would be turned from the theme subject to the person of his Saviour. I remember his relating to me how he had been rebuked by a listener for using the story of Abraham's offering of Isaac as an illustration of believing faith instead of using it to speak of Christ. Although in a sense he did not accept the rebuke, I detected also a genuine grief that he should have been adjudged guilty of failing to exalt Christ in his preaching. Notice his sudden turn of direction in commenting on the parable of the wedding feast in Luke 14.

'To take the lowest seat is not only the wise course, it is the safe one. There is only one direction in which a man can be moved from it – by promotion. He who is our Teacher in this is also our Example. He took the lowest of all low places and is now exalted to the highest (Phil 2.8,9).'

But although my father's objectives in unfolding Scripture were undeviatingly to exalt Christ, he did not pursue that course in an unbalanced way. There were many themes of Scripture that did not bear directly upon the Person of Christ or His work but provided the background against which his Saviour's glories would shine. The example which I give shows this all-round balanced exposition at its best. He takes a broad subject, as he loved to do, and looked at it from every angle showing all the reflected glory of the divine author but, among all the bright facets of this Bible story, none are made to shine more brightly than points 6 and 7 which bear directly upon Christ Himself.

AN AFRICAN COURTIER
(Acts 8.26-40)

Introduction. First individual conversion recorded in Acts. A member of the race of Ham. An instance of 'there are last that shall be first'. Also a rebuke to 19 centuries of Christian witness – God's care for backward peoples. Gospel takes account of racial characteristics but despairs of none. Readiness of oppressed and backward peoples to embrace the gospel. 'Ethiopia will soon stretch out her hands to God' (Ps 68.31).

The story given its place in Scripture because of *abiding* principles embedded in it. What lessons may we gather from this first century story?

(1) *That God seeks men in order that men may seek Him.*

    (a) 'None that seeketh after God' by unaided nature.

    (b) The initiative lies with God. 'Salvation is of the Lord.'

    (c) A great promise. Ps 50.23.

(2) *That God's ways of revealing Himself to sincere seekers are Sovereign.*

    (a) His disposal of small circumstances.

    (b) His choice of instruments and agents.

    (c) His preparations in servant and seeker.

(3) *That formal religion leaves the soul unsatisfied.*

    (a) A Proselyte?

    (b) Still seeking (v.31). *hodēgō* = to guide.

    (c) Peace not to be earned.

(4) *That he who desires to know God does well to consult Holy Scripture.*

    (a) The Book for wisdom.

    (b) The need for the Preacher. 'Understandest thou?' (v.30).

    (c) Blessing through reading the Scriptures.

(5) *That a teachable spirit is indispensable in the search after God.*

    (a) Welcoming a helper (v.31) 'A hungry man will eat off a common plate'.

    (b) Bunyan and the wives of Bedford. Earthly distinctions dwindle when God grips the soul.

(6) *That Christ Jesus is the key to open every door of truth.*

    (a) A road to Christ from every text.

    (b) A Spirit-filled and Spirit-guided servant will guide along that way.

(7) *That a suffering, sin-bearing, dying Christ who lives again in endless, victorious life is the sum of God's message to mankind.*

    (a) 'Preached' (v.35). *euaggelizō*

    (b) A humbled Man.

    (c) An unjustly condemned Man.

    (d) A Man 'cut off'.

    (e) A sacrifice for sins.
    (f) Reconciliation to God through Christ.
(8) *That finding is better than seeking.*
    (a) When faith is born.
    (b) Cromwell's dictum: 'The only better sect than seekers are the finders'.
(9) *That when the soul finds salvation, the fact should be confessed openly.*
    (a) The true impulse.
    (b) How to confess.
    (c) The ordinance of discipleship.
    (d) The loss of secret discipleship.
(10) *That God is able to make such as trust Him stand alone.*
    (a) Philip removed.
    (b) Difficulties ahead.
    (c) What he had – The Word of God; the Spirit of God. Why North Africa became the land of the vanished Church.
    (d) Forward with God. Tomorrow will bring its own grace for it own difficulties.
    'Yea, and he shall be holden up, for God is able to make him stand' (Rom 14.4).

How many in his audience would have been able to avoid the conviction of all ten of his arrows?

In one of his talks my father gave this advice to the Christian about his personal use of the Bible – 'Read. Pray. Compare. Believe. Obey.' These were the steps he followed himself as he used the Scriptures and this daily exercise equipped him to be the balanced expositor he became.

Behind his exposition lay a profound respect for the text of Scripture in the original languages of Hebrew and Greek. Although he knew no Hebrew and had only a slender knowledge of Greek he was always careful, where he was in any doubt, to consult written or living authorities with an understanding of the Hebrew or Greek text. It was solely on the grounds of textual accuracy that in his later years he used the 1881 English Revised Version of the New Testament since he knew it to be based on a sounder Greek text than the Authorized Version. But he was never a champion of any one English version and when studying a particular passage he would refer to all available versions and make use of any insights which they might give.

As I look through the notes of some of his most moving addressed, full of application and point, I am struck with the care taken in the early stages to explain key Bible words in the text. The foundation of what he taught must be absolutely loyal to the Scriptures and he could not be happy with teaching that did not rest squarely upon what was written. In one address on the Virgin Birth of Christ he faces the problem of the Hebrew word *almah* used by Isaiah in his prophecy of Christ's birth (7.14).

'The Hebrew word *almah* does not necessarily mean a virgin but indicates a young woman of marriageable age, although the Septuagint translates by *parthenos* – a virgin. But Matthew carries back the truth from Bethlehem to Isaiah's day and sees in Mary's son the guarantee of the perpetual dominion of the house of David.'

Such honesty was typical of his exposition and it gave him, I believe, a greater sense of authority than if he had been dogmatic in style. Here is an example of the way in which his humble and reverent approach to Scripture gave power to his ministry. It comes towards the close of an address on 'Peter and the Scriptures' in which he had referred to Peter's statement (2 Peter 3.16) that Paul's letters contained 'things hard to be understood'.

'There is nothing better than the devout study of Holy Scripture to keep a man humble. "We know nothing yet as we ought to know." Even Paul might have retaliated that brother Peter's epistles were not all milk for babes.

But there are only *some* things hard to be understood while there are many exceeding great and precious promises in embarrassing profusion to be picked by the hand of simple faith. There are some necessary bones in the body of Scripture but also meat in abundance. There are some hard knots in the timber of this living tree but from its branches hang clusters of luscious fruit for the gathering.

We must learn to wait for knowledge of the things hard to be understood until it please the divine teacher to conduct our souls into understanding of them. In the meantime, draw freely of the sweet succulence of the precious things whose abundance invites us "Eat! O friend".'

> *Bread that camest down from heaven,*
> *Fruit of the Eternal Tree,*
> *Banquet which my God hath given*
> *Even unto me.*

Lo, before a world that scorneth,
I give thanks and eat
At the table in the desert
Filled with heavenly meat.

Another conviction of my father's that had a profound effect upon his exposition concerned the divine unity of Scripture. To him the Bible was a whole and every part of it was the living word of God.

'...all parts of Scripture are necessary. It may be said of Scripture as of the body, "the uncomely parts are the more necessary". But, you ask, would the Bible be incomplete without Esther? Yes, for there is taught that God is behind the seeming hap of history. The book without His Name is nevertheless full of His anonymous mercy. Would the New Testament be marred without Philemon? Yes: it would lack a supremely beautiful object lesson of God's care for the under-dog, His providence in the mending of our follies and worse, and of the way Christianity deals with evils such as slavery.'

'Life is in the whole. The word is quick and living. Is it a mirror? Yes, but such a mirror as the living eye. Is it a seed? Yes, but a seed enfolding the vitality of God. Is it a sword? Yes, but a sword that omnisciently discerns and omnipotently pierces the human heart. Hold it reverently, for you have a living word in your hands.'

His teaching of the fundamental truths of the gospel was based on the whole of Scripture and he regarded such doctrine as the unarguable teaching of the Bible from end to end. Even when expounding a doctrine from a particular passage he would bring to bear upon it insights and illuminations from other parts of Scripture.

'The doctrine of the Deity of Christ does not depend on a dozen or a score or fifty proof texts. It is inwoven to the fabric of Holy Writ. It is implied in thousands of places, assumed in innumerable passages, histories and situations. Most convincing are the indirect allusions that peep out of passages where it is not in question. Lacking recognition of it we have lost the key of knowledge; without it the bottom falls out of the Apostolic gospel; it is necessary to the whole redemptive scheme revealed in the Bible.'

My father's understanding of the unity of Scripture gave him great freedom when preaching from Old Testament themes since here he found not simply prophecies of the coming of Christ but foreshadowings, types, principles and illustrations of the truth of God that was later to be revealed in Christ. Some of his friends had revolted against extreme forms of typology based on the Old Testament but he would never stand completely with them although he rejected any systems that 'turned the Bible into a book of puzzles'.

'God's thoughts centre upon His Beloved Son. Christ is everywhere in the Word; His face looks out of every page of the Old Testament – typical men, histories, rites and objects. All the Old Testament says "There cometh One".

In the New Testament types are sometimes actually so called or, at least, indicated to be so. Adam is specifically named in Romans 5 to be a type of the Lord. Melchisedec in Hebrews 7 is shown to depict the order of Christ's priesthood, both the positive statements and the significant omissions of the Scripture narrative being adduced by the writer...But objects such as the tabernacle furniture are also indicated to be types. Hebrews 9.1-8 are sufficient warrant to encourage us to find truth about Christ in the lampstand, the table of shewbread, the veil, the censer, the ark, the cherubim and the mercyseat. "Of which we cannot now speak particularly".'

His handling of Old Testament Scriptures pointing to Christ was never fanciful or clever. He used them to extol his Saviour in a simple relevant way that meant much to the simple believer. I therefore bring this article to an end where he would himself have wanted to bring us – to a place of reverent adoration of the Person of Christ.

THE TREE OF DELIGHT
(Song of Songs 2.3,4)

'As the apple tree among the trees of the wood.'
The apple, or perhaps the orange or apricot tree, is the most conspicuous tree in the wood with its golden fruit peeping from under the leaves; it is different, attractive, conspicuous and beautiful.
'So is my Beloved among the sons.' This is how the church sees Christ; this is how the individual believer views his Lord.

Fairer than all the earth-born race,
Perfect in comeliness Thou art.
Replenished are Thy lips with grace
And full of love Thy tender heart.
God ever blest, we bow the knee
And own all fulness dwells in Thee.

'I sat down under His shadow with great delight.' He is a tree with a deep inviting shadow affording refuge from the scorching tropical sun. His shade draws as if it said 'Come sit here and be at peace'. Here at his table we are under His shadow and we find it delightful.

It is the foliage of the tree that affords the restful shade but more – the fruit of the tree offers itself for our enjoyment. It is within reach as we sit, for the lower branches stoop to us with their luscious burden.

'And His fruit was sweet to my taste.' Never was a fruit-laden tree to match our Lord Jesus. The fruit of the Spirit hangs in plentiful profusion upon Him. Here are love, joy, peace, long-suffering, gentleness, goodness, meekness, faithfulness and self-control, in profusion and without measure.

To meditate on Him in all His pathway is to eat His fruit and find it sweet to our taste.

'He brought me into His banqueting house, and His banner over me was love.' Here, in the manner of one of those dissolving views we have seen projected, the outlines of one picture fade and melt into another. We see the shade of the apple tree give place to the brilliance of the banqueting hall, the fruit of the tree to the laden table, the over-arching branches to the folds of the King's banner emblazoned with His new best name of Love.

And the supreme wonder is to find myself in this place of all delights – a wonder not lessened when I find that I am there because He, under Whose banner I rest secure, brought me there.

He brought me! May His Name be for ever praised!

On special occasions

My father's gifts of lucid and balanced exposition, coupled with his rare gifts for presenting truth in a captivating way, soon led to his receiving invitations to minister at Christian conferences and conventions throughout the country. In addition his skill in suiting the word to the occasion resulted in a stream of invitations to give addresses on special occasions in local churches and on behalf of Christian societies. He responded to as many of these as he could fit into his busy life.

On such occasions he would seek an appropriate scripture and expound it with reference to the special event, for he well knew that special occasions brought special opportunities which could not be better used than by unfolding the mind of God from the Scriptures. One such occasion was the 'opening of a new Gospel Preaching place' at which he ministered on the phrase 'the work of the Lord' (1 Cor 16.10). His four simple points were:

(1) Work in Faith
(2) Work in Humility
(3) Work to the Pattern
(4) Work Steadfastly

This simple framework provided the opportunity for giving much powerful godly advice some of which is well-worth quoting today. Here are some of his words on humility.

'Make a serious effort to esteem others better than yourself in the matter of public ministry. If you find it hard, start by esteeming them as good as yourself and remember that your work could not be done except in connection with what others do...

Do not have too liberal an estimate of the quality and value of your own contributions to the work of the Lord. Think over how it ought to be done and might be done; you will have to ask forgiveness for its poorness...

Seek readiness to sink self for the Lord's cause. More wreckage is caused by dwelling on our rights than from any other cause. Dwell rather on your obligations...

No man is humble who is prayerless. The bowed head, bent knees and uplifted hands are all signs of self-distrust and consciousness of want of wisdom. Prayer kills pride or pride kills prayer. Prayer opens channels for the inflow of God and is the open secret of effective service.'

The same address contains one of his flashes of humour which he used sparingly but effectively. It comes in the passage on steadfastness.

'There is sometimes an effervescence about a new work; some are always ready for a change from the old to the new seeing an excuse for throwing off old obligations which have become irksome. Be sure of your guidance before you dare to transfer your activities to a new quarter. Make certain of your marching orders and, if in doubt, stand still where you are until the cloud moves.

A work such as is being inaugurated needs quiet doggedness as a quality in those who will take it up. Do you recollect Dryden's lines about one of the King's favourites of his day?

"A man so various that he seemed to be
Not one, but all mankind's epitome.
Stiff in opinions, always in the wrong,
Was everything by starts and nothing long;
But in the course of one revolving moon,
Was chymist, fiddler, statesman and buffoon."

This is an unlovely trait and never more so than in the work of the Lord. Avoid it.'

But my father's gifts shone perhaps most brightly on domestic occasions in the local church for he allied with his ability to expound the Word a warmth of human understanding that made him acceptable to his hearers. Here was no remote Biblical scholar whose lofty teaching awed his hearers but a man among men who could understand human frailty and guide others in the steps of God where he himself had already trodden. Listen to his comments on Matthew 18.10: 'Take heed that ye despise not one of these little ones'. His words combine exposition and humanity in fine balance:

'There is a good deal in the Bible about reverence. We are all aware that God is to be feared but reverence looks in two directions – towards God and towards man. We are enjoined to love the brotherhood but before that we are told to honour all men (1 Peter 2.17). We are to entertain a respect for the soul of the individual and among them is the little child.

We are in an irreverent world, and where God is not feared it is not long until man is not regarded. The world has a poor opinion of the value of the individual...

But Christ says, take heed that you do not think lightly of even one of these little ones. High heaven sets a value on the soul of the child and he is represented before Him in that high court.

The good work in which we are interested today is marked by reverence for the soul of the little one and this is in line with the expressed will of the Saviour.'

There were occasions when he seized these opportunities to present Christ to those present who did not know Christ as Saviour but he could do this with courtesy and acceptance yet with a directness that would have left his audience in no doubt of God's word to them.

'It is not enough that you should give your children the advantages of education and physical soundness; see that they are fed, clothed, housed and protected as well as your means will allow. We know you already do this. But you should give your children the provision for the soul that no Sunday School teacher can give – that spiritual advantage that a godly home life alone can supply; the most potent influence the world knows.

It is a great thing to send the young folks to Sunday School; we thank you for your trust in us; it is a good thing to be sympathetic towards them being taught about Jesus Christ. But it is not doing the best possible for them. The best thing would be to go the same road yourself that you would like them to take. Example is better than precept. If it is your desire that John or Mary should become a truly useful godly man or woman, first do the one thing needful to start on that path of life yourself – turn to Christ, receive Him into your life as Saviour, Friend, Guide and Master. He will give you the power, the vision and the grace to lead your own little ones to Himself.'

Upon my shelves is a well-worn loose leaf book containing the marriage service which he used and the names of 25 couples whom he joined in marriage between 1933 and 1946. The book contains several sets of notes of talks given on these joyous occasions and elsewhere I have found several more. I am struck by the essential similarity between most of these marriage talks and can see that his chief concern was to lay a sound spiritual basis for a Christian marriage. There is however a freshness about each talk revealing that he prepared each time a presentation of Christian marriage with each couple and their circumstances in mind.

'Marriage depends for success on the continuance of mutual love. Love is essentially unselfish. Its nature is to give, spend and serve, keeping no accounts, acquiring no rights, but always showing readiness to meet obligations. "By love serve one another."

This might be said to non-Christians for altruism is an accepted good in human philosophy. But this is a Christian wedding and the glory of the Faith is its supply of the means to meet its own demands.

The secret of serving each other in love is for each to serve Christ. For devotion to each other's interest is to be devoted to Christ; loyalty to each other is loyalty to Him.'

My father's marriage addresses always carried practical advice about home life and such advice almost invariably covered in various ways four basic principles.

'Christ in the home is the secret of successful home-building. If He is staying with you there will be a place of honour for His word, a place of prayer together and apart, a place for His people   and a place for His interests. Begin as you intend to go on. Press Him to stay with you through all your life-day.'

Perhaps the most moving of his addresses on family occasions were his words of comfort and hope given at the funerals of humble folk in his own local church or of Christian friends of long standing. In these talks his Christian hope shone at its brightest as he ministered the Word of the Lord regarding life eternal.

'Let me remind you of the figures by means of which the Word of God emphasises the vast change that Christ's triumph has made to the Christian's view of death.

It is likened to striking a tent. "We know that if our earthly house of this tabernacle were dissolved" (2 Cor 5.1). The tabernacle was a temporary structure made for the housing of those on pilgrimage. It was not a permanent abode. With the experience of life it became the worse for wear, until the time came when it had to be taken down for the last time. So with these bodies in which for the present our redeemed spirits are housed. They too suffer with the passage of the years and finally have to be laid aside. The Scripture goes on to show that instantly the tent is struck the pilgrim himself, erstwhile housed therein, is "at home with the Lord". What is there of fear in such a view of death?

It is likened to a ship setting sail. "The time of my departure [literally, setting sail] is at hand" (2 Tim 4.6). To the Philippians Paul confesses an eagerness to set out on this new voyage because the haven of desire to which it swiftly leads is Christ Himself. "To depart and to be with Christ is far better" (Phil 1.23). So that death to the Christian is but a loosing away from a familiar roadstead and the raising of a sail that bears unfailingly to bliss. What is there of dread or sorrow in this?

Death is also spoken of commonly as a "falling asleep". Just as after the toil of a long day we lie down and lose ourselves in sweet sleep, so at the close of our appointed life-day we "fall asleep". I grant you that sometimes it is a strange lullaby that rocks many a one into this slumber (it was a hail of stones in Stephen's case: an executioner's axe in Paul's); yet the end of the day brings to the tired body rest – "Our friend Lazarus sleepeth". What can be less a thing of dread or sorrow than this?'

Among my father's papers are a number of prayers written out for these occasions and I close with one which he must have used towards the end of his life when already he strongly felt the beckoning hand of the Lord whom he had faithfully served for so long. It expresses his own living faith and certain expectation of being for ever in the presence of the Lord Jesus Christ.

'Father, one by one Thou art breaking the ties that hold our hearts in this present world, and one by one Thou art adding to the cords that draw our hearts to the invisible and eternal world. We stand here today and lift our souls to Thee. Some have lost a dear friend, some a relative, some a loved mother, and one the dear partner of his life.

We feel keenly the snapping of the tie. Give Thy consoling grace to each as Thou dost know and see the need.

We praise Thee for the knowledge that our loved one is with Thee; that she henceforth dwells in that world where pain and tears are not; that she rests in perfect blessedness at home with the Lord.

So, in our sense of present loss we yet are able to thank Thee that it has pleased Thee to call her to Thyself and we now reverently commit her earthly house to the ground, assured that she will share gloriously in that resurrection which will be granted to the dead in Christ at our Lord's return. For then shall we who have come in this life to trust and love Him, be together caught up to His presence and together be for ever with the Lord.

With the comfort of this great promise in our hearts we turn our steps back to our appointed duties.'

Counsel to Preachers

During his ministry my father had very few opportunities of speaking to young men collectively about all that is involved in preaching the Word although he was constantly looking out for young men whom he could encourage to exercise the gift of public ministry. There were, however, a few occasions when he spoke to groups of young men about preaching and the notes he left of these occasions reveal a great deal of those God-inspired ideals which he himself pursued for over forty years. On such occasions he evidently spoke with some reluctance for he had no high opinion of his own ability that had bloomed through years of dedication and application.

'I have said nothing so far about the techniques of preaching. I speak with diffidence about this for I am too acutely aware of my limitations to presume to be an authority.'

Such modesty was typical for he knew that pride would deny the Lord whom he was called to exalt. In this connection he quoted Denney:

'No man can bear witness to Christ and to himself at the same time. No man can give the impression that he himself is clever and that Christ is mighty to save.'

To him oral preaching ability was secondary to the preparation of the minister's heart in the presence of the Lord whom he served. His first task must be to show Christ through the Scriptures; until he had an all-round knowledge and understanding of the Book of all books he could never adequately speak of Christ and no other kind of preparation or advice would be worth anything. His advice on knowing the Scriptures was given under five headings.

'*Read.* Familiarize yourself with the contents for this will be an education in itself. Read it regularly and methodically using the time and method best suited to your circumstances. Aim at acquaintance with every part of the Bible and give it your full attention for there is no padding in Scripture. *Think.* There is no value in skimming over the Bible but meditation will make your reading profitable. Raise questions out of your reading and think out the answers. Make comparisons with other passages of Scripture with a kindred subject. Note prominent words, striking phrases, significant omissions and similes used to illustrate truth.

Pray. Reading and meditation are both ways of affording the Lord the opportunity to speak. Prayer is the illuminating secret even of the intellectual eye. Pray for a right motive in the use of Scripture which is "that I may know Him"; pray too that Scripture will make you to know your own heart in its workings; pray about difficulties met in your reading and wait for the answers.

Believe. The Christian is a believer since this is his habitual attitude to God's word which becomes such to him in effectual power as it comes from His mouth and is meekly received. Apply the results of your reading, meditation and prayer to your own life.

Obey. You never learn a second lesson from God until you practise the first. When you see a command put it into conduct; when you see a precept put it into practice. You may get through man's universities not knowing much more than when you went in; not so in God's. Obey what God teaches you and He will lead you into larger knowledge of Himself.'

Such advice, valuable as it is, gives little guidance about methods of Bible study for my father was fully aware of the danger of stereotyped systems and he wanted each aspiring preacher to seek and find God's way for himself.

'The Golden Rule is that there is no golden rule...Get a method that helps *you.* Daily reading and prayer for one's own soul is indispensable whether a man is a preacher or not. Our ministry can rise no higher than the level of our own enjoyment of divine realities.'

He regarded a preacher's general preparation to be a task that was continuous as he read not only from the Scriptures but also from works of reference, written ministry and daily secular reading.

'Read and think; think and read; pursue ideas; follow up lines of thought; work out illustrations; catch aphorisms. Gather material, not necessarily for immediate use, and find some way of retaining it.

You are never off duty at this phase of your preparation for not only in set times of study but in conversation, by observation, from your newspaper and other reading, fresh ways of stating old truth will come to you.'

My father had himself developed the art of continual meditation and at all times and places his thoughts would turn as opportunity came to Christ and His Word.

'Let meditation develop into a habit. Think on your feet and when you are about your routine duties. Habituate your mind to turn to its own company when set free for a very short time. Meditation is second nature to those who have become men of the Bible.'

My father was most insistent that the aspiring preacher should have an accurate knowledge of the text of the Bible and he encouraged young men to gain a working knowledge of New Testament Greek. But he recognized that many young men with the natural and spiritual gifts to minister might never be able to achieve this goal and for them he advocated the careful use of concordance and lexicon to ensure a right understanding of the text of Scripture.

When it came to particular preparation my father's advice was to keep among the great themes of Scripture which he declared would demand a lifetime of study and would occupy a lifetime of preaching. His lists read like a three year syllabus of a Bible College as he emphasized the worthlessness of pursuing other lines.

'Keep among these mighty matters. Do not become a trifler with pretty little texts with dainty morals, or a clever weaver of wordy nothings hung on out-of-the-way phrases stolen from their contexts in the minor prophets. "Suburban preaching" is a plague. To men asking for bread it gives a sugary wafer; to souls asking for light it offers a farthing squib. Have none of it – do not waste precious time at it. Get to the citadel and from its noble towers cry aloud the things that matter. Preach Christ; preach the Word; proclaim Salvation...'

In his talks to preachers my father dwelt mainly on spiritual preparation and aims but he did refer to the mechanics of preaching in advice that is both humorous and direct. He warned against faults of manner and urged that the preacher should avoid using an unnatural voice, extravagant gestures and distracting habits like nervous coughs, hands in pockets or sniffs and snorts! – 'Anything that gets in the way of your message – cut it out.' Equally he warned of faults in the presentation of the preacher's message.

'Avoid circumlocution, idle repetition and hackneyed phrases. Practise the clear crisp sentence and try to present truth in a new way avoiding phrases and expressions which you would have difficulty in explaining were you challenged about them. Do not be satisfied with anything short

of the best of which you are capable. It is reprehensible to offer anything
short of the best to the Lord.'

In the advice he gave, my father was clearly conscious that the preacher's
divine message was held in an earthen vessel and we find him warning young
preachers of the dangers that come from within the vain heart of man. The
following quotation incidentally reflects the long years he spent in his secular
occupation on London's riverside.

'The channel of London river has the dredgers for ever at work in it,
counteracting the equally constant silting up that proceeds with every tide
that sweeps it. So the channel of the preacher's heart must be dredged
again and again by honest self-examination that it may be kept clear for
the passage to and fro of the stately ships of the thoughts of God laden with
power from afar. Strange filth is raised from the deep channels of the heart
thus; things surprisingly base, humiliatingly mean. The process of getting
rid of them is not pleasant but the alternative is the terrible one of being
rendered useless. Be honest with yourself. Be real. Your God hates all
sham.'

As I close this brief series of recollections of my father's ministry, I must end
where he would have ended – with Christ whose glory he sought from the
beginning to the end of his ministry. He would not want to be remembered for
himself in spite of all the light and joy which God channelled to his hearers
through him but he would be glad that there were some who spoke of him as an
English merchant once spoke of Samuel Rutherford: 'I heard a little fair man
and he shewed me the loveliness of Christ'.

'The spouse in the Song of Songs says of the Beloved "He is altogether
lovely". So speaks the soul of Christ, but only the soul that knows Him.
Long ago we were introduced to Him and since then our acquaintance has
become friendship, whose fellowship has deepened, whose converse has
become closer and more constant, until we cannot think of life without
Him, and say with Faber:

>"My blessed Lord; my precious Lord;
>Forgive me if I say
>For very love Thy blessed Name
>Ten thousand times a day"!'